Negotiating
the
Numbered Treaties

§

Negotiating
the
Numbered Treaties

An Intellectual and Political Biography

of Alexander Morris

§

Robert J. Talbot

PURICH
PUBLISHING
LIMITED
SASKATOON, SK. CANADA

Purich Publishing Ltd.
Box 23032, Market Mall Post Office, Saskatoon, SK, Canada, S7J 5H3
Phone: (306) 373-5311 Fax: (306) 373-5315 Email: purich@sasktel.net
www.purichpublishing.com

Library and Archives Canada Cataloguing in Publication

Talbot, Robert J., 1982-
    Negotiating the numbered treaties : an intellectual and political biography of Alexander Morris / Robert J. Talbot.

Includes bibliographical references and index.
ISBN 978-1-895830-36-1

    1. Morris, Alexander, 1826-1889. 2. Indians of North America – Canada – Treaties – History. 3. Indians of North America – Canada – Government relations – 1860-1951. 4. Indian land transfers – Canada, Western – History. 5. Manitoba – History – 1870-1918. 6. Northwest Territories – History – 1870-1905. 7. Canada. Dept. of Indian Affairs – History. 8. Lieutenant governors – Manitoba – Biography. 9. Lieutenant governors – Northwest Territories – Biography. 10. Manitoba – Biography. 11. Northwest Territories – Biography. I. Title.

FC3217.1.M67T34 2009   971.05'2092   C2009-901942-6

Edited, designed, and typeset by Donald Ward.
Cover design by Duncan Campbell.
Index by Ursula Acton.
Map by Donald Ward.
Cover image of Alexander Morris (LAC, PA-025468).
Cover image of Treaty Medal by Bob Michayluik Photography.
Treaty Medal courtesy Saskatchewan Office of the Treaty Commissioner.
Cover image of page 1 of Treaty 6 (LAC, E-004156541).

Purich Publishing gratefully acknowledges the assistance of the Government of Canada through the Book Publishing Industry Development Program and the Government of Saskatchewan through the Creative Economy Entrepreneurial Fund for its publishing program.

Printed on 100 per cent post-consumer, recycled, ancient-forest-friendly paper.

for Sheila

Acknowledgements

THIS BOOK IS BASED ON RESEARCH that was originally conducted for a master's thesis in history at the University of Ottawa under the supervision of Dr. Jan Grabowski. Dr. Grabowski provided invaluable insight, constructive criticism, and encouragement throughout the research and writing process, and I am deeply grateful for his guidance. Drs. Michael Behiels, Jeff Keshen, and Rich Connors were also generous with their time and counsel. Dr. Barry Cottam, of Indian and Northern Affairs Canada, provided early inspiration and directed me to key archival and primary sources, for which I am immensely grateful. I also thank the teaching staff and personnel of the Department of History, in particular Suzanne Dalrymple, Francine Laramée, and Manon Bouladier-Major.

I am grateful to the Social Sciences and Humanities Research Council of Canada and the Ontario Graduate Scholarship Program, who provided generous financial support during my studies at the University of Ottawa. Hopefully they will continue to do so for aspiring historians and patrons of the humanities.

Many thanks are also owing for the diligent efforts and patience of the good people at Purich Publishing Ltd., including Don Purich, Karen Bolstad, Donald Ward, and Ursula Acton. They identified important "problem" points that would otherwise have escaped my notice, and, more generally, have helped transform the text into what I hope will be a pleasant read. Any errors that remain are my own.

I must reserve the greatest gratitude for my wife, Sheila, my parents, Lloyd and Peggi, and my siblings, Carolyn, Mary Ann, and Jonathan, for their love and constant support in this and all of life's endeavours.

FRONTISPIECE. *Alexander Morris in Ottawa, December 1869, at the beginning of his two-year term as John A. Macdonald's Minister of Inland Revenue* (Library and Archives Canada, PA-025468).

Contents

PART IV: Indian Affairs

Introduction

ALEXANDER MORRIS (1826-1889) IS BEST REMEMBERED for his service as Lieu-tenant-Governor of Manitoba and the North West Territories, and as the chief Canadian negotiator for Treaties 3 – 6 with the First Nations of Western Canada. Ideologically, Morris was a conservative, an imperialist, and a devout Christian. Historians have traditionally argued that Euro-Canadian officials such as Morris failed to appreciate the significance of the treaties they were negotiating or the long-term reciprocal relationship they entailed for Aboriginal peoples. Morris's understanding of the treaty relationship, however, was likely much-closer to the Native perspective than has previously been believed.

The convictions of the individual are, to a significant extent, the product of social formation. The individual's capacity to transcend his or her social forma-tion and think or act outside the constraints it can impose is a subject of ongoing debate. In the case of 19th-century treaty making between Canada and the First Nations of the North West, historians have yet to agree on how far treaty negotia-tors such as Alexander Morris were able to understand and empathize with the Aboriginal peoples they encountered.

Many historians have argued that treaty negotiations were not grounded in mutually understood terms; the parties held disparate conceptions of the mean-ing and significance of the treaties and the long-term relationship they entailed. The earliest treaty historiography asserted that the treaties were entered into on the initiative of the Canadian government, acting out of a sense of paternalism to protect the Native population. Euro-Canadian historians have traditionally portrayed the treaties as tragedies of history — land surrenders forced on the bands by government negotiators in exchange for paltry compensation. Since the mid-1980s, however, ethno-historians, anthropologists, and social historians have emphasized Aboriginal agency, convincingly arguing that the original inhabitants of the land were not merely passive observers; rather, they used treaty negotiations as a means of securing autonomy and a relationship of reciprocity with the larger white society. It was the Euro-Canadian negotiators, encumbered with an allegedly incompatible world view, who failed to understand the deeper significance of the relationship to which they had committed their government.

The new historiography has been crucial in providing an Aboriginal-centred perspective, but it tends to reduce government officials to the category of "classic imperialist." Moreover, it operates on the assumption that little distinction need be made among the various officials, like Morris, whose ideological convictions and social formation had limited their capacity to understand Aboriginal people. While this historiography provides the crucial structural and institutional contexts under which government officials operated, it does not capture the individual experiences of those involved in shaping and applying the government's policies. The unique contributions of key actors, and their capacity to demonstrate intellectual flexibility in their encounters with Aboriginal people, remain obscured.

Over the past two decades, new frames of analysis have emerged that better incorporate an Aboriginal understanding of the treaty relationship. With the increasing articulation of the Aboriginal perspective, a more systematic comparison and intertextual analysis with the Euro-Canadian understanding of the treaty relationship is now possible. Alexander Morris served as Lieutenant-Governor of Manitoba (1872-1877) and the North West Territories (1872-1876), and was the principle Treaty Commissioner for the renegotiation of Treaties 1 and 2 and the negotiation of Treaties 3, 4, 5, and 6. It is argued here that his understanding of the significance of the treaties was much closer to Aboriginal understandings than his critics until now have credited him with. Over time, and through his many interactions and intellectual exchanges with First Nations leaders, Alexander Morris was able to transcend his social formation and empathize significantly with their viewpoint. This is not to say that all Aboriginal people viewed the treaties in the same manner. Nonetheless, Morris was able to reach a common understanding with a number of their principle negotiators.

Morris's apparent ideological transformation can best be understood with an examination of how his world-view and personal convictions developed over time. Beginning with his early life, social formation, and professional and political career, this book analyzes the ideological influences that would have informed Morris's understanding of the treaties and his overall view of the North West before he moved there in 1872.

Morris's ideological formation and political activities provide an insight into Canadian ambitions in the North West. An ardent proponent of Confederation, Morris played a limited role in achieving the union of 1867; he was a confidant of John A. Macdonald, and shared the latter's vision for the expansion of the country. He was also a long-time advocate of the annexation of the North West. He is possibly the only Father of Confederation who actually went West to impose the new nation's vision, the only one of those otherwise well-studied individuals who dealt personally and extensively with the First Nations of the North West. He understood the treaties he helped negotiate, and he tried to communicate his understanding to the government and the public. Despite his conservative, imperialist convictions, Morris came to sympathize with the peoples who were so misunderstood by his contemporaries in Ottawa. He demonstrated a remarkable ability to understand and even adopt certain aspects of the world view of the Aboriginal people. That he took these principles to heart is evidenced in his approach to the question of treaty implementation, and also his publication of *The Treaties of Canada with the Indians of Manitoba and the North West Territories*.[1]

A biography of one of the major actors in the treaty-making process that applies these new frames of analysis can contribute to our understanding of the process as a whole. By understanding Alexander Morris, we may discern how he and others of his position might have viewed the treaties. Morris's personal development may shed light on the degree of intellectual flexibility that others of his social formation might have been capable of. Morris's example can also serve as a reminder of the reciprocal intellectual relationship that existed at various levels of Native-Newcomer relations. Newcomers to the North West no doubt projected their values and perceptions on others, but in some cases they may have been equally informed by the world views of the individuals they encountered.

PART I

§

The Man in the Making

1

Morris's Place in Canadian Historiography

ALEXANDER MORRIS'S PLACE IN CANADIAN HISTORIOGRAPHY must be understood in the context of general developments in the field of treaty history. Up until the early 1980s, non-Aboriginal historians continued to overlook the founding principles of the treaties, portraying them instead as tragedies of history — mere instruments of subjugation. In 1932, G. F. G. Stanley set the tone that would dominate the next half century:

> In the first place they were not really negotiated treaties in the proper sense of the word. The concessions granted to the Indians were never made in deference to the Indians. Discussion was confined to an explanation of the terms. . . . The fact is that the Indians never understood what was happening.[1]

Fifty years later, historians were still making generalized assumptions about the numbered treaties. Reading Treaty 4 (1874), for instance, one historian was taken aback by the agricultural implements promised to the bands, and assumed that they had been provided as a way of imposing the white man's way of life on the nomadic plains dweller: "That these Plains Indians had neither interest in nor tradition of farming seemed to be beside the point. . . . Treaty No. 4 is so similar to all the others concluded in the 1870s that one cannot avoid the conclusion that they were imposed rather than negotiated."[2] Such literal readings of treaty texts foster the assumption that the First Nations were overwhelmingly disadvantaged and largely ineffective as negotiators; they overlook Aboriginal agency.

In the mid-1980s, however, Jean Friesen and John L. Tobias published two important scholarly articles arguing that the First Nations had not been passive observers, but, rather, the driving force of the treaties:

Men who had for at least a century dealt with the economic demands of the Hudson's Bay Company or American free traders and the political demands of the new nation of the Métis, men who had experienced dislocation, epidemics, and the revolutions of horse and gun, are widely viewed as children in arranging their treaties with these same Europeans.[3]

Friesen offers the logical consideration that, quite simply, the "Indian leaders took this difficult situation and, in most cases, made the best deal they could." As Tobias explains, "the Cree were both flexible and active in promoting their own interests, and willing to accommodate themselves to a new way of life."[4] In other words, treaty was a means of adapting to changing circumstances: "they manoeuvred, stalled, debated, compared offers, and with some success played upon the commissioners' desire to win their friendship and peaceful acceptance of white intrusion into their lands."[5] This willingness to make treaty, to work within the diplomatic framework presented to them, Friesen continues, derived from their political and legal "concept and practice of reciprocity," or the entering into of relationships of mutual obligation and benefit in the interest of establishing security.[6]

Making up for past inaccuracies, however, has resulted in overcompensation; the new analysis has led to another simplification whereby the Indians are now portrayed as the only party in the negotiations who understood the significance of the treaty:

An important component of the Indian treaty-making framework was the concept of reciprocity. By offering food and gifts and agreeing to annual payments (the annuities) to the Cree, the treaty commissioners, consciously or not, agreed to a mutual obligation of reciprocity. It is apparent that the treaty commissioners did not understand what kind of an agreement they were entering when they signed the treaties.[7]

The Euro-Canadian negotiator, Friesen argues, was "a classic imperialist," bent on assimilating the Indians and fulfilling his assumed burden of "Christian duty."[8] Curiously, in Friesen as in Stanley, the reader is still required to accept the assumption that the parties simply did not understand each other, and thus held irreconcilable understandings of the meaning of the relationship they were negotiating.

Morris's position as the chief Crown negotiator, and his subsequent publication of a book on the making and administration of the treaties, have made him something of a lightning rod for much of the criticism aimed at the treaties and the bureaucrats responsible for their lacklustre administration. Morris's *The Treaties of Canada with the Indians of Manitoba and the North-West Territories* remains arguably the most important written source for the treaties of the 1870s. In focussing on the flawed treaty implementation of the 1880s and later, some historians have operated on the assumption that the treaties negotiated a decade earlier were themselves inherently flawed, and that the poor implementation that followed was an inevitable product of them. In short, they were reading history in reverse. Under this interpretation, much of the blame for the failed implementation of the 1880s and later has, by default, been placed at the feet of the Crown negotiators. By extension, general criticisms aimed at "the government" have often been applied to its most recognizable figure, Alexander Morris. As Lieutenant-Governor and chief Crown negotiator, and given that the most extensive textual records relate directly to him — including archival sources as well as his book — Morris has become the most recognizable individual of that monolithic government, and thus the target of much of the criticism.[9]

The problem is that the government was not monolithic. Much has been made of the internal divisions that existed in the various Aboriginal groups who signed the treaties, but the situation in the government was not dissimilar. It included a number of actors of disparate backgrounds and varying degrees of experience with the North West, its people, and the treaties. Historians must distinguish among those in government who generally favoured a more faithful implementation of the treaties — such as Morris, James McKay, or W. J. Christie — and those who were inclined to more parsimonious arrangements, such as J. A. N. Provencher, E. A. Meredith, and David Mills.

Many researchers have focussed on the lacklustre implementation policies of the late 1870s and into the early 20th century, *after* Morris had left the North West.[10] There is less discussion about treaty implementation issues during the 1870s, when important divisions arose within the government over how best to proceed on the issue — divisions that increasingly marginalized Morris and his position. A closer look at treaty implementation during the mid-1870s, before the notorious Dewdney era, serves to draw the distinction between such actors, and helps explain the internal struggle that resulted in the victory of the fiscally conservative policy.

Morris's understanding of the treaties can be discerned from three areas. First, a look at his earlier life can help identify Morris's intellectual development and transformation over time; this can serve to trace the development of his appreciation for the treaties, to the extent of altering his former beliefs and convictions. Second, an analysis of the treaty negotiations applying new frames of reference, including oral history, can serve to compare Morris's understanding of the treaties with that of his Aboriginal counterparts. Third, an examination of Morris's role in treaty implementation reveals his expanded understanding of the treaties through his actions.

Alexander Morris is no stranger to Canadian historiography, but he has seldom been the primary object of study. Few historians have bothered to place his treaty-making years in the context of his early life and formative experiences. He has appeared in a number of collective biographies, such as Geo. Maclean Rose's 1886 *Cyclopaedia of Canadian Biography.*[11] Lila Staples in 1928[12] and R. G. Babion in 1945[13] each completed biographical works that offer important information on Morris's career, but neither focussed specifically on his dealings with First Nations. Both were effusive in their praise. "Whether scholarship and political genius came to Alexander Morris from his Scottish forebears, or were gifts from the gods, may be mere conjecture," wrote Staples. "Certain it is he possessed both."[14] Babion called his own study a "pioneer work," but his analysis follows much the same line as that of his predecessor. Nonetheless, both historians provided important factual information on Morris's education, business career, and politics that place his other activities in a broader context. The most balanced sketch — and the most recent — appears in Jean Friesen's entry in the *Dictionary of Canadian Biography*, in which Morris's career is presented in the context of class and financial interests, reminding readers that, while ideologies are derived in part from abstract personal beliefs, they are equally subject to the individual's material circumstances.

Advances in the fields of Aboriginal and oral history have served to articulate Aboriginal perspectives and understandings of the treaties, making comparative and intertextual analyses of the discourse of Morris and the Aboriginal negotiators possible. The language applied at treaty time by Morris and his counterparts, including articulations of the treaty relationship and the establishment of an atmosphere of trust between the parties, were just as important to the successful completion of the treaties as were the material promises and negotiating tactics applied by both sides. The discourse of reciprocity and equality, which often involved speaking in metaphor, were applied by both parties.

There are many significant works that place Morris in the larger context of 19th-century political and intellectual developments in Canada, the British Empire, and the Western world in general.[15] Other works on treaty history place him in the context of those events and provide an Aboriginal perspective.[16] This is not the first time it has been suggested that Morris had sympathy for his Aboriginal counterparts. As Mary Fitz-Gibbon noted, Morris

> showed a great understanding and sympathy for the plight of the Indians. For this he gained the respect of all who had contact with him. It was

partly through the vision of Alexander Morris that the government of Sir John A. Macdonald was persuaded to establish the North West Mounted Police force in 1873 to bring law and order to the West and to end tribal warfare — thereby preventing the wholesale slaughter that occurred in the United States.[17]

What has not been attempted so far is the tracing of his intellectual transition over time, culminating in his experiences in the North West.

2

Morris's Intellectual Development

Politics and Identity

Alexander Morris was born into a family of Upper Canadian entrepreneurs and politicians, and from an early age demonstrated a keen interest in Canadian politics. His father, William, was an affluent merchant and prominent Conservative politician. He and his brother, Alexander's namesake, settled in Upper Canada in 1806, in part to pay off debts their father had accumulated. William took great care with his finances, and he imparted this outlook to his children. The two brothers opened a store in Elizabethtown, becoming, "two more of those small merchants in Upper Canada who served as middlemen between the mercantile houses of Montreal and the Indians, loggers, and settlers peopling the edge of the wilderness."[1] William served with the loyalist forces in the War of 1812, and again during the 1837-1838 rebellions, gaining renown for leading a successful charge at the Battle of Ogdensburg in New York, in February 1813. Following the war, William and his brother moved to the Scottish settlement of Perth, the military, judicial, social, and political centre of Lanark County and the Ottawa Valley region. He soon became a Justice of the Peace, and in 1820 he was elected to the Upper Canada House of Assembly as the member for Lanark County, a post he would occupy until 1836, when he was appointed to the Legislative Council. William's brother James also enjoyed a successful political career, becoming Postmaster-General of the United Canadas. It was at Perth, in the familiar company of other transplanted Scottish settlers, that William decided in 1823 to marry Elizabeth Cockhran, herself of Scottish extraction, and raise a family. Here, he could make a comfortable fortune in commercial enterprise and frontier land speculation — practices that would be taken up by his children, and most skillfully by his first son, Alexander, born in 1826. The birth was celebrated by friends and family, some having come from as far away as the Scottish Highlands "to drink to the health of the 'wee young lad'."[2]

The young Alexander Morris loved the natural abundance of his home region. It was with some heartache that, at fifteen years of age, he left for Scotland, at his father's behest, to receive a higher education. Morris spent two years with his mother's family attending the prestigious Madras College in St. Andrews, and later registered in Arts at the University of Glasgow, although he did not complete a degree. He developed an affinity for his parents' homeland, visiting Scotland's historic manors and castles and its ancient battlefields, and wandering through Glasgow and Edinburgh, "the grey old town . . . with its University of historic ruins."[3] He even caught a glimpse of the young Queen Victoria, who was visiting Edinburgh at the time.[4]

Alexander excelled at his scholarly pursuits,[5] but public speaking proved a challenge he would have to overcome. After reciting a passage from Homer before his peers and professors, he "felt as if a twenty four pounder had been taken off his chest."[6] He came to admire people who had the gift of oratory.

Canada was never far from the young scholar's mind, despite the many distractions his parents' homeland had to offer. As one acquaintance wrote,

> the project of a General Canadian Confederation was the dream of his boyhood. At an age when most boys are to be found at the skating-rink or in the cricket field, he loved to bury himself in the pages of Lord Durham's "Report," or in some of the many works treating of that wonderful, far-away region then nominally known as the Hudson's Bay Company's Territories.[7]

One of Morris's final assignments at the University of Glasgow was a short paper, "An Incident in the Rebellion in Canada in the Years 38-9 [sic]."[8] It was a rather sensational account of the Battle of the Windmill, a skirmish between Upper Canadian loyalists and American-backed rebels in November 1838.

The short essay reveals much about the young Morris's intellectual and ideological development. It demonstrates the extent to which he had internalized the imperialist, anti-American, and anti-French-Canadian rhetoric of the day. The essay is equally telling of the insecurities borne by Canada's anglophone Tories as they struggled to assert their loyalty in the wake of two rebellions, and in the face of the success of their southern, republican neighbour. From boyhood, Morris had a strong sense of patriotism and loyalty to Britain, coupled with anti-American sentiment. He was deeply concerned with the country's image and political future. He used the essay to belittle the significance of the rebellion and assert the loyalty of the majority of Canadians:

> Canada was it is well known the scene of a civil war, caused by the machinations of a few designing, discontented men, such as Mackenzie, Papineau, Bidwell; who sought their own aggrandizement at the expense of their countries [*sic*] peace. The rebellion, insignificant in itself, would soon have been crushed by the loyal British-hearted Canadians, had not bands of Yankee "boufers" and reckless villains, reckless Sympathizers, flocked to the assistance of the discontented few, who had forsooth assumed the lofty title of Patriots.

Just cause lay entirely with the loyalists, he insisted, who were determined to defend their territory and property rights. Applying the rhetoric of the militia myth,[9] he gave credit to the Anglophone Canadians for fighting off the annexationists and keeping the colony in British hands, and cast doubt on the loyalty of the French Canadians:

> Much praise is due to the Canadians for the prompt manner, in which, independent of the military (there was but one regiment in the province) they rose to a man to demonstrate to their misguided brethren — the French population — and more especially to the 'free and enlightened citizens' of the New World, that they were not yet tired or ashamed of their Mother country, but were ready to repell [*sic*] any invasion of their rights and territories. The lesson has been, it is believed, an effective one, so that it will probably be long ere the peace of the country is again disturbed, as the policy of the government towards the French Canadians has been quite changed.

The policy to which the young scholar referred was that of the Durham Report: union of the Canadas and eventual assimilation of the troublesome French-speaking population.

In 1843, Morris, now seventeen, returned home from Glasgow with the intention of studying law. His father wanted him "to follow a business life,"[10] but a three-year placement with Thorne and Heward, commission merchants in Montreal, proved that "he was not cut out for this sort of thing and . . . he reverted to his original intention of studying law."[11] Before leaving, Morris spent three months in a small community north of Montreal to learn French — an ability that would prove useful in future legal practice in the city and, later, in dealing with the diverse population of the North West.[12] In 1847, perhaps as a favour to Morris's father, a Kingston lawyer named John A. Macdonald took on the aspiring young man as an articled "student at law."[13] In Macdonald's office Morris worked alongside the future Liberal premier of Ontario, Oliver Mowat. While there, Morris also took up studies at Queen's College, but "'worked so hard his health gave way,'" and he returned to Montreal.[14] Undeterred, he began studies toward an Arts degree at McGill University the following year. By 1851, he had completed a law degree and was admitted to the bars of both Canadas.

Late in that same year, on November 6, Morris married Margaret Cline of Cornwall, Ontario (then Canada West). Like Alexander, she was from a well-connected family and of a religious inclination. Margaret took an active role in her husband's public life, especially when it came to hosting social gatherings aimed at smoothing over partisan differences between the many political guests who came to the Morris household.[15] Alexander and Margaret had eleven children over the course of their marriage, eight of whom survived childhood.[16] There is every indication that Morris cared for his children dearly;[17] later in his career he took several of them on treaty trips in the North West.

Morris may have had many children, but he was not a physically healthy man. He suffered throughout his life from a series of afflictions, including bronchitis, "hereditary rheumatism of the head," "malarial symptoms," "severe attacks of fever," and "other nervous disorders."[18] He was often told by doctors that he should avoid over-exertion and take bed rest — advice that he did not always follow, especially in the North West where his duties would require him to travel long distances, often in difficult conditions, to meet with First Nations leaders.

Morris's legal education in Kingston and Montreal contributed to his indoctrination into Canadian conservative politics and provided an outlet for his burgeoning personal ambitions. While at McGill, he studied under William Badgley, a "powerful and effective partisan of the institutions of neo-classical liberalism, British immigration, the abolition of seigneurial tenure, and cultural harmony between Canada's two major ethnic groups." Badgley had been involved in the court martial of French-Canadian rebels, had "campaigned in favour of legislative union of the Canadas in the wake of Lord Durham's report of 1839, and drafted the Common School Act of 1841 that introduced a centralized, autocratic system of public education for Canada West." He believed firmly in the "expansion of the state's role in securing investment, and unification of the legal institutions of the two Canadas." As a student and apprentice, Morris had taken an active role in this project of centralization, helping draft "Badgley's revisionist 800-article code of criminal law and procedure, and assist[ing] with his principal's work on the Legislative Committee on Railways, Canals, and Telegraph Lines."[19]

While articling with Macdonald in Kingston, Morris had also been exposed to the ideas of conservatism, British imperialism, and confederation. He attended

Negotiating the Numbered Treaties

the founding convention of the short-lived British North American League in Kingston in late July 1849. The league had a profound impact on the ideological development of the impressionable 23-year-old. A number of people close to him — including his father, John A. Macdonald, P. M. Vankoughnet and Hugh E. Montgomerie — were prominent in the proceedings. The league brought together over 150 conservative anglophone lawyers, politicians, and businessmen from Canada West, Montreal, and Quebec City. They were disillusioned by their party's recent electoral defeat, and the new Reform administration's 1849 Rebellion Losses Bill, which promised to compensate anyone not convicted of sedition who had suffered property damages during the 1837-1838 rebellions, regardless of what side they had supported. The self-proclaimed loyal conservative anglophone population was outraged by the prospect that their tax dollars would be used to compensate the rebels. Some saw the bill as proof of the "French domination" in the ruling Reform coalition of Robert Baldwin and Louis-Hippolyte LaFontaine.[20] A series of riots in April 1849 by conservative anglophone sympathizers resulted in the destruction of the Montreal parliament buildings. Critics alleged that the league "advocated extreme Toryism and extreme disloyalty and finally threatened to drive the French into the sea."[21]

The situation amounted to an identity crisis for the Tories. After decades of maintaining a British presence in North America, they argued, loyal English-speaking Canadians were being rewarded with British indifference. To make matters worse, Britain's Liberal government had adopted the economic philosophy of Manchester liberalism, which called for free trade and an end to imperial preference. For Canada's agricultural and manufacturing interests, especially, this spelled disaster. A few individuals advocated "an Union of all the British North American Provinces" as a means to overcome French domination and the country's economic woes. It would create "a large home market for the consumption of agricultural products and domestic manufactures, and . . . consolidat[e] the interests and strength of the British population of North America."[22]

Earlier that year, Alexander Morris and Hugh E. Montgomerie had co-authored an anonymous diatribe against the Rebellion Losses Bill, pointing out that its support came "all from French districts."[23] To them, the bill was nothing short of a betrayal of that population, primarily British, that had remained "nine-tenths" loyal:

The loyal population of Canada had seen insult after insult showered on their heads from the Ministerial Benches in the Legislative Assembly — insults, the grossest and most revolting, added to what they felt to be a tyrannous injustice. These insults . . . were heaped upon them, because they had borne arms to uphold the Sovereignty of the Gracious Lady. . . .

While failing to appreciate the circumstances that had led to rebellion, the authors nonetheless assumed the role of apologists for the destruction of the Provincial Parliament in Montreal by a conservative mob:

> . . . the occurrence can scarcely be a matter of surprise to those who remember that the British of Montreal had, but eleven short years before, risen as one man to quell a "foul unnatural Rebellion," and now . . . suddenly found themselves called upon to contribute towards the indemnification of those who had aided and abetted in that Rebellion. Throughout the British population of the Province, the announcement that the Loyal were to be taxed to pay the Rebel was received with universal indignation.[24]

In closing, the authors took inspiration in quoting the 1841 assessment of British Prime Minister Lord John Russell: "We have only to consider the means of binding Canada more firmly to this country — of developing her resources — of strengthening her *British* population — of defending her territory — and of supporting and encouraging the loyal spirit of her people."[25] For Morris and Montgomerie, then, the loyalty of French Canadians was to be held in suspicion, and Canada's future would be best secured by the guaranteed political dominance of its British population. Only time would tell what impact such prejudices might have on Morris's attitude toward the diverse population he was to encounter in the North West.

The project of a British North American union "to lay the foundations for making this country a great nation upon a solid and enduring basis"[26] appealed to Morris's sense of patriotism, and he was one of the league's earliest converts to the idea.[27] By the mid-1850s, he clearly saw himself and his peers in the "mercantile classes" as the future commercial and political leaders of a great country. Overcoming his initial difficulties about speaking in public, he took great pleasure in giving patriotic speeches to rally the energies of these future leaders to the cause of building that country:

> Let me as a young man call upon my contemporaries in life to remember that as time speeds on and years begin to tell on us and youth ripens into manhood we will find ourselves occupying the position and called to perform the duties which their elders now occupy and perform. Resolve then, future Merchants of Canada, that you will be found sustaining the character of British merchants — intelligent, educated, honourable, independent merchants. Resolve that while sedulously devoting yourselves to your business you will yet find opportunities for strengthening and developing your mental faculties. . . .[28]

Negotiating the Numbered Treaties

Canada was rife with opportunity, and it was up to the young ambitious men of the mercantile classes to develop that potential. "Let us push our way up hill then, for in this country in our Parent land, there are no weights to press us down, no obstacles which cannot be overcome by persevering diligence combined with honesty and uprightness."[29] The patriotism of Morris's youth had blossomed into a mission of nation-building. He would soon engage directly in shaping Canada's legal structure, and make his first forays into political life.

Beliefs and Convictions

Morris's exposure to Conservative Canadian politics had been facilitated by his education and extracurricular activities while living in Montreal. He inserted himself into that class of lawyers and mercantile and industrial capitalists who dominated the economy and social structure of Canada's leading city. Many of these individuals were supporters of the Mercantile Library Association of Montreal, which was essentially a young men's club for wealthy anglophones. The association aimed to foster debate and discussion on the pressing topics of the day as part of a general effort to direct the energies and attentions of the colony's future leaders away from the unsavoury diversions available to young men in mid-19th-century Montreal. By 1848, Morris had been named vice-president of the association, a position he shared with Montgomerie.[30] It was here, on the lecture circuit, that he gave expression to the religious and moral convictions he had assumed from childhood.

During his time with the association, Morris developed a great deference for those who displayed oratorical skill, and a belief in the value of the spoken word, by which "the spirit of inquiry may be enkindled."[31] Morris saw the association as a means of diverting the idle time and energies of impressionable young men from vice. The association, he asserted, "fortifies [our] moral principles and gives [us] a distaste to the ephemeral pleasure of empty frivolity or gay dissipation."[32]

Alexander Morris was raised a member of the Presbyterian Church. His father had lobbied his entire life for the interests of the church, most notably for a share in the clergy reserves and in establishing the church-affiliated Queen's College at Kingston. The "clergy reserves for [William] Morris, and for many other Scots," explains William Morris's biographer, "were the symbolic battleground in a struggle over whether the British empire would be uninational or binational in character."[33] Alexander Morris inherited his father's devotion to the church. By 1856 he had succeeded his father in becoming a ruling elder of the synod of the Presbyterian Church in Canada. Morris corresponded with other church leaders in British North America and in Scotland in support of missions, establishing new churches and colleges, and in identifying potential clergymen to fill the necessary posts. By 1857 he had been elected to the Board of Trustees of Queen's College and had gained a reputation as "the Procurator of the Church" and a man with true "zeal for the Church."[34] He even inherited the family pew after his father's death: number 40 at St. Andrew's Church, Montreal.[35] He remained active in the business of the church most of his life.

Morris was active in supporting missionary work, and he helped edit the *Presbyterian*, "a missionary and religious record of the same branch of the Presbyterian Church in Canada."[36] He also became the first editor of the *Juvenile Presbyterian*, a "Missionary record and Sabbath Scholar's magazine."[37] Morris's involvement with the magazine is indicative of his convictions, idealism, and missionary zeal. The journal covered Presbyterian missions to peoples around the globe, including Sikhs and Hindus in India, Jews in Europe and Turkey, and Indigenous peoples in New Zealand, North America and elsewhere. The tone of the magazine was one of concern for the material and spiritual well-being of the children attending the international missions.

Morris's sympathy for other religions was limited. He referred to "the stern contest between light, civilization and liberty, on the one hand, and the fierce fanaticism and blind hate of the proud Mussulman and the cringing but subtle and cruel Hindoo on the other," which, Morris insisted, would "still more and more be moulded by the influence of British energy and enlightenment."[38] He viewed other Christian denominations with suspicion as well. In the 1850s, he supported missions aimed at converting French-Canadian Catholics,[39] and discussions on religion often turned to "the absurd pretension of the Romish Church to infallibility."[40] He was also sceptical of other non-Catholic denominations, and as a member of the association's executive he helped block its subscription to the *Christian Inquirer*, a Unitarian journal.[41]

Morris's religiosity extended to a preoccupation with morality. The temptations of mid-19th-century Montreal would have been many, including alcohol and illicit sexual behaviour, especially for wealthy young men of the anglophone mercantile classes who had the means to indulge. "It will at once be admitted," he told a gathering at the association, "that young men are placed in circumstances of peculiar temptation when their lot is cast in a city such as this."[42] Even the most upstanding of citizens, Morris warned, was susceptible to such vice. To avoid temptation, Morris believed that young men like himself should spurn idleness and dedicate their time and effort to productive pursuits and morally sound diversions. He believed that it was incumbent on every man to "make a right use of the time and talents given us"[43]: "[W]ith ourselves rests humanly speaking our future and . . . upon ourselves it wholly depends whether that great work of self-improvement which we owe it as a duty to our maker, to society and ourselves to carry out, is furthered to the extent it might be."[44]

To this end, Morris glorified the mythical figure of the "self-made" man who overcame disadvantage and circumstance, and, through hard work, the rejection of idleness, a desire to learn, and a focussed goal, made something of his life. Morris was particularly enamoured of the great men of history,[45] and from an early stage in his career, he aspired to build such a legacy for himself. He criticized those who failed in achievement despite the God-given advantages they possessed, and who instead dabbled in frivolous interests without ever focussing on a singular purpose in their lives. He acknowledged that some individuals were burdened by circumstance and deprivation more than others, but at the end of the day, he argued, people under all variety of circumstances had proved capable of uplifting themselves and making something of their lives.[46] It remained to be seen whether Morris would follow the example of many of his colleagues and condemn the First Nations of the North West for their alleged "idleness."

Early Perceptions of Indigenous Peoples

Morris demonstrated an early interest in Indigenous peoples, stemming from a combination of religious moralism, paternalistic altruism, and academic curiosity. Morris's earliest interest in Indigenous peoples may have originated from a number of personal experiences. As a youth visiting family in Glasgow, he was struck by his uncle Matthew Cochran, "a silk merchant who in his early years had lived in Peru and had many ancient Indian relics."[47] Morris's father, having traded with Indians in his early days at Brockville, even employing a few, would have had his share of stories to tell. Indeed, William's relations with those trading partners left a lasting impression on young Alexander. "[W]e have the Saulteaux [Ojibwa] where I came from," he would tell First Nations negotiators at Treaty Number 4, decades later. "They were my friends. I was the son of a white Chief who had a high place among them, they told him they would do his work, they called him Shekeishkeik. I learned from him to love the red man."[48]

Morris's first public lecture, given to the Mercantile Library Association of Montreal at an evening session in January 1849, was entitled, "The North American Indians; their Origin, Customs, and Oratory."[49] It was, as Friesen has suggested, "an early indication of one of the consuming passions of his later life."[50] But at this stage in his life, Morris could only pretend to have an expansive personal knowledge of the subject. Nervous that his audience might catch on, he approached his uncle, the Hon. James Morris, for advice. James told his nephew "to look his audience in the face and believe he knew more about his subject than any of them."[51] Morris's approach to the topic combined academic curiosity with a limited measure of respect for the people being discussed.

"The peculiarity of their customs, and the rich originality of their oratory," he told his audience, "are subjects in which much information and amusement may be expected." The origin "of these wandering tribes," he said, "is still involved in considerable doubt and difficulty, and the result of any investigation into the subject must prove of much interest to the public generally." He acknowledged that the Indians were "at one time the sole occupants of this extensive region"[52] — a statement that would, in future, provide Morris with a basis for recognizing Aboriginal title.

As the empires of Europe expanded around the globe and made contact with foreign cultures, the study of Indigenous peoples became increasingly fashionable. Popular novels such as Herman Melville's *Typee* (1846), and Jean-Jacques Rousseau's notion of the "noble savage" served to draw a romantic link between the seemingly utopic lives of Indigenous peoples and their relationship with nature. "For those with such ideas," writes Douglas Owram, "the Indian was a natural representative of wilderness life. His nomadic existence and warlike appearance made him a natural symbol of the freedom inherent in a primitive way of life."[53] Morris's speech coincided with the publication of a number of popular works of the day by authors and organizations, such as the Aborigines' Protection Society, which was concerned with the future of Indigenous peoples.[54]

Morris's interest in Indigenous peoples corresponded with a fascination with the natural world. He kept his own garden and found great joy in the "innocent amusement" and "simple pure pleasure" of horticulture.[55] He believed that the health of the mind and body were intimately connected, and admiring natural beauty was, for him, a necessary antidote to the demands of everyday life. While an advocate of development, he also lamented the destruction of natural beauty:

> The farmer [seeks] to get from the soil as speedy a return as may be, in utter disregard of [its] exhaustion, which will be the necessary result. His remorseless axe too, deals destruction among the noble monarchs of the forest. Not one does he spare and soon a smouldering log-heap or a few charred blackened stumps are all that remain to tell the hapless fate which befell the venerable trees. Wide-spreading maples or majestic oaks, which had a wise and judicious discrimination been exerted would, when in process of time, [have provided a] solitary break in the almost universal loneliness.[56]

This lament was reconciled, in part, by a perception that the development of natural resources was a necessary step on the road to progress and civilization, and by an equally romantic view of the settler.

Morris's romantic understanding of nature lent itself to a nostalgia that combined admiration with religious paternalism. He equated the Indian with Adam — alone with nature's bounty, blissfully ignorant, and unencumbered by the potentially corrupting tree of knowledge:

Negotiating the Numbered Treaties

It may be a lingering trace of that better nature . . . that primeval state of innocency and bliss, when the first of our race majestic in his likeness to the Creator, dwelt in the earthly paradise — the Garden of Eden "where out of the ground made the Lord God to grow every tree that is pleasant to the sight and good for food". . . . no taste is so generally diffused, so innocent and yet so easy of gratification as the love of plants and flowers.[57]

Morris theorized that civilized man's love of nature was a throwback to his primeval origins. He believed, somewhat condescendingly, that the "innate admiration of the beautiful in nature, which, a living, abiding principle dwells in every heart," was "common alike to the untutored savage and to the richly cultivated mind, though differing in degree — all are endowed with the aptness for perceiving and appreciating this sentiment."[58]

While Morris maintained that Indigenous people were an interesting and exotic subject for discussion, he depicted them as deprived: "The manners, the customs, the foibles and the follies of the inhabitants of other lands, who have not been favoured, as we have, but who still remain sunk in worse than midnight darkness, are depicted in lively colours and we depart wiser, if not better men."[59] Indigenous peoples and their picturesque, aesthetically pleasant customs provided an interesting subject for anthropological study, he suggested, but theirs was an example to avoid. Beyond the lessons of a symbiotic relationship with nature, there was little the white man could learn from them that would lead to the improvement of his own life. Rather, it was a burden incumbent on the white man to uplift Indigenous peoples through missionary work and teaching.

Despite his condescension, Morris's interest in Canada's First Nations was rooted in a genuine concern for their future and well-being. At Treaty 6, in 1876, he told the negotiators of his early interest in their people, recalling his first foray into public life:

I have come seven hundred miles to see you. Why should I take all this trouble? . . . . [The] reason is a personal one, because since I was a young man my heart was warm to the Indians, and I have taken a great interest in them; for more than twenty-five years I have studied their condition in the present and in the future. I have been many years in public life, but the first words I spoke in public were for the Indians, and in that vision of the day I saw the Queen's white men understanding their duty; I saw them understanding that they had no right to wrap themselves up in a cold mantle of selfishness, that they had no right to turn away and say, "Am I my brother's keeper?" On the contrary, I saw them saying, the Indians are our brothers, we must try to help them to make a living for themselves and their children.[60]

Confronting the issues faced by Canada's Native peoples first-hand would force Morris to reconcile his love of nature and "the Indians" with his profound belief in the necessity of development and territorial expansion. Reconciliation would be found in his desire to see them prosper within the framework of this development by providing them with a means to survive. This would emerge as one reason Morris would advocate so strongly for treaty implementation, to ensure not only that the Indigenous peoples did not hinder development — this is all some government officials were interested in — but that they benefited, reciprocally, from it as well.

Part II

§

Business and Politics

3

Morris's Business Career

Land Speculation

Morris dealt heavily in land speculation, a practice he learned from his father. Throughout his life, the buying and selling of land provided him with a continuing source of income, allowing him to live at a level of comfort unknown to most 19th-century Canadians. Additionally, Morris's land dealings helped him develop a set of shrewd and often aggressive negotiating tactics, skills that he would later apply at the treaty negotiations. Finally, as Morris developed a greater personal acquaintance with the Canadas' impending land shortage, he became acutely aware of the need to find a new source of national wealth and prosperity, and looked increasingly to the agricultural potential of the vast and "empty" North West.[1]

Morris's father had made a handsome profit in land speculation. William Morris's preferred strategy was to buy undeveloped Crown land — referred to as "wild lands" — and sell when the advance of settlement and infrastructure had boosted its value. Such lands were plentiful in the 1820s and '30s in Upper Canada. Renting out "wild lands" could be especially advantageous, as tenant farmers increased the value of land by clearing trees and stones for planting — at no extra cost to William, who remained the lawful owner. By 1851, however, William Morris's health had taken a turn for the worse, and he could no longer manage his affairs. Alexander moved into his father's Montreal home to live with him "during his last few years of suffering."[2] Caring for his father also meant gradually taking over his business affairs. By 1853, Alexander had become an executor of his father's estate, and in 1855 William officially gave his son power of attorney over his affairs.[3]

Alexander Morris was not new to the practice of land speculation. At 21, he had been introduced to the business when his Uncle James sold him 200 acres in Essex County "with all houses, outhouses, woods and waters thereon," for the modest sum of £10.[4] Alexander Morris paid local agents to expand his operations, with each one assigned to a specific collection of townships or counties. They provided advice as to the quality of a given lot and its potential to appreciate or depreciate in value; they kept a record of the tenants living on each plot, collected rents and mortgages, and identified potential buyers and sellers, often negotiating on Morris's behalf or closing the deal themselves.[5] They reported on improvements tenants made to the land, so that the tenant would often have to buy it at a higher price than Morris had originally paid. They also reported on tenants' temperament, circumstances, and willingness to buy at a favourable price.[6] Morris used his agents to enforce his ownership by controlling the ways in which tenants used the land,[7] watching for potential trespassers, and removing squatters.[8] He expected them to go to court when necessary to assert his title.

Asserting clear title to a given plot of land could be rife with costly complications. The histories of title were often complex and difficult to trace. Documentation proving ownership was not always readily available, especially when multiple parties retained an interest in a given lot; copies of deeds were not consistently produced for each interested party. If one party wanted to prove his stake in a given piece of land, he would have to acquire the deed, or search through county records to prove his case. It was not uncommon for disputes to go on for decades. Frequent unwritten understandings or conditions to agreements added to the complicated histories.[9] With hundreds of transactions being made, often on lots that neither father nor son had visited, such "outside promises" were difficult to track or verify.[10]

In a culture ruled by the notions of property rights, the legal wrangling and uncertainty over title made for difficult business. Buyers would not purchase land without knowing the history of its title, and owners risked being sued if they sold a plot without informing or compensating another party that had a partial interest in it. Society at large suffered as uncertainty of ownership retarded development. On a personal as well as practical level, Alexander Morris came to believe in the importance of clarity of title, of the ultimate need for agreements to be mutually understood by all parties, and of the importance of meeting the terms of an agreement. He acted on this principle throughout his career.

The importance of clarity of title and mutually understood terms of agreement could not have been made more clear to Morris than in the execution of his father's estate. When William Morris died in 1858, Alexander, along with one of his father's closest friends, a man named Hugh Allen, was left with the responsibility of dividing the assets equally among the four Morris children. The earth on William's grave had barely settled before his children began bickering over the details of the inheritance. By November of that year, Alexander was soliciting the costly advice of his former Kingston colleague, Oliver Mowat.[11] Alexander's brother-in-law, William Lambe, was unhappy about certain restrictions of access to his wife's share of the inheritance. It seems that William Morris had little faith in his son-in-law, but Alexander's brothers sided with Lambe, and what began as a squabble among siblings turned into a three-year legal battle that was eventually resolved in name only.[12] The action demonstrated Alexander Morris's willingness and capacity to drive a hard bargain, even when it came to family.

Legal disputes aside, William Morris had left his children a handsome inheritance. Evaluating the estate was no small task, and Alexander soon found himself contacting agents throughout the province to collect from his father's debtors and gather estimates on plots of land in order for the inheritance to be evenly divided. In all, each of the four children received money, stocks, and lands valued at £8,822, 11 shillings and 4.5 pence.[13] Morris apportioned to himself more of his father's lands than any of his siblings, including lots that had been used to secure debts. When it came time to collect, William's son had few qualms.

Not all of Alexander Morris's properties proved as lucrative as he might have hoped. By late 1855, the last of Upper Canada's good agricultural Crown lands had been bought up, and speculators like Morris increasingly had difficulty turning a profit. Land that he was able to acquire often turned out to be of limited value and poor accessibility. Morris found that even the lots that had some agricultural value were difficult to sell at a profit, for prospective buyers were interested only in the arable sections of a lot, leaving Morris with the rocky or marshy sections. Much of the land he inherited from his father had been purchased in recent years in and around the frontier regions of Lanark and Renfrew Counties. The land, reported one agent,

> is of very little value. It is nearly all Rock and the most valuable timber all plundered off. . . . There is no Road by which teams can pass within two miles of it and not likely to be better for years to come as the land for that distance around is all about the same quality and unfit for settlement. . . . And I think if the land were sold at one dollar per acre, the Interest of the money would amount to as much or more than the rise of the land for three generations to come.[14]

Morris's home region felt the crunch especially: "These counties were on the edge of the shield and residents of the area had to fight a stubborn and often rocky land in order to make a living."[15]

The significance of the emerging land shortage went beyond the interests of a few speculators. As Douglas Owram explains,

Immigration from Europe and the settlement of the wilderness had been the basis of trade and prosperity. Canada, however, needed not only land but an abundance of it. If it was to attract immigrants from Europe and prevent its own population from emigrating to the United States, it had to be able to offer a surplus of good land at nominal prices.[16]

Morris, then, was acutely aware of the waning potential of the country's frontier, and of the general threat to its economy. By the mid-1850s, a dependence on wheat, the devastating effects of the wheat midge, and the problem of soil exhaustion were already showing their effects in Lower Canada, and the problems appeared to be spreading to Upper Canada. Morris travelled to rural Upper Canada to express to farmers his concern with the Canadas' agricultural trade deficit with the US, and the devastating corollary effect this would visit on the country's fledgling industry. Farmers could do their bit, he urged, by practising crop rotation and diversification, so as to appeal to British markets, and by buying from local industry and manufacturing, as opposed to their often-cheaper counterparts south of the border. "A Home market is not to be despised," he asserted in language that evokes the National Policy of later decades. "Nor harmful to think how systematically we have undervalued ourselves and depreciated our own industry."[17]

The country's agricultural and manufacturing woes presented a threat not only to Morris's own interests, but to his sense of economic nationalism. He lamented the fact that Canada lagged far behind the US in manufacturing, despite his belief in the country's superior natural potential:

> Our country could take a high stand as a Manufacturing country. We have lavish waterpower, we have men of energy and skill, we have aptitude for mechanical pursuits. We have beaten the world in edge tools, but we use them to disfigure our own faces. . . . We go to other markets for boots and shoes . . . and send away hides . . . to be manufactured for us and to help to create a home market for American farmers. . . . Living alongside the Great Union we must feel the influence of this policy and no Canadian can go to the States without being struck with the extent of their Manufactures.[18]

The young country, only now coming of age with the passing of the first stages of settlement, was ready to mature:

> [T]he whole country is with all its interests on the highroad to manhood and feels as all youths must out of their teens do very independent. In that condition then "this Canada" is at present and we have begun to boast a little of our progress. Public sentiment has assumed a healthy tone. We feel

somewhat of the incipient strength of a people and a national sentiment in a feeling of interest in our resources and a desire to advance and turn them to practical account has arisen. It is right to cherish such a feeling. There is no earthborn sentiment more pure and excellent than patriotism.[19]

The future of Canada's agricultural and industrial interests nevertheless remained uncertain. Anxious economic nationalists like Morris would have to look further afield if their country's future was to be secure.

Morris's Legal Career

In many ways, Morris's legal work was an extension of his ongoing experiences in land speculation and business. His education had imparted a belief in the state's ultimate purpose of fostering growth and development. He gave expression to this belief by lobbying for a legal system conducive to commercial enterprise. Shortly after graduating in law from McGill in 1851, and being admitted to the bars of both Canadas, Morris accepted a partnership in the Montreal firm of Frederick William Torrance. He remained with the firm for ten years. Torrance was an old acquaintance of Morris's father. A member of a well-connected Montreal family, he was also one of the city's leading lawyers. The Torrance-Morris partnership was in essence a commercial law firm, which included the two lawyers, a clerk and bookkeeper, and the occasional law student. Its day-to-day business involved the "service or management of a large portfolio of family business enterprises and investments in the Montreal-based forwarding, retail, transportation, and financial sectors."[20] This included providing legal advice and drafting legal agreements for commercial enterprise and land speculation. The firm occasionally engaged in criminal law.

The partnership proved both profitable and ideologically formative for Morris. Torrance was a proponent of the Mercantile Library Association. He also oversaw the establishment of the Fraser Institute, to which he named Morris a member of the Board of Governors. Torrance started the institute as "a centre for political literacy and intellectual leadership. His goal was better imbrication of institutional reform into lay consciousness."[21] Like Morris, Torrance was a "dyed-in-the-wool Presbyterian and Manchester liberal." He was also a confederationist. Torrance campaigned throughout his career for "a fusion of the laws of Upper and Lower Canada" as part of the larger goal of "standardization of social institutions, business practices, and legal culture." Soon, the lawyers gained a reputation "as the foremost exponents of commercial law in Canada, patriarchs of the Montreal bar and business community."[22]

The firm concerned itself with creating a stable environment that would protect businesses from problems of liability and uncertainty of ownership. They sought a system of clear, rigidly codified commercial laws that would allow for a more narrow and thus a more predictable interpretation. A codified system imported from the legal traditions of Upper Canada, they hoped, would supersede Lower Canada's old customary law, which had its origins in the *Coûtume de Paris*. The latter tended to allow for a more flexible interpretation — an inconvenience for business people who preferred operating in an environment in which they could better anticipate legal risks.[23]

Torrance and Morris communicated their message to political colleagues and the public: "The firm influenced that process of state formation and legal change through pamphleteering, law school lecturing, and publishing in legal and other periodicals."[24] The greatest perceived institutional obstacle to a business-friendly legal environment was the old French seigneurial system. From their perspective, the seigneury was an impediment to development and created an "insecurity of title in Canada East."[25]

Morris's time with the firm reinforced his existing convictions, but it also exposed him to different ideas. Torrance and Morris shared an extensive library that included volumes on history, religion, and current events, but primarily legal reference materials that contained a variety of opinions. "[D]eeds and instruments which condence (*sic*) the agreements of men with one another," read one revealing opinion,

> must be construed according to the true intent and meaning of the parties who make them. To find out this intention is often very difficult: for when agreements are committed to writing, all extrinsic evidence of intention is shut out; and words being the only marks of that intention, it happens that sometimes from the imperfection and poverty of language and sometimes from the barbarous and inaccurate application of it much doubt arises with respect to the ideas which the parties decide by the words they employ to express them.[26]

While promoting a rigid, literalist interpretation of land ownership, Morris also came to understand that contractual agreements could not always be constrained to the written word of a legal document. Such flexibility in this regard would prove central to Morris's interpretation of the treaties over a decade later.

4

The Politics of Annexation

Developing the Platform

In 1855, at the age of 29, Alexander Morris contributed an essay, "Canada and Her Resources," to the Paris Exhibition Committee of Canada. The Canadian exhibit — funded by the government at the considerable cost of £10,000 — promoted Canadian industry and resources.[1] Morris's paper was aimed at potential investors. He used descriptive language and favourable statistics to depict Canada as a land of advanced infrastructure, commercial development, social and political sophistication, and unlimited economic potential. The essay won second prize from Governor General Sir Edmund Walker Head, himself an ardent supporter of British American union, and was published for distribution. Jean Friesen described it as a "plodding, descriptive pamphlet" that "predicts a glorious future for this 'fertile British Province.'"[2] But the essay reveals as much about Morris as it does about his subject. It gives a sense of his economic nationalism and his utilitarian view of the natural world, a view that increasingly subsumed Morris's original love of unspoiled nature and his concern for Indigenous peoples. The country's perceived economic successes and future potential validated Morris's sense of patriotism. Finally, Morris used the essay to consolidate his ideological beliefs and build a profile for himself back home in Canada in anticipation of his first run for political office.

Morris's piece was fittingly patriotic. He wrote the essay "to contribute his mite to the advancement of his native country" and dedicated it "to THE PEOPLE OF CANADA."[3] The author framed his patriotism in imperialistic terms. Mindful, perhaps, of lingering doubts with respect to the colony's loyalty, Morris insisted that Canadians were proud British subjects, and that their British heritage ensured the colony's glorious future. Canadians were "destined yet to be a great people," he insisted, "on whom is entailed the rich inheritance of our civilization, our freedom, and our glory." It was the Empire's most important colony — "the brightest jewel of the British Crown."[4] With a view to eliminating the perception that Canada was little more than a rugged frontier society, Morris insisted that the colony was home to as civilized a lifestyle as could be found elsewhere in the Empire. He took particular pride in the active and informed citizenry, which had been formed out of a sound educational system, its public press, and a strong tradition of local self-government.[5]

Morris's pride of country was explicit in his descriptions of the Canadas' natural bounty. But for this aspiring capitalist, commercial development had become increasingly more important than maintaining the natural world. The trees of the Ottawa Valley, for instance, were at once beautiful and ready for exploitation: "a luxuriant growth of red and white pine timber, making the most valuable forests in the world, abundantly intersected with large rivers, fitted to convey the timber to market, when manufactured." Canada's natural products, he assured readers, provided "an almost inexhaustible source of wealth."[6] Morris believed that nature's bounty was a gift from God, given to man that it might be exploited.[7] Indeed, if Morris held a romantic view of the country's natural beauty, he held an equally romantic view of industry's destiny in conquering it.[8] He pointed to the unspoiled lands of "the western portion of Canada West" as the future of an even greater lumber trade. For all his enthusiasm, Morris was still clinging to the hope that the rugged shield country held enough promise to ensure the country's future. His essay did not speculate on the agricultural potential of the vast Hudson's Bay Company territories.

Morris appeared to give little consideration to the colony's original inhabitants. He did inform his readers about a treaty with the Saugeen of Huron County in western Upper Canada, but explained it in terms of extinguishing Aboriginal title for the purpose of opening the land to settlement.[9] To Morris, the treaty seems to have represented little more than a profitable land transaction, merely an extension of the larger legal policy of guaranteeing security of ownership. At the very least, he recognized that the extinguishment of Aboriginal title was sometimes a necessary precursor to settlement.

Morris believed that the first responsibility of the state was to provide a stable environment conducive to commercial development. He promised potential investors that the colonial government was "patriotic and attentive to the commercial and industrial interests."[10] Commercial development could not proceed without a proper transportation infrastructure, and Morris took pride in describing the country's network of railways and navigable waterways, envisioning the development of a massive extension of the Ottawa Valley line to the Pacific Ocean. It would open access to more mining and timber resources, and make Canada Britain's stepping stone to trade with the Orient and the American Midwest.[11]

The essay contains Morris's first official endorsement of British North American union:

> It would be very desirable that free trade in its fullest extent should be established between [the colonies], as the more their interests are assimilated, and a congeniality of feeling created, the more advantages will their intercourse prove to the whole of these important colonies, whose eventual union is beyond doubt desirable, and in fact is only a matter of time.[12]

Morris's belief in the idea was borne of economic ideology. He argued that the economic strengths of one province would compensate for the weaknesses of another, and, like other union-minded Tories of the first half of the 19th century, he believed that the creation of a larger political entity would help Canada extend its credit and capacity for taxation, and alleviate its substantial debt. This would, in turn, help finance public works, like the railway, and economic development in general. A greater British North America would also provide a meaningful counterweight to American power on the continent, and offer an object worthy of political pursuit for aspiring young Canadian men of standing, including the 29-year-old Morris himself.[13] From childhood, Morris had been enamoured with visions of empire, and he now saw an opportunity for building a mighty arm of that empire in North America.

Inspired by the success of his essay, and emboldened by his prominence as a lawyer, Morris made his first formal bid for political office that same year. Family, friends, and colleagues had already made the transition into politics, and so the move was a natural progression in the career of a young man of Morris's circumstances and background. But it was also a sign of his rising personal ambitions and his sense of self-importance. Morris opted to run in Renfrew County, next to Lanark County "of which my father . . . was for twenty four years the faithful representative."[14]

The aspiring politician ran on a platform of commercial development that corresponded to his economic nationalism and personal interests. He presented himself to electors "as one whose sympathies and interests are identified with your own," declaring that he possessed, "as do also several of my relatives, a considerable property" in Renfrew to assert that his own financial well-being depended on the prosperity of the county. He reminded voters that he was a native of Lanark County, but beyond riches and family standing, he wished to be perceived as a patriot, and he equated that patriotism with the pursuit of economic development:

A Canadian by birth and sentiment, I shall, whether in a private or the public capacity to which I aspire, ever consider the advancement of my country in all her interests, as a matter of the highest importance, demanding the earnest co-operation of all true patriots. I shall therefore be found steadily and independently supporting all such measures [that] conduce to the development of the resources, the extension of the industry, the growth of the trade and the promotion of the general prosperity of my native country.

Morris's electoral platform repeated many of the calls for economic development he had made in his prize-winning essay. The Ottawa territory, especially, he argued, was "deserving of greater attention than [it has] yet enjoyed." He promised voters that, as a member of the Legislature, he would lobby to develop the dreamed-of Ottawa route to the American Midwest to promote trade and settlement. Speaking to his own land interests, Morris called for "a further extension of the free grant system . . . and the gradual survey of the great tract lying between this County and Lake Huron."[15]

When Morris lost his first bid for political office it was a great disappointment, both for him and his politically successful family. Years spent learning the legal trade in Kingston and Montreal had left him out of touch with the local electorate. A few years later, Morris declined a second opportunity to run, ostensibly because of "family affairs."[16] Still smarting from his previous defeat, he was perhaps avoiding what might have been another humiliation. "It is a pity you had not been able to visit Renfrew this winter," wrote political supporter David Campbell in March 1857. "Our prospects are *apparently* not so favourable."[17] But Morris was not completely deterred. He continued to build a political profile and preach his ideology at clubs and on the lecture circuit. When he campaigned, it was on the issue of annexing the North West.

The movement to annex the North West had been a minor one until 1856, when discoveries of the region's fertility became public. Practically overnight, it seemed, the country's agricultural woes appeared to have been solved. For Morris, the revelation was significant, for it served both his business interests and his economic nationalism. By the late 1850s, he was one of a small but influential group "who continually spoke or wrote of the potential of the West and of the crucial need for Canadian expansion." The group, explains Douglas Owram, "were very quickly able to effect a profound shift in public and official opinion."[18]

For some, the annexation of the North West appealed to their patriotic zeal and ideological beliefs, and their desire to secure Canada's political future. Chief among them was George Brown, future Father of Confederation and editor of the popular Toronto *Globe*. "A distrust of the monopolistic Hudson's Bay Company and a fervent enthusiasm for the spread of British institutions gave the movement a particular appeal to Brown," Owram explains. More importantly, perhaps, adding a North Western appendage to Ontario would "ensure the dominance of English Canada and the Reform party."[19] Another prominent advocate was Philip M. Vankoughnet, a relative of Morris and President of the Executive Council and a future Commissioner of Crown Lands. Vankoughnet helped ensure that "the Liberal-Conservatives of John A. Macdonald accepted the idea of expansion, albeit more cautiously."[20] Many of these men had vested economic interests. Allan Macdonell, "the most committed of all these early expansionists," had applied repeatedly to the Canadian Legislature for a Pacific railway charter, without success. Macdonell went on to form the North West Transportation, Navigation and Railway Company, "the first substantial commercial attempt to reopen trade with the region."[21] The Brown family was also involved in the company.

Morris consolidated his place in the movement for North West annexation and British North American confederation with two successful public lectures given in the late 1850s. The first, entitled, "Nova Britannia; or, British North America, Its Extent and Future," he delivered in the familiar setting of the Mercantile Library Association of Montreal, "as part of its special course, on the 18th of March, 1858."[22] He made an impassioned case for uniting the colonies, and concluded with an argument for the annexation of the North West. His audience was so impressed by the speech that they moved for its publication. Within ten days, some 3,000 copies had been sold. Morris delivered another lecture later that year, entitled, "The Hudson's Bay and Pacific Territories," that focussed on the vast resource potential of the North West and called for its prompt annexation. It, too, met with a warm reception, and was published. What becomes apparent in the intensity of Morris's language in the lectures is that his desire to see a united British North America annex the North West originated in a personal need to see his national vision completed. "Surely it is a noble destiny that is before us," he told his audience, "and who, as he reflects upon all these things, does not feel an honest pride as he thinks that he too may, in however humble a sphere, or by however feeble an effort, aid in urging on that great destiny?"[23] Taking part in this grand scheme provided a means to validate his patriotism and, among other things, lay to rest his nascent inferiority complex regarding the United States. The treaties he later negotiated with the First Nations of the North West would come to occupy an important place in the fulfilment of Morris's dream.

Whereas the somewhat defensive "Canada and Her Resources" had been an attempt to counter pessimism over the country's economic potential, Morris's new lectures seized on the optimism stemming from the discoveries in the North West. He described British North American union as a great patriotic project that would ensure the colonies' survival from absorption by their southern neighbour, and secure for Canada a prominent place in the Empire "and amid the ranks of nations."[24] In language that foreshadowed the high imperialism of the 1880s,

Morris saw Nova Britannia as one of the pillars of the Empire, the "built up great colonies" or "New Britains in all parts of the habitable globe" that were "destined eventually to be great kindred nations, bound together by the ties of origin and by parental and filial affection."

Morris's lecture was consistent with other patriotic speeches of the day. "Long before the surge of imperialism in the late nineteenth century," writes Carl Berger, "British North Americans had looked upon the Empire as the vehicle and embodiment of a progressive civilization which was designated by Providence to spread its culture, religion, and political institutions across the face of the earth."[25]

In great detail and with an array of statistics, Morris catalogued the colonies' collective economic potential, and asserted that the population would find unity in a common British character and nationality. He foresaw a fusion of races: "Inheriting, as we do, all the characteristics of the British people, combining therewith the chivalrous feeling and impulsiveness of France, and fusing other nationalities which mingle here with these, into one, as I trust, harmonious whole."[26] Having inherited the principles, national characteristics, institutions, rights, and liberties of the mother country — including, especially, the principle of self-government — a united British North America was destined by Providence to be a great country. With its vast territorial and resource potential, Nova Britannia would be an empire unto itself.[27]

At the heart of building "the Great Britannic Empire of the North"[28] was the annexation of the North West. Canada needed the territory, he said, lest the country continue to lose settlers and immigration to the United States or, worse, lose the entire territory to American expansion. He painted a generous picture of the North West.

> The great valley of the Saskatchewan should form the subject of immediate attention. . . . there is a vast region well adapted for becoming the residence of a large population. Once the Red River settlement is opened to our commerce, a wide field extends before our enterprise; and those who recollect or have otherwise become familiar with the struggles, forty years ago, of the settlers in Western Canada [Ontario], and the painful, toilsome warfare with which they conquered that rising portion of the Province from the wilderness, will regard the task of colonization as a comparatively light one.[29]

For a seasoned speculator like Morris, the prospect of buying up land that was completely cultivable and thus 100 per cent saleable must have been enticing. He recounted in romantic language the caravanesque voyage of George Simpson's 1841 expedition to Fort Edmonton, describing the lush prairie, meadows, and

An Intellectual & Political Biography of Alexander Morris   43

forests, likening it to an endless English countryside.[30] He seized on the findings of the Hind and Mackenzie expeditions as proof "not only [of] its adaptation for settlement, but that it is adapted to take the highest rank as a grazing-country."[31] It was merely a matter of providing settlers with a means of moving in:

> Introduce the European or the Canadian element into the settlement, and in a very few years the beautiful prairies of the Red River and the Assiniboine would be white with flocks and herds, and a large and flourishing centre of civilization, liberty, and progress planted, and another link . . . in British territory between the Atlantic and the Pacific.'"[32]

He repeated in even stronger terms his conviction that a Pacific railway would make Canada the link or throughway of the Empire, connecting Britain with India, Australia, New Zealand, and, most importantly, China. The new country, he boasted, would be "an English Russia":

> with free institutions, with high civilization, and entire freedom of speech and thought — with its face to the south and its back to the pole, with its right and left resting on the Atlantic and the Pacific, and with the telegraph and the iron road connecting the two oceans! . . . . [S]uch is the vision which is present to us, and to many others "to the manner born," whose all and whose destiny is here. . . . Let us each and all, then, do our part in our respective spheres, however humble they may be, toward the accomplishment of so noble an enterprise. . . .[33]

The Chinese trade would make Canada rich, to the point of eclipsing the United States: "Thus, British America, from a mere colonial dependency, would assume a controlling rank in the world. To her other nations would be tributary; and in vain would the United States attempt to be her rival. . . ."[34] The North West was the solution to all the Canadas' economic woes. It was also the means of his own ideological, patriotic, and financial salvation.

Morris attempted to rationalize the annexation in religious and moral terms. Canada's motivation for annexing the North West should not be "a mere grasping thirst of territorial aggrandizement, but a large-spirited and comprehensive appreciation of the requirements of the country, and a proper sense of the responsibilities to be assumed in regard to the well-being of the native and other inhabitants, and the due development of the resources of the territory." The moral argument conveniently extended to the interests of the Canadian Province: "To a large portion of the territory we have an indubitable legal claim; . . . all that is adapted for settlement should be placed under the jurisdiction of representative government."[35] It was the duty of the country to take what God had provided, he argued: the Hudson's Bay Territories were to Canadians what Canaan had been to the Israelites.[36] Moreover, it was Canada's duty to help spread British civilization and liberty throughout the world:

> Surely it is plain to the most superficial observer that there is an overruling purpose in all this. Surely these English-speaking nations have a mission to discharge to the human race. . . . [T]his British race, with its energy and intelligence, its political liberty, its freedom of speech and of conscience, and its earnest religious character, is fast disseminating itself throughout the habitable globe.[37]

Morris claimed to be upholding the rights and considerations of the people who already lived in the country. The Red River colony, he asserted, was "a petitioner at the portals of our Legislature for admission to those inherent rights of free self-government which every Briton inherits as a birthright."[38]

The greatest barrier to the spread of civilization, he maintained, was the Hudson's Bay Company. Seizing on recent discontent in Red River, Morris accused the company of trying to hide the region's potential so as to maintain its trade monopoly, which he characterized as "wholly indefensible," as it stifled trade and forced it "out of its natural channels."[39] He dismissed the Company's Charter of 1670 as a "relic of antiquity" full of "all sorts of right lawyerly phrases," and asserted that Canada had a superior legal claim to the territory by way of the historic French presence in the North West.[40] At the very least, title to the land was confused: "The words of the grant are vague and indefinite in the extreme."[41]

Morris also appears to have made a passing reference to the unextinguished Aboriginal title: the company's "right of exclusive trade with the Indians over what is known as the 'Indian Territories' . . . is not disputed, and is at present held under . . . [an] Act of Parliament. . . . This license expires during the present year."[42] Some fifteen years later, Morris came to recognize that both the Aboriginal peoples and the Hudson's Bay Company had a claim to the land, and that each would have to be settled if Canada's tenuous legal claim was to be placed on a more certain footing.

Legal arguments aside, Morris believed that it was simply unjust that the interests of a commercial company should take precedence over the interests of the empire, the colonies, and countless future settlers. "Should such a 'Paradise of fertility' as this remain longer locked up?" he asked. "Will the gathering of a few peltries compensate for the withdrawal of such a region from the industry of our race? Assuredly not."[43]

Morris accused the Hudson's Bay Company of being fixated on "its own aggrandizement, as companies generally are," and went so far as to suggest that it be dissolved. Once "the tenacious grasp of the huge *main mort* of the Hudson's

Bay Company is relaxed," he declared, "so will these fair Territories stand before us and present to the attention of the human family vast expanses of rich arable country — goodly habitations for the residence of civilized man."[44]

Morris's lectures contained passing references to the original inhabitants of the territory, but they were clearly an afterthought. His first public lecture a decade earlier had been on "the North American Indian," but now he seemed to be describing a land that was virtually empty, "lying idle, and unoccupied to any extent by civilized life."[45] The presence and economic activities of the First Nations were deemed insignificant; they were part of the natural scenery, he seemed to suggest, and the Hudson's Bay Company's relationship with many of them was exploitative and unjust.[46] He recognized that removing the Company would create a politically ambiguous situation for the Aboriginal population, but argued for it nonetheless:

> The rights and the position of the Indians are to be thought of and protect-
> ed. Still, the fact is obvious and indisputable, that the power of the com-
> pany, if it continue to exist, must be restrained, and subjected to colonial
> control; and that, moreover, the rights of colonization and trade, at least in
> all the habitable territories, must be free and unfettered.[47]

Aboriginal rights were an afterthought, a caveat to the larger interests of Euro-Canadians. Implicit in Morris's argument was the notion that the rights and concerns of the majority should take precedence over those of the Hudson's Bay Company and the territory's nomadic, "uncivilized" population, and the assumption that First Nations bands would be moved to less favourable territories to continue their hunting and trapping.

In Office, 1861-1872

Morris's reputation as a booster for confederation and territorial expansion served him well. In 1861, he made another bid for political office, and won as a Liberal-Conservative in his father's old riding of Lanark South. He campaigned as a fiscal conservative, and promised to challenge the government's corrupt and extravagant spending. He urged his electorate not to push for the dissolution of the Province of Canada, but rather pledged to lobby for some form of representation by population — which would have favoured the larger Canada West — and to make Ottawa the capital of the United Canadas.[48]

Morris's political career in the 1860s saw him drop some of his early radicalism in favour of a less partisan pragmatism, but the goals of confederation and North West annexation remained close to his heart. His first speech to the Assembly, in March 1862, addressed the divisive question of representation-by-population. Morris confessed that his views had softened somewhat on the issue since he took his seat in the House and had witnessed first-hand the bitter divisions that persisted on this and other issues. He had been especially impressed by the non-partisan, pragmatic approach taken by one Lewis Thomas Drummond — a *Rouge* from Canada East who had defended the rebels of 1838 and later allied with LaFontaine[49] — to help settle the issue of seigneurial tenure. Morris called for a similarly non-partisan approach to address the "rep-by-pop" issue.[50] He suggested that the answer lay in his old source of inspiration — Confederation — which, he insisted, "'would give to the people of each Province the right to manage their own internal affairs, while at the same time managing in common matters of common concern so as to secure the consolidation of the Britannic power on this continent.'"[51]

During this early period in his political career, Morris took inspiration from other pragmatic political figures of differing backgrounds, such as the Irish Catholic and one-time-Fenian-turned-confederationist, Thomas D'Arcy McGee. McGee commended Morris's "Nova Britannia" lecture, and the two became fast friends, even spending their free time rowing down the Ottawa River together. Morris was one of the last people to see McGee alive: on the day of his assassination, April 7, 1868, when "poor D'Arcy was shot to death by one of the Fenians, for he had denounced their visionary and wicked schemes."[52]

As his views moderated, Morris quickly developed a reputation as a broker politician, contributing indirectly to the achievement of Confederation. His best-known act of political compromise came in June 1864, during the height of political instability in the Canadian Assembly. The Macdonald-Taché administration, having come to office only a few weeks earlier, was facing defeat at the hands of a group of Reformers led by Macdonald's bitter rival, George Brown. Morris, friends with both Macdonald and Brown, along with J. H. Pope, another Liberal-Conservative member, helped broker discussions between the rivals, ultimately leading to the so-called "Great Coalition" that advocated and achieved Confederation. Over the course of the next few years, he quietly urged Macdonald to maintain the coalition "in order that the cause of Confederation could be more rapidly advanced."[53] He also came to view the "alliance that so long existed between the Conservatives and French" as being in "the best interests of the Dominion."[54] Morris's time in Ottawa had exposed him to the diverse groups that made up Canada's political community, allowing him to meet and interact with Catholic French Canadians and Reformers alike, and his views toward all of them had softened accordingly.

Morris made his own contribution to the Confederation debates in February 1865. He argued that the goals of Confederation and North West annexation were inextricably linked by the larger objective of creating a country strong enough to resist absorption into the United States. "We have either to rise into strength and wealth and power by means of this union, under the sheltering protection of Britain," he told his fellow members, "or we must be absorbed by the great power beside us."[55] It was, above all, a matter of pride: "We will have the pride to belong to a great country still attached to the Crown of Great Britain, but in which, notwithstanding, we shall have entire freedom of action and the blessings of responsible self-government."[56]

After Confederation, Morris continued to lobby for the annexation of the North West. By the late 1860s, it had defined his political platform, and he was studying every scrap of information on the territory that he could find. In December 1867, he vigorously defended Public Works Minister William McDougall's resolutions calling for "the acquisition of the North West Territories by the Dominion." He elaborated on the country's historical claim, taking inspiration from the French and Jesuit missionaries who had already made the "fertile belt" their home: "The country is ours by right of inheritance," it was "our manifest destiny."[57]

Morris acknowledged the issue of Aboriginal claims to the territory, but seemed to assume that this title would be extinguished with relative ease, as it had in the old Upper Canadian treaties. For the moment, he was more interested in discussing the immediate steps he would take to promote the region's development, such as the creation of a rail and steam transportation route connecting it with Canada, and an immediate land survey to begin divvying up the territory. As for the Hudson's Bay Company, he declared that what little rights the company might have should be promptly bought out.

Two years later, during the Red River Resistance of 1869-70, Morris took greater notice of the question of Aboriginal rights, telling electors that "these obstructions would pass away before a firm and conciliatory course, and a thorough respect for the rights of the present inhabitants of the Red River country, who would come to see that their interests and ours were one and identical," adding that "a wise and kind policy would be pursued towards the Indian population of the North West. We in Canada could place in proud contrast to the conduct of the American people our dealings with the Indian race during the last fifty years."[58] Contrasting American and Canadian policies would become a favourite tactic.

As early as 1867, Morris began to take a more direct personal role in the region's future. He would "throw open the fertile glades and prairies of the fertile belt, and give actual settlers free grants of land," he told the House of Commons. He would "organize a local government there, and give the people the benefit of a constitutional authority, and so aid them in the great work of colonizing that fertile region."[59] To his dismay, the appointment of Lieutenant-Governor of the North West Territories went to William McDougall, but Morris got what he considered a just reward for his services when Macdonald appointed him Minister of Inland Revenue in late 1869, a post he would occupy for two years.

5

"Retirement" in the North West

THOUGH NOT YET TAKING A DIRECT HAND in the administration of the North West, Alexander Morris certainly had a finger in its budding land speculation. His land and business interests had been quietly expanding since the late 1850s, and his holdings now included a handsome fortune in mining, forestry, and transportation interests in Ontario.[1] He was a shrewd and sometimes unforgiving businessman. Joint ventures with family and friends that turned out to be especially lucrative often resulted in disputes over ownership and percentages, and Morris did not shy away from pressing his case, even against those closest to him.[2]

When the Canadian government bought out the Hudson's Bay Company in 1869, and subsequently annexed the territories and created the province of Manitoba, it was only a matter of time before Morris began buying up lots in the region. His political responsibilities in Ottawa, meanwhile, had begun to take their toll on his health, and he began exploring options for early retirement. A move to Manitoba appealed to him on various grounds. The open air and natural setting could serve his ailing health, but even more, it would put him in close proximity to his commercial interests. Most significantly, however, the move appealed to his dream of witnessing the realization of the region's development.

"If I must retire," he wrote Macdonald in May 1871, "I would like you to send me to Manitoba as Judge. The work would be light & though an exile, the country has a future & I could be of use."[3] The Prime Minister eventually granted Morris's request, and in mid-1872 he and his family moved to Manitoba to begin what could hardly be described as "retirement."[4]

By all accounts, Morris fulfilled his responsibilities as Chief Justice of Manitoba's Court of Queen's Bench competently. He soon found that he would have to strike a balance between the oft-feuding segments of the population, including the French and English Métis, the old settler population, and the growing number of recent arrivals from Ontario. As Jean Friesen explains, "Morris's goal

ALEXANDER MORRIS IN OTTAWA, APRIL 1871. *Ill and overworked, Morris had begun to contemplate early retirement, and the North West seemed a good place to settle down to a quiet life and further land speculation* (Library and Archives Canada, PA-026335).

was to see a peaceful, stable Manitoba based largely on the Ontario model, with an acquiescent and cooperative French population." As Chief Justice, Morris wrote that he "quietly enforced . . . English practice & English law . . . and have carried with me the French Bar." During his first year in the province, Morris pushed "for a speedy settlement of Métis land claims to divert support from Riel . . . and to provide assistance for the substantial number of Métis he expected would desert Riel for the leadership of the more moderate Pascal Breland," a respected trader and property owner.[5]

In December 1872, Macdonald appointed Morris Lieutenant-Governor of Manitoba and the North West Territories. The new role would require an even more delicate diplomacy, as Macdonald warned him:

> I hope that long ere this reaches you your Commission will have arrived, that you will have been sworn in, and that the Ship of State under your skilful guidance will be making great progress. You are strong enough now [to show] rather a stiff upper lip to Bishop Taché and to . . . Mr. Riel. You have got the law abiding and orderly people all in your favour, both French and English, and you have 300 good men at your back. You are therefore quite at liberty to steer an independent course, though of course you will have to use more than your usual amount of *suaviter* in keeping the discordant elements from quarrelling.[6]

Morris's many responsibilities and achievements in this capacity have been documented by Lila Staples, R. G. Babion, and Jean Friesen. As Lieutenant-Governor, Morris was "responsible for the administration of federal moneys . . . crown lands, and customs," and he also initially "served in a private capacity as Macdonald's own representative."[7] He facilitated the work of an often fractious and inexperienced provincial legislature and cabinet, and sat as head of the Executive Council of the North West Territories. As he became more sympathetic to local concerns and interests of Manitoba, and as the provincial government gained in experience, Morris advocated for increased provincial responsibility. This corresponded with his belief that local self-government was an inherent right of all British subjects.

With much tact he also managed to broker the formation of a single university, the University of Manitoba, with the principle Catholic, Anglican, and Presbyterian Churches, thus avoiding the religious divisions that had encumbered Ontario's university formation experience. This was an indication that Morris's religious conservatism had softened somewhat by way of his earlier political interactions and his new experiences in a small Red River community that could ill afford bitter religious division.

Morris's "brilliant wife and most attractive daughters," living with him at Government House in Fort Garry, played their part to provide the diverse peoples of

Manitoba with "a delightful neutral ground," in which "the harshness and bitterness of political and religious differences" could be "sensibly assuaged." Alexander and Margaret taught their children to respect the poor as well as the wealthy, Indians and Métis as well as whites:

> The poor Indian was always received with a smile," wrote one observer, "and the suffering Half-breed with kindness. They listened with patience to the tales of distress, which were not few, and . . . taught each race and every religion that there existed at least one place in Manitoba where they were all welcome, at all times, and under all circumstances.[8]

The situation Morris inherited in Manitoba was nothing short of volatile, especially with regard to the land question. Tensions between French-speaking Catholic Métis and the recently arrived anglophone Orangists from Ontario had only intensified after the Red River Rebellion of 1869-1870. The Ontarians pressed claims for property damages and wrongful imprisonment allegedly suffered during the rebellion. The Métis were increasingly anxious over the rhetoric of the Orangists and the flood of new arrivals in general, and wanted the lands promised them under the 1870 *Manitoba Act* to be promptly delivered. Many Métis lots, despite being long established, "were rejected out of hand because of insufficient cultivation."[9] The federal government refused to recognize some Métis altogether, because they had failed to register as citizens in the 1871 census. The land rights of Métis who had settled farther afield in the North West Territories remained ambiguous. They maintained that Morris's predecessor, Adams Archibald, had promised them compensation for having ended the old hay privilege — the cutting of hay on the commons, which was now occupied by settlers.[10]

On balance, Morris proved sympathetic to Métis concerns. He believed they had a prior claim to the land, especially to those lots they had occupied as earlier inhabitants of the region. He was driven by practical considerations as well. He lobbied Ottawa to grant land to the Métis to head off support for Louis Riel — who was gathering support in Manitoba for a federal by-election — and prevent another outbreak. Morris recommended that each family be given 140 acres, and that the federal government "disallow any act passed by the Manitoba legislature regarding the sale or seizure of Aboriginal lands to whites," so as to prevent speculators from cheating the Métis out of their land.[11]

Ottawa delayed its decision on the hay privilege and land grant questions, but Morris had land set aside for the Métis in any case, pending the government's decision. He "recommended that the Canadian government intervene and offer an even more flexible package to the Métis in way of compensation."[12] He tried to buy time in Manitoba, meanwhile, by restricting the sale of lands earmarked for the Métis. Despite his efforts, the government officially announced in July that

"Métis farmers would no longer have the right to cut hay on areas recently settled by whites, in spite of the fact that they had done this for years."[13] They would be offered no compensation. The federal government also continued to refuse to recognize the land claims of Métis who had failed to register in the 1871 census, having concluded "that the Métis had already received more land than they were entitled to receive as a result of the census."[14] Morris "reminded Ottawa that the *Manitoba Act* guaranteed the Métis right to [a portion of the] land," and that, if not fully recognized, more unrest might ensue. Lacking any other apparent solution, Morris suggested that the government offer the Métis scrip — certificates that could be redeemed for cash or land — instead of providing land directly.[15] The scheme that was eventually devised was woefully inadequate. As scrip could be exchanged for Crown lands or money, most Métis opted for the latter, many preferring to settle farther west in Saskatchewan country. Other scrip was bought off cheaply by speculators. As Olive Dickason explains, "ninety per cent of the land ended up in the hands of persons other than Métis."[16]

While using his office to advocate on behalf of Métis land concerns, Morris nonetheless took advantage of the Métis "sell-off" to further his own interests. By early 1873, he had gained a reputation as one of the busier land speculators in

GOVERNMENT HOUSE, UPPER FORT GARRY, CA. 1876. *Morris frequently met with visiting First Nations representatives in the circular court in front of the residence* (Library and Archives Canada, C-007620).

Winnipeg. As he had in Ontario, Morris employed agents to identify potential buyers and sellers, and to manage his holdings. By January 1873 he had acquired no fewer than ninety-two lots in the city, valued collectively at $26,000. Among his interests were ten Métis river lots. In early 1873, as Lieutenant-Governor, he withheld his assent from the *Half-Breed and Grant Protection Act*. As R. G. Babion explains, speculators had "bought lands from Half-Breeds at low prices. The bill was designed to cancel all these sales and to give the vendor an action to recover the price."[17] In many things, Morris was sympathetic to Métis concerns, but only insofar as they did not conflict with his personal interests.

Morris cast his glance on the lands he believed would best appreciate in commercial, as well as agricultural, value. In late 1872, he attempted to purchase the south-western corner of the junction of the Assiniboine and Red Rivers, which lay directly opposite the entrance of the strategic Upper Fort Garry. The attempt failed, but around the same time he acquired the south-western corner of what would become the busy Portage and Main intersection, and set about constructing a series of buildings. Rents on the land and its buildings alone would net him $5,500 a year. The lot was the subject of some controversy, however, as the old Council of Assiniboia had reserved in its minutes the right to a section to widen the road for the public good — land on which Morris's new buildings now stood. Morris pressed his own interests against those of the public, arguing that the old Council's jurisdiction and minutes were *ultra vires*, beyond the power of the council to decide. The legal wrangling endured into the 1880s.

Morris made his mark as Lieutenant-Governor in the local politics, land speculation, and Métis-settler relations of Manitoba, but his most significant role as Lieutenant-Governor — and in Canadian history — came in Indian Affairs and treaty negotiation.

Part III

§

The Negotiator

6

An Overview of the Numbered Treaties

By the time of his "retirement" to the North West in 1872, Morris's fixation on the economic potential of the region had eclipsed his earlier concern for its original inhabitants. The new atmosphere of optimism seemed to validate, at long last, his life-long economic nationalism, and his legal and political career had put him in contact with the visionaries and nation-builders of the day, fuelling his own dreams of national glory. Actually moving into the territory, however, forced him to rethink his positions and eventually reconcile his nationalism with the plight of the First Nations. During his time in the North West, the "Indian question" became more and more present in his mind. The goal of building a transcontinental empire, easily conjured up in distant Perth, Montreal, or Ottawa, lost some of its immediacy. The realities of the First Nations' plight could no longer be dismissed or ignored. As Morris invested more personal time and energy in the treaty-making process, he gained a personal stake in the treaties themselves and in their long-term outcome. They took on a huge significance for Morris, and he became increasingly disillusioned with Ottawa as he realized that his colleagues and superiors were not of the same mind.

Morris's early interest in the First Nations of the North West provided him with a starting point for sympathizing with the ones he encountered. He paid close attention to the language of their conversation, especially in negotiations, and often appropriated their symbolism and imagery in his attempts to reach an understanding. Developing a genuine concern for their situation and circumstances, his sympathy turned to empathy. His goal of seeing the territory settled and its resources developed remained ever-present, but he recognized the threat this posed to the future of the Native people. By the end of his tenure, he had come to admire them in many ways, and he sincerely hoped they would survive as distinct, self-sustaining communities.

To reconcile his goal of territorial development with Aboriginal survival, Morris attempted to integrate the Indigenous peoples into the process of development, to make them co-beneficiaries with the settlers who were sure to enter their ancestral territories. The treaties were central to this strategy. Morris came to the North West with a view of the treaties as another necessary step in legitimizing Canada's territorial expansion; by the end of his tenure, he had come to realize that they entailed much more than a mere land transaction. While extinguishment of title remained a principle goal of the treaties, Morris came to view them as the basis for a positive, reciprocal relationship between the Crown and the First Nations of the North West.

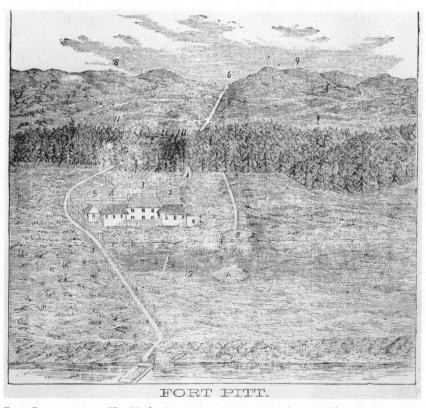

FORT PITT.

FORT PITT, CA. 1876. *This Hudson's Bay Company post was the second location for Treaty 6 negotiations, after Fort Carlton. It was here that the influential Cree Chief Sweetgrass, among others, signed the treaty.* "This sketch of Fort Pitt by Cst. Smith appeared in the special Rebellion number of the *Winnipeg Daily Sun*, undated" (HBCA 1987/363-F-90/10).

7

The First Nations and the Treaties

History and Precedents

Morris was to play a central role in the making of the numbered treaties, but treaty making itself was nothing new to the First Nations of the North West. The principle of establishing relationships of friendship and reciprocity with outsiders had long been an integral element of the Cree and Ojibwa value systems. As one treaty elder explained, "it was decided long before the white man arrived that the First Nations would treat the newcomers as relatives, as brothers and sisters. The First Nations had decided that they would live in peace and that they would share the land with these newcomers."[1] Historian Stephen Sliwa makes the case that the fluid membership and flexibility of Cree communities "allowed for the formation of close relationships, not only among the multi-band organization within their own nation but also with other Aboriginal plains nations, European fur traders and, later, the Métis." Indeed, "the reciprocal responsibilities and obligations associated with being considered 'kin' were far from symbolic."[2] The Cree and Ojibwa of present-day Western Canada had developed their own traditions of alliance and treaty generations before the numbered treaties:

> For generations, diplomacy was a means through which the Plains Cree sought to capitalize on opportunities and to cope with change. . . . prior to 1870, the Cree had established close relations with a number of Aborigi-

nal plains nations — first with the Blackfoot during the late seventeenth century and later with the Mandan and Assiniboine peoples — as a means of achieving a defined group of self-interest. Consequently, an alliance with "the Great Queen Mother" was a continuation of this practice and represented to the Aboriginal inhabitants of the parklands a wealth of opportunity.[3]

In his study of the Plains Cree, J. S. Milloy notes that the Cree, Ojibwa, and Assiniboine were being referred to as "the allied tribes" in the mid-1800s.[4] Historically, the three nations had been allied against a common foe, the Sioux.[5] In the years leading up to the numbered treaties, they once again found common interest as they shifted westward toward Blackfoot territory[6] where the diminishing buffalo remained in significant numbers.[7] Aboriginal negotiating teams were not without internal and inter-tribal divisions, but their common diplomatic practices and principles and their history of alliance building made it possible for them to negotiate in some cases under a single treaty an agreement with the Crown. This shared diplomatic tradition accounts for the similarities between the negotiating processes of Treaties 3 - 6, in which Morris was involved.

Centuries earlier, the Indigenous tradition of building relationships of reciprocity played a prominent role in ongoing diplomatic interactions and agreements conducted with European newcomers, specifically, the Hudson's Bay Company.[8] The Company conformed early on to Aboriginal diplomatic precedent in the North West. In 1680, for instance, Company officials in London instructed their James Bay Governor to "endeavour to make such contracts with the Indians in all places where you settle as may in future times ascertain to us all liberty of trade & commerce and a league of friendship & peaceable cohabitation."[9] Over time, it became commonplace for trading sessions to open with elaborate pomp and ceremony. First, the Indians would designate a leader to receive a suit of clothing from company officials — given to recognize his authority. Such displays of friendship and mutual respect always closed with the symbolic exchange of gifts and smoking of the pipe, a sign of friendship and thanks to the Creator.[10] Carried over to the treaty making of the 19th century, the "pipe-stem" or "medicine pipe" ceremony was considered sacred by the Aboriginal peoples:

For Aboriginal people, only truth could be spoken by all taking part in this ceremony . . . for the First Nations, everything that was said once the pipe was smoked would be considered part of the agreement. Once the pipe had been smoked, a spirit of trust and friendship was established, and as a result it was the "spirit and intent" of all the discussions that constituted the agreement, not just the signed document.[11]

The spoken exchange and the negotiations as a whole were considered part of the agreement, in addition to what had been written down.

The Aboriginal diplomatic tradition carried over into the formalized treaty-making process with the Crown. Laura Peers explains the Ojibwa understanding of making alliances in terms of the 1817 treaty with the Selkirk settlers of the Red River:

> [Ojibwa Chief] Peguis was conforming to traditional Native ideas about alliances, which were based on the metaphor of kinship and involved reciprocal aid, including military aid. Thus, the Ojibwa readily offered assistance to the settlers in the full expectation that they would themselves receive aid from the Europeans some day. . . . [Colony administrator] Alexander Ross recalled that . . . receiving aid from the Indians "tended to foster kind and generous feelings between the two races."[12]

The Ojibwa came to expect military assistance in the event of attacks from the Sioux, while the settlers were convinced the Ojibwa would aid them against the Yankees. Ojibwa peoples later negotiated the Robinson Treaties and the Mani-

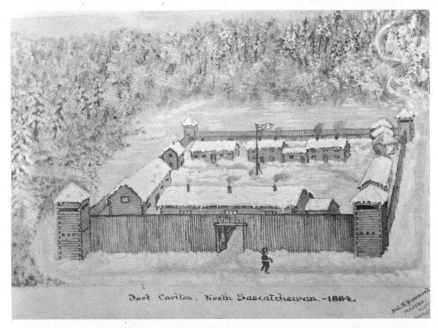

FORT CARLTON, 1884. *The bulk of Treaty 6 negotiations took place near this Hudson's Bay Company post.* "Fort Carlton, North Saskatchewan – 1884. Photograph of a sketch of Fort Carlton by H. B. Hammond, who was stationed there in 1884-85 and served with the N.W.M.P. during the Rebellion" (HBCA Album 8/65).

toulin Island Treaty with the Crown in 1850 and 1862, respectively. The time-honoured diplomatic traditions and legacies of these treaties would inform the making of the numbered treaties.

Understanding the Oral Record

For Aboriginal peoples, the treaties involved the establishment of a new relationship between Euro-Canadians and themselves, based on the principles of equality and mutual assistance. The current understanding of the treaties among Saskatchewan elders stresses the notions of mutual assistance and equality under the Crown. Cree elder Simon Kytwayhat invokes a language of kinship not unlike that employed by Morris:

> When our cousins, the White man, first came to peacefully live on these lands with the Indigenous people, as far as I can remember, Elders have referred to them as *kiciwâminawak* (our first cousins). I have heard from my Elders that the Queen came to offer a traditional adoption of us as our mother. "You will be my children," she had said.[13]

Elder Jacob Bill sums up the treaty relationship, expressing the principles of mutual respect, obligation, benefit, and equality:

> It was the will of the Creator that the White man would come here and live with us, among us to share our lives together with him, and also both of us collectively, to benefit from the bounty of Mother Earth for all time to come and for himself so that there is enough for him to make a living from the bounty, but equally with the Indians. That is the value and the true nature and spirit and intent of the treaty on both sides, and it's on both for both to benefit.[14]

The late Gordon Oaks, a Treaty 4 Cree chief, inherited the story of a young, multilingual Cree man named Sewepiton who was present at the negotiations. His recollection of the treaty also stressed the principle of equality between the two parties: "Sewepiton understood that it was two nations bargaining. It was one nation asking for the approval and right to enter the land and the other nation agreed but only in exchange for certain rights."[15] According to Plains Cree oral history, the Native signatories sincerely accepted Morris's gestures for reciprocity: "His words signify a treaty of peace and friendship, and not [simply] the land terms set out in the written treaty."[16] Elders in Alberta remember the treaty history in similar terms. They, too, recall that their negotiators trusted the word of the commissioners.

Our Elders and Treaty and Aboriginal Rights research efforts have established that the spirit and terms of the treaties Indian peoples signed was to share the land with the Europeans. In return, Indian peoples were to receive protection for the use of their lands, as well as provision of such services as would enable our survival on smaller territories and alongside European settlers. Indian peoples signed the treaties in good faith. We trusted the word of the "Great White Father" given to us by his negotiators. . . . We trusted the Commissioners when they promised we could continue to use the lands assigned to the Crown for our traditional economic purposes.[17]

Throughout the negotiations, the Indian leadership repeatedly sought verification of Morris's sincerity, which he repeatedly demonstrated.

Saskatchewan First Nations in particular have consistently interpreted the treaty relationship not only to be based on the principles of reciprocity, equality, and trust, but also to have entailed a promise of internal self-government and economic self-reliance flowing therefrom.[18] From the Aboriginal perspective, this promise entailed three elements: first, the authority to make decisions that determined the conditions of their lives; second, economic self-reliance, which, at the time, entailed the promise for a continuation of traditional hunting, trapping, and fishing activities, as well as the new economic opportunities involved in agriculture; third, a relationship of reciprocity: "Because we share this land with people of other origins, we must forge a new relationship characterized by mutual recognition, respect, sharing and responsibilities."[19]

Pragmatic Considerations

In addition to historical practice, the First Nations sought treaties for pragmatic considerations. The traditional plains way of life underwent drastic changes during the second half of the 19th century. By the 1870s, the buffalo — the mainstay of their economy and way of life — had dwindled dangerously. Morris wrote to the Minister of the Interior in 1873 that the "buffalo are rapidly diminishing," and the "slaughter is such that within 5 or 6 years few will be left."[20] Other factors drove the Indian leadership to secure a relationship of mutual assistance, including the decline of the fur trade economy, smallpox epidemics, the illicit trade in alcohol by American free-traders, and the anticipated westward expansion of Euro-Canadian settlers and Métis. As a result, many chiefs and councillors were anxious to sign treaties with the Crown to achieve stability and a new means for survival. The rumoured sale of Rupert's Land to Canada, conducted with little consultation or compensation, also alerted them to the need to act quickly if they hoped to secure protection and a fair deal and resolve a politically ambiguous situation. As early as 1871, the Cree Chief Sweetgrass petitioned the government:

Great Father, I shake hands with you, and bid you welcome. We heard our lands were sold and we did not like it; we don't want to sell our lands; it is our property, and no one has the right to sell them. . . . Our country is getting ruined of fur-bearing animals . . . . We want cattle, tools, agricultural implements and assistance in everything when we come to settle — our country is no longer able to support us. . . . We have had great starvation the past winter, and the small-pox took away many of our people. . . . We want you to stop the Americans from coming to trade on our lands. . . . We invite you to come and see us and to speak with us.[21]

Others were less diplomatic in their language: "Do not bring settlers and surveyors amongst us," warned the Ojibwa near Lake of the Woods, "until a clear understanding has been arrived at as to what our relations are to be in time to come."[22]

It was the First Nations, not the Canadian government, who took the initiative in making treaty. The Macdonald government had shown itself extremely reluctant to enter into any such obligations west of Portage la Prairie, where its authority was weak.[23] The call for agricultural implements also originated with the Indians, as many believed they would inevitably have to turn to the farm economy to survive. In the earliest treaty negotiations in the North West, the government initially offered only land reserves and cash annuities to the Ojibwa, but in each instance the Indians refused and, "much to Treaty Commissioner Wemyss Simpson's chagrin, farm animals, horses, wagons, and farm tools and equipment" had to be promised.[24] Similar promises would be made in Treaties 3, 4, 5, and 6, which Morris would negotiate.

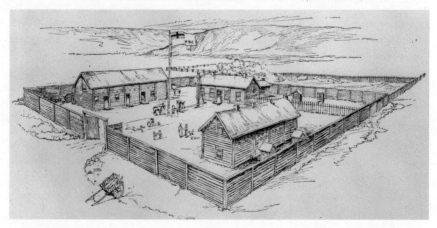

FORT QU'APPELLE, 1867. *Treaty 4 negotiations were conducted here in September 1874.* "Hudson's Bay Company's Fort Qu'Appelle in 1867. Drawn by Leonard Lowson, *Manitoba Free Press* artist, from sketches and diagrams by Isaac Cowie, 1913" (HBCA 1987/363-F-50/8).

8

Morris the Negotiator

ALEXANDER MORRIS WAS KNOWN TO DRIVE a hard bargain in business, and he did not soften his stance when negotiating a treaty. That the Aboriginal negotiators secured the concessions they did is a testament both to their skills and to a negotiating position that was perhaps stronger than historians have previously asserted. By the early 1870s, it was imperative that Canada secure friendly relations with the original inhabitants of the North West. The government was anxious to establish order and a measure of authority over a vast region where the North West Mounted Police had not yet established themselves. Even so, Morris was under pressure from a cash-strapped federal government to negotiate modest terms, and he took pride in his ability to stay within the means of the government — although he and the government ultimately agreed to relatively costly terms.

Morris had come to appreciate how seriously the First Nations took any promise made at treaty negotiations, and he was aware that the terms agreed to at one treaty would inform the others. Any breech of the terms was considered a breach of faith, rendering the treaty null and void and, by extension, creating a threat both to the legitimacy of the government's claim on the land and to settlement. Morris was anxious to avoid any promise he did not believe the government could honour. He was especially unyielding on the reserve land question, a reflection of government priorities and Morris's own history with land transactions. During the latter half of his tenure as Lieutenant-Governor, he did demonstrate a certain flexibility as to reserve location, and occasionally size, but this would seldom be repeated by later administrators.

Credit for the successful outcome of the negotiations must be given in part to Morris, who was much more conciliatory than the other government officials directing treaty negotiation and implementation, and especially more so than Department of the Interior officials in Ottawa. He applied Aboriginal ways of speaking, symbolism, and concepts of diplomacy in his own speeches and explanations of the treaty relationship. He evoked the principles of reciprocity, equality, and mutual trust that persist today in Aboriginal understandings of the treaty relationship. While misunderstandings did occur — individual provisions remain topics of contention today — what remains consistent between the written and oral records is the intended new relationship.

Morris's approach to treaty making was informed by precedent. He took pride in British conceptions of justice and the rule of law, and long before moving to the North West he had recognized that the First Nations had, in British law and practice, an inherent claim to the land. The Royal Proclamation of 1763, for instance, recognized Aboriginal title in the hope that "the Indians may be convinced of our Justice and determined Resolution to remove all reasonable Cause of Discontent."[1] As the Canadian government attempted to secure the 1869 transfer of Rupert's Land from the Hudson's Bay Company, Colonial Secretary Lord Granville reminded the Canadian Governor-General that "the old inhabitants of the Country will be treated with such forethought and consideration as may preserve them from the dangers of the approaching change, and satisfy them of the friendly interest [of] their new Governors."[2] The terms for the land transfer accordingly called for "compensation for lands required for purposes of settlement [to] be disposed of by the Canadian Government in communication with the Imperial Government."[3] The government agreed to resolve such matters "in conformity with the equitable principles which have uniformly governed the British Crown in its dealings with the aborigines."[4] Decades earlier, these principles had been put into practice at the Selkirk, Robinson, and Manitoulin Island Treaties. In each case, the Canadians sought to secure land for Crown ownership and settlement, but only after first establishing friendly relations with the First Nations. The Robinson Treaties guaranteed traditional hunting and fishing practices, which were also recognized in the numbered treaties. Morris took inspiration from these earlier examples of diplomacy.[5]

His approach to treaty making was also informed by Treaties 1 and 2. The numbered treaties of Western Canada were distinct from their predecessors. George F. G. Stanley writes that they were

more formal, ceremonious, and imposing; the areas to be ceded were larger; and the number of Indians to be treated with more numerous and warlike. Moreover, the early negotiations involved only a simple surrender for cash or annuities, with perhaps, the promise of a reserved area. The later treaties contained, not only the details of the cession, but the expressed obligation of the Canadian Government to make provision for the instruction, health and civilization of the native tribes.[6]

The formality and ceremony of the numbered treaties would involve a specific type of discourse — the discourse of reciprocity. In developing the first two numbered treaties, the government followed the objectives of securing land and friendly relations with the Natives, operating in consultation with the Hudson's Bay Company. Significant authority devolved to the negotiators.[7] These first two treaties were renegotiated a few years later, but the language of reciprocity and kinship was present to some degree in the initial negotiations. "Your Great Mother, the Queen, wishes to do justice to all her children alike," Lieutenant-Governor Adams Archibald had promised. "She will deal fairly with those of the setting sun, just as she would with those of the rising sun. She wishes order and peace to reign through all her country. . . . She wishes her red children to be happy and contented."[8] In the years to come, Morris would expand on the use of such language, and take a greater role in directing the negotiations.

Archibald's record in dealing with the peoples of the North West was mixed. He had a hand in Treaties 1 and 2 in late 1871, at Lower Fort Garry and at the Manitoba Post, but left most of the actual negotiating to Indian Commissioner Wemyss Simpson. During his brief tenure, Archibald advocated for a faithful implementation of Treaties 1 and 2, but his attitude was at times condescending and unsympathetic. When initially confronted by First Nations' requests to make treaty in 1870, he delayed, citing doubt as to their claims to the land. "Besides," he confided to Secretary of State Joseph Howe, "a treaty with savages to whom time is of no value, can only be made after much talk and great delay."[9] The term "savage" had been part of Morris's lexicon in the 1850s, but he had dropped it by the early 1870s; it appears in none of his correspondence of the period. Unlike Archibald, he appreciated the fact that time was precious, especially in light of the increasingly desperate circumstances among many First Nations.

The handling of Treaties 1 and 2 left much to be desired. Archibald resented having to meet with the Aboriginal negotiators at two separate locations, but ultimately assented out of logistical considerations and as a sign of good will. He failed to explain the reserve system properly, and his negotiating party made a number of promises, pertaining largely to agricultural implements, that they did not include in the text of either treaty. These would later be known as the "outside promises." Simpson, responsible for implementing the treaty promises, resolved that the bands should not be given any agricultural implements until the government decided they were ready to use them. His response to the just complaints of Aboriginal leaders was to avoid them by spending the better part of the year in Ottawa.[10]

Archibald complained to Secretary of State Howe about Simpson's absence and his mishandling of treaty implementation. He argued that the government should fulfill its obligations, if only for strategic considerations, maintaining friendship and trust. He complained "that the Indians were bringing their grievances to him even though he had no authority or responsibility for dealing with them."[11] Archibald wanted someone else to fulfill the task, suggesting that, if Simpson was unwilling to live in Manitoba, he should at least have a representative who could meet with the Indians and field their complaints. He failed utterly to appreciate why the First Nations leaders preferred dealing with the office of the Lieutenant-Governor over officials of the Department of the Interior. Morris, by contrast, came to appreciate both the diplomatic and the pragmatic reasons for insisting on a direct relationship with the representative of the Queen.

Cross-Cultural Understanding

With each experience of treaty negotiation, Morris's approach became increasingly informed by the Aboriginal peoples themselves. He attempted to explain his position in language consistent with their understandings of the principles of reciprocity and equality. According to Morris, the whites and Indians were entering into agreements to coexist peacefully, as equals, under the sovereignty of the Queen (the Great Mother), whose authority had been mandated by God (the Creator or Great Spirit).

"Who made the earth, the grass the stone, and the wood?" he asked at Treaty 4 negotiations. He answered himself:

The Great Spirit. He made them for all his children to use, and it is not stealing to use the gift of the Great Spirit. The lands are the Queen's under the Great Spirit. . . . In this country, now, no man need be afraid. If a white man does wrong to an Indian, the Queen will punish them.[12]

Morris and First Nations leaders spoke in terms of kinship. "The red and white man must live together," said Morris, "and be good friends, and the Indians must live together like brothers with each other and the white man."[13] Cree Chief Kakuishmay at Treaty 4 acknowledged this relationship: "We see the good you wish to show us. . . . Let us join together and make the Treaty; when both join together it is very good. . . . Just now the Great Spirit is watching over us; it is good, He who has strength and power is overlooking our doings."[14]

Morris's use of kinship language corresponded to traditional understandings of kinship among the First Nations. According to the Cree doctrine of *wâhkôhtowin*, an unwritten code of conduct, the symbolic relationship of mother and child (the Queen and her subjects) is based on "the principle of mutual respect which entailed the reciprocal duties of nurturing, caring, loyalty, and fidelity." Family members, or brothers and sisters (the Queen's white and red children), hold "relationships regulated by the laws of kinship, which recognized the close yet separate and independent existence of each and which provided for the principle of non-interference." [15] Thus, the Great Mother represents the state, under whose sovereignty the whites and Indians, although remaining independent from each other, are to coexist in a relationship of mutual assistance. "The Queen cares for you and for your children," Morris said, "and she cares for the children that are yet to be born. She would like to take you by the hand." The new relationship was to last forever, maintained and renewed annually through the symbolic gift of five dollars to every Treaty Indian "as long as the sun shines and water flows." [16] Morris learned the significance of the annuity when the signatories of Treaties 1 and 2 began refusing it on the principle that the treaty had been broken when the government failed to meet the "outside promises."

Morris and other Canadian negotiators held true to the time-honoured practice of gift-giving at each treaty. The First Nations of the North West had, on several occasions, refused to receive presents or cash gratuities from the government before making a treaty, as they believed doing so might bind them to conditions or commitments that they had not yet agreed upon. [17] Only after making a treaty were the presents and gratuity accepted. "If you shake hands with us and make a treaty," Morris promised,

> we are ready to make a present at the end of the treaty, of eight dollars for every man, woman and child in your nations. We are ready also to give calico, clothing and other presents. We are ready to give every recognized Chief, a present of twenty five dollars, a medal, and a suit of clothing. [18]

Morris understood the significance of such gifts, the likes of which had been exchanged at diplomatic encounters with Indigenous peoples throughout the preceding centuries, by both the French and the British. The annual gratuity and suits of clothing, he later explained, made the chiefs and their counsellors "in a sense officers of the Crown." The medallions were given

> in conformity with an ancient custom, and are much prized and cherished by the Chiefs and their families. On one occasion a young Chief was decorated in my presence with the old King George silver medal, by one of the band, to whom it had been entrusted for safe keeping by the young man's father, who was a Chief, with the charge that on the boy's coming of age, it would be delivered over to him. [19]

One side was engraved with the image of a chief and a Canadian official, with right hands clasped (signifying friendship and the compact of treaty), the sun shining in the background (signifying eternity), and a hatchet buried in the ground (signifying peace). The other side of the medallion depicted Queen Victoria. The medallions held a symbolic significance for both sides.

Treaty 3

Treaty 3 was signed in October 1873 at the North West Angle on Lake of the Woods, just east of the present Manitoba-Ontario border. It was significant for the treaty-making process as a whole, as it would set many of the terms for future treaties and the renegotiation of Treaties 1 and 2. For Morris, the experience was formative, as he learned firsthand about the diplomatic traditions and negotiating skills of his Aboriginal counterparts. All the same, he approached the negotiations with the firm hand he felt his position as an official of the government demanded. Having long been interested in First Nations' languages and customs, he attempted to meet them on their own terms.

Negotiations in the Lake of the Woods area had been an outstanding issue since 1870. With the beginning of the construction of a road-waterway passage in 1869, the region was to become a crucial link between Canada and the North West. It was also through this region that the future Canadian Pacific Railway would pass, and good relations with the local Ojibwa were essential. In 1870, the Canadian government had become especially anxious to secure the safe passage of troops to quell the Red River Resistance.

The Ojibwa had no interest in interrupting the passage of Canadian troops, but refused the diplomatic overtures made by Wemyss Simpson at Fort Frances,

TREATY MEDAL *used for Treaties 3 – 8.* (Bob Michayluik Photography; medal courtesy Office of the Treaty Commissioner, Saskatchewan.)

Ontario in mid-1870 and again in 1871 and 1872. They preferred to wait and see how the government treated the First Nations in Manitoba before making any commitments of their own. "We want to see how the Red River Indians will be settled with and whether the soldiers will take away their lands," declared the Chief of the Fort Frances band. "We will not take your presents, they are a bait and if we take them you will say we are bound to you."[20] The Ojibwa considered Simpson's treaty terms parsimonious; the Woodland Ojibwa on the American side of the border had secured far better.[21] Both Simpson and Lieutenant-Governor Archibald believed that the government should not expend more than the absolute minimum, considering the land to be of little agricultural value.[22] Simpson's tactlessness could not have been conducive to successful negotiations. He had long considered the Ojibwa "with obvious distaste," commenting that "they had refused Christianity, were extremely filthy in their habits, and like all Indians were incapable of gratitude."[23] Neither Archibald nor Simpson "gave credence to the Indian point of view, if indeed the Indian point of view was fully comprehended or appreciated."[24] Additionally, the Ojibwa insisted on negotiating with a representative of the Crown, which Simpson was not.[25]

The Woodland Ojibwa desired a treaty in anticipation of the gradual encroachments resulting from the construction of the road-waterway passage through their lands, but they had little reason to rush into an agreement on unsatisfactory terms. The livelihood of most was based on trapping and fishing, and while the supply of game and the state of the fur trade had suffered somewhat by the early 1870s, they had not been nearly as affected by the decline of the buffalo as the peoples of the plains. Nor was there any immediate threat of mass immigration, given the limited agricultural promise of most of their lands.

Chief engineer Simon J. Dawson, who was directing the construction of the road, was more sympathetic to the Ojibwa perspective than Simpson or Archibald. He lobbied the federal government to consider more generous terms if it hoped to secure a treaty that included the cession of Aboriginal title. He also recommended that this time the negotiations be attended by the Lieutenant-Governor of Manitoba, a representative of the Crown. Minister of the Interior Alexander Campbell consequently instructed Morris to travel to the North West Angle in the fall of 1873 and make a treaty. The Privy Council approved a maximum payment of $15 per person, along with a maximum annuity of $7. Morris was urged to keep the payments as low as possible to avoid complaints or additional demands from the signatories of Treaties 1 and 2, and in consideration of future treaties.[26]

Morris was given little instruction beyond this. The maximum size of the reserves to be granted (one square mile per family of five) was communicated to him only a few days before he left for the Angle, and the policy as to the granting of schools was unclear. He was told that, "because the cash payment and

Negotiating the Numbered Treaties

annuities had been raised, presents such as agricultural implements should not be granted."[27] Dawson and the newly appointed Indian Affairs Commissioner, J. A. N. Provencher, would serve as treaty commissioners. James McKay, Robert Pither, and Molyneux St. John would also attend.

Morris set off for the Angle in September, his daughters Christine and Elizabeth in tow. The negotiations opened with pomp and ceremony. Where Simpson had disliked dealing with the First Nations, Morris approached the opportunity with both curiosity and enthusiasm:

> On arriving, the Indians, who were already there, came up to the house I occupied, in procession, headed by braves bearing a banner and a Union Jack, and accompanied by others beating drums. They asked leave to perform a dance in my honour, after which they presented to me the pipe of peace.[28]

If he had not already been aware of it, Morris saw for himself that this was no mere land transaction. Rather, it was the entering into of a new relationship between the Crown and the Ojibwa people that would entail responsibilities and obligations on both sides. Morris made a point of appearing in a manner befitting the significance of his office and the task that lay before him. He brought along a small military contingent from Lower Fort Garry, after the practice of Archibald and on the advice of Dawson. The Indians, Dawson explained,

> feel and know that the treaty is a matter of the greatest importance to them, and when they see the Commissioners coming unattended, as they have so far done, to treaty with them, and observe the utmost parsimony, manifested even in dealing them out a few days rations, as has hitherto been the case, they are led to the belief that the Government of Canada attaches but little importance to negotiations which are to them the gravest moment.[29]

Morris found the presence of the troops useful, as they helped prevent the illegal trade of alcohol and "exerted a moral influence which contributed to the success of the negotiations."[30]

Pomp and circumstance aside, he approached the negotiations with typical firmness. He soon learned that the Ojibwa were equally resolute. Once assembled, they made the commissioners wait while they convened among themselves to develop a common negotiating position. They were determined to ensure their physical and cultural survival, and to improve their material well-being. In the course of the negotiations, Morris was forced to give way on several issues.

The Ojibwa opened the negotiations on October 1 with a demand for compensation for the Dawson road. Morris had a much more general project in mind, and told them that "he had come as a representative of the Queen and the

Government of Canada to treat for their land and settle all other matters, past and future."[31] The Ojibwa reminded Morris that he was in their country, not his, but after conferring among themselves they agreed to hear what Morris had to say. Morris and the commissioners, meanwhile, had concluded that the Ojibwa would likely accept no less than a $5 annuity. He made this offer, in addition to a one-time $10 per person payment, $20 annuities for chiefs and councillors, and reserve lands amounting to one square mile per family. The chiefs made a counter-proposal that included increased payments, annuities, and a variety of agricultural and domestic implements which Morris estimated would come to some $125,000 annually. He peremptorily refused, and tried to pressure the chiefs into accepting his terms, imploring them to think of their children's future. If the treaty were to fail, he warned, the blame would rest with them: "If we do not succeed today I shall go away feeling sorry for you and for your children that you could not see what was good for you and for them."[32] The chiefs were unmoved. Their spokesmen informed him, Morris wrote, "that the Chiefs, warriors and braves were of one mind, that they would make a treaty only if we acceded to their demand."[33] Morris threatened to end the conference immediately, and to treat separately with those bands who were willing to treat. This brought matters to a crisis.

It was at this point that divisions in the Ojibwa leadership began to show. Despite pressure from his colleagues, Chief Ka-Katche-way of the Lac Seul band came forward to state his willingness to treat, but not without making additional demands for a schoolmaster, seed, agricultural implements, and cattle. He was soon joined by Chief Blackstone. Morris had known all along that the bands were not as unified as they presented themselves, and the new circumstances greatly strengthened his hand. Indeed, as Wayne E. Daugherty explains, "there is every indication that Morris had prior knowledge of the attitude of this particular chief and the people he represented."[34] A document dated October 1, 1873, purportedly recounts a communication between Morris and Ka-Katche-way. According to the document, Morris wrote:

> He is prepared on the part of himself and people he represents to enter into a Treaty with the Government on the terms [that] may be proposed. His Band, he says, have little farms on English River about a day's journey below the outlet of Lac Seul, and they are particularly anxious to get things necessary for these farms.[35]

Expressing his desire "to treat with them as a nation," and suggesting some willingness to consider the question of schools and agricultural implements, Morris urged the other chiefs to take an additional day to take counsel among themselves. They reluctantly agreed.[36]

Negotiating the Numbered Treaties

The turning point appears to have come at this council, during which the chiefs were joined by four Métis advisors, including James McKay and John Nolin, who were familiar with both the government and the Ojibwa. The Métis were "men of their own blood," recalled Morris, who gave the Indians "friendly advice,"[37] and they proved crucial to the success of the negotiations. "You owe the treaty much to the Half-breeds," said Mawedopenais, Chief of Fort Frances and principle spokesman for the Ojibwa. "I know it," Morris replied. "I am proud that all the Half-breeds of Manitoba, who are here, gave their Governor their cordial support."[38] Morris expressed his appreciation in his official report:

> I have much pleasure in bearing testimony to the hearty cooperation and efficient aid the Commissioners received from the Métis who were present at the Angle, and who, with one accord, whether of French or English origin, used the influence which their relationship to the Indians gave them, to impress them with the necessity of their entering into the treaty.[39]

While the Ojibwa were convening, Morris and the commissioners decided to raise the cash payment to $12, and to offer certain agricultural implements, cattle and seed, along with an annual sum of $1,500 for ammunition for hunting and twine for fishing nets. They also offered schools to those bands that requested them.

When the parties reconvened the following day, the chiefs welcomed the new offer, but it took five more hours of negotiations to resolve their additional demands and concerns. Their demands included a $50 annuity, a medal, and and an "official suit of clothing" for each chief, a flag for themselves and their headmen, "suits of clothing every year for all the bands," free passage on the future railway, a treaty provision banning alcohol on reserve lands, assurances that they would not be conscripted in war, assurances that those responsible for implementing the treaty would be held to account, treaty status for relatives living in the United States, assurances as to reserve locations and mineral rights, the inclusion of a number of resident Métis families in the treaty, the employment of John Nolin as Indian Agent, and, finally, the removal of Hudson's Bay Company claims on their reserve lands.

Morris conceded on a number of items in an attempt to meet the chiefs halfway. He refused the annual clothing for all the bands, the chiefs' $50 annuity, and free passage on the railway, which he did not have authority to grant. He offered to give "presents of clothing and food . . . at the close of the treaty," agreed to write the alcohol ban into the text, assured them that "the Queen was not in the habit of employing the Indians in warfare," and that "the ear of the Queen's Government will always be open to hear the complaints of her Indian people, and she will deal with her servants that do not do their duty in a proper manner."[40] As to reserve lands, Morris promised "that enquiry would be made into the matter" of Hudson's Bay Company claims in the vicinity of Fort Frances, but he did not commit to an outcome, promising only that justice would be done to both the First Nations and the Company. He told the Ojibwa that they would have mineral rights on their reserve lands, but not on Crown land. Provencher promised that the reserves would be selected in consultation with them and include those lands already under cultivation. Morris promised that members of their bands living in the United States would have up to two years to return to Canada and be considered part of the treaty. He also promised to recommend that resident Métis identified by the chiefs "should be permitted the option of taking either status as Indians or whites."[41] Finally, Morris promised to provide the chiefs and headmen with official suits of clothing, flags, and medals. After reaching an understanding on these items, the final text of the treaty was written out, and then explained to the Ojibwa in their language by James McKay. Not all of these items made their way into the treaty text, but they were included in Morris's report and in the transcribed proceedings submitted to the Department of the Interior in Ottawa. The parties made their final remarks and signed the treaty, after which the payments were made and provisions distributed, bringing an official end to the proceedings.

The experience had been both physically and emotionally exhausting for Morris. The final day's negotiations had been especially taxing. He was relieved at the conclusion, but also proud of the accomplishment: "On the whole," he wrote, "I am of opinion that the issue is a happy one."[42] With significant assistance from Dawson and the Métis, Morris had succeeded where Simpson had twice failed, and peacefully secured a crucial section of territory for the Canadian government on terms he deemed acceptable.

The treaty was the result of hard bargaining, but it was also owing in part to the language used by Morris and the other commissioners. Simon Dawson, who was most familiar with the people of the region, opened for the commissioners by "reciprocat[ing] the expression of pleasure used by the Chiefs through their spokesman." He hoped that the treaty would "fix permanently the friendly relations between the Indians and the white men," and described the Queen as the "Great Mother," and the governor as "representative of Her Majesty."[43] In his own opening address, Morris also explained the treaty relationship in kinship terms: "We are all the children of the same Great Spirit, and are subject to the same Queen. I want to settle all matters both of the past and the present, so that the white and red man will always be friends."[44]

As Dawson had anticipated, Morris's position as the representative of the Queen was important to the Ojibwa. The authority of his position and his direct link to the Crown lent credence to his use of the language of reciprocity and kinship. "We think it a great thing to meet you here," Mawedopenais had told Morris. "What we have heard yesterday, and as you represented yourself, you said the Queen sent you here, the way we understood you as a representative of the Queen." He had challenged Morris to use this authority to grant their initial terms: "We have understood . . . that Her Majesty has given you the same power and authority as *she* has, to act in this business; you said the Queen gave you her goodness, her charitableness in your hands." When he added that the land was theirs by right, under the Great Spirit, Morris was forced to clarify his position:

> I wish to tell you that I am a servant of the Queen. I cannot do my own will; I must do hers. I can only give you what she tells me to give you. . . . I ask you not to turn your backs on what is offered to you, and you ought to see by what the Queen is offering you that she loves her red subjects as much as her white.[45]

Morris reminded the chief that the annuity would be given forever: "What I offer you is to be while the water flows and the sun rises." Mawedopenais repeated Morris's expression, asserting that he wanted assurances that his community would have the means to sustain itself long into the future: "Our hands are poor but our heads are rich, and it is riches that we ask so that we may be able to support our families as long as the sun rises and the water runs."[46]

Gaining the chiefs' trust and establishing a dialogue had not come easily, however. Chief Powhassan, who acted as assistant spokesman, cast doubt on Morris's authority and wisdom when he refused their initial offer:

> We understood yesterday that the Queen had given you the power to act upon . . . and that the riches of the Queen she had filled your head and body with, and you had only to throw them round about; but it seems it is not so, but that you have only half the power that she has, and that she has only half filled your head.[47]

Morris once again clarified his position: "You can understand very well; for instance, one of your great chiefs asks a brave to deliver a message, he represents you, and that is how I stand with the Queen's Government." An atmosphere of trust was still wanting, however. "The white man has robbed us of our riches, and we don't wish to give them up again without getting something in their place," said Mawedopenais.[48]

The Ojibwa had good reason to suspect the good will of the white man, and the promises of government officials, from their own experience and also from what they had heard with regard to the unkept outside promises and poor treaty implementation of Treaties 1 and 2.[49]

The subsequent impasse, and the government's strengthened bargaining position when Ka-Katche-way broke with his colleagues, gave Morris another opportunity to establish an atmosphere of trust. Mawedopenais challenged him to show his power, and it was at this point that most of the discussion as to the treaty relationship occurred. Morris explained the government's offer, and couched it in terms that he hoped would express his good will and distinguish this agreement from any past transgression that might have contributed to their distrust:

> I hope we are going to understand one another today. And that I can go back and report that I left my Indian friends contented, and that I have put into their hands the means of providing for themselves and their families at home. . . . we are anxious to show you that we have a great desire to understand you — that we wish to do the utmost in our power to make you contented, so that the white and the red man will always be friends. This year, instead of ten dollars we will give you twelve dollars. . . . I wish you to understand we do not come here as traders, but as representing the Crown, and to do what we believe is just and right. We have asked in that spirit, and I hope you will meet me in that spirit and shake hands with me today and make a treaty forever.[50]

The $2 added to the one-time gratuity and the additional promise of certain implements may have led to a turning point in the negotiations, but Morris's words, and his expression of the treaty relationship, may have contributed equally to the change in perception among the Ojibwa negotiators. Mawedopenais cautiously accepted Morris's overture: "Depending upon the words you have told us, and stretched out your hands in a friendly way, I depend upon that." The chief proceeded to make additional demands, but his speech became more cordial, at times deferential, and at times alluding to or reminding Morris of the promise of good will that he had made. When, on the issue of Métis membership in the treaty, Morris promised to recommend it, Mawedopenais reminded him of the relationship of trust that was now being established, and that he was taking Morris at his word to follow through: "I hope you will not drop the question; we have understood you to say that you came here as a friend, and represented your charitableness, and we depend upon your kindness."[51]

Mawedopenais sought assurance that those responsible for administering the treaty would be both trustworthy and familiar with the proceedings. "I begin now to see how I value the proceedings," he told Morris:

> I have come to this point, and all that are taking part in this treaty and yourself. I would wish to have all your names in writing handed over to us. I would not find it to my convenience to have a stranger here to transact our business between me and you. It is a white man who does not understand our language that is taking it down. I would like a man that

Negotiating the Numbered Treaties

understands our language and our ways. We would ask your Excellency as a favour to appoint him [John Nolin] for us.[52]

Morris agreed that Nolin would be a good choice as Indian Agent, and he would recommend his appointment. Mawedopenais also wanted assurance that those responsible for the treaty's implementation would be held to account:

All the promises that you have made me, the little promises and the money you have promised, when it comes to me year after year — should I see that there is anything wanting, through the negligence of the people that have to see after these things, I trust it will be in my power to put them in prison.[53]

Morris replied: "The ear of the Queen's Government will always be open to hear the complaints of her Indian people, and she will deal with her servants that do not do their duty in a proper manner."[54]

It was important to both parties that they understand each other fully. Dawson assured the Ojibwa that they would have answers both during and after the treaty: "When we arrange the general matters in question, should you choose to ask anything, I shall be most happy to explain it, as I am here all the time."[55] Later into the treaty, Mawedopenais declared to Morris, "Why we keep you so long is that it is our wish that everything should be properly understood between us." To which Morris replied: "That is why I am here. It is my pleasure, and I want when we once shake hands that it should be forever."[56]

The chief was obviously moved by Morris's cordiality and manner of speech:

You have come before us with a smiling face, you have shown us great charity — you have promised the good things; you have given us your best compliments and wishes, not only for once but forever; let there now forever be peace and friendship between us. . . . I will tell you one thing. You understand me now, that I have taken your hand firmly and in friendship. I repeat twice that you have done so, that these promises that you have made, and the treaty to be concluded, let it be as you promise, as long as the sun rises over our head and as long as the water runs.[57]

Mawedopenais's statement brought the treaty to a close, as he declared for the first time the cession of lands and his acceptance of the treaty, in addition to his acceptance of the friendship Morris had offered:

Now you see me stand before you all; what has been done here today has been done openly before the Great Spirit, and before the nation, and I hope that I may never hear anyone say that this treaty has been done secretly; and now, in closing this Council, I take off my glove, and in giving you my hand, I deliver over my birthright and lands; and in taking your hand, I hold fast all the promises you have made, and I hope they will last as long as the sun goes round and the water flows, as you have said.[58]

Morris took Mawedopenais's hand and promised that he would keep his word, believing that the treaty he was signing would "bind the red man and the white together as friends forever."[59]

The observer from the local newspaper, the *Manitoban*, transcribing the proceedings, remarked that the treaty had succeeded in large part because of the dignity with which it had been conducted. "One very wonderful thing that forced itself on the attention of everyone was the perfect order that prevailed throughout the camp, and which more particularly marked proceedings in the council." Despite the difficulty of the negotiations, "there was no petulance, no ill-feeling evinced; but everything was done with a calm dignity that was pleasing to behold, and which might be copied with advantage by more pretentious deliberative assemblies."[60]

DAVID LAIRD, OTTAWA, MARCH 1874. *Laird was Minister of the Interior from late 1873 to October 1876. He accompanied Morris to Fort Qu'Appelle in September 1874 as a Treaty Commissioner for the negotiation of Treaty 4, and led the negotiations at Treaty 7 in 1877* (Library and Archives Canada, PA-025478).

The completion of the treaty was followed by celebration. Before departing, Morris "presented an ox to the nation, and after it had been eaten a grand dance was indulged in."[61]

After the treaty, Morris recommended implementing the treaty promises as soon as possible. He advised making Nolin an Indian Agent, recommended an inquiry be made into the issue of Hudson's Bay Company lands on reserves, and called for a speedy identification of reserves in consultation with the Ojibwa. For this task, he recommended Simon Dawson out of consideration for his knowledge of the land and its people. It was clear to Morris that the Ojibwa had first claim to the land. "No patents should be issued, or licenses granted, for mineral or timber lands, or other lands, until the question of the reserves has been first adjusted," he told the Minister of the Interior.[62] He presumably made this suggestion on the basis that the Ojibwa had first claim to the territory and might desire lands that had mineral value, but ultimately officials in Ottawa would make policies to the contrary.

Morris also learned of the great significance the chiefs placed on the suits, flags, and medals they had requested, particularly the medals: "Mawedopenais produced one of the medals given to the Red River chiefs, said it was not silver, and they were ashamed to wear it, as it turned black, and then, with an air of great contempt, struck it with his knife." As one observer recalled, "The result was anything but the 'true ring,' and made every man ashamed of the petty meanness that had been practised." Morris promised to report what Mawedopenais had said, "and the manner in which he had spoken."[63] Only silver medals "shall be worthy of the high position our Mother the Queen occupies."[64]

Treaty 4

Buoyed by his success at Treaty 3, Morris increasingly involved himself in the treaty making process. The Plains Cree west of Manitoba had for some time been lobbying for a treaty. Morris himself had been lobbying Ottawa since early 1873, without success. Macdonald had not been keen on extending the responsibilities of his government. He preferred to wait for the demand for settlement to increase before making any treaty.

The country was far from secure. American traders had established fortified posts across the Canadian prairie and were effectively in a state of open warfare with the plains nations. This was especially apparent after the Cypress Hills Massacre of June 1873. The spectre of American annexation of the territory was not far from Morris's mind. "We are exposed to constant eruptions of American desperadoes" he warned Ottawa late in 1873; the "matter was likely to lead to serious trouble and possible Fenian invasion."[65]

Canada's claim to sovereignty over the lands west of Manitoba was uncertain at best. As Wemyss Simpson had warned in 1871, making treaties in the North West was "essential to the peace, if not the actual retention, of the country."[66] First Nations-Métis relations were also tense at times as the two groups competed for the remaining buffalo. Settlement in the "fertile belt," then, was a peaceful strategy for maintaining a measure of stability in the west, but little could be accomplished before order had actually been established. Morris and other officials began lobbying Ottawa for the establishment of a military police force.[67] Securing Canadian sovereignty and establishing any such force with its necessary infrastructure, however, would first require the consent of the original inhabitants.

Many Canadians believed the First Nations would actively disrupt government plans if good relations were not established through treaty. Already in the early 1870s, the Ojibwa had refused passage to settlers attempting to move west of Portage la Prairie, posting a notice on a church door warning other parties "not to intrude on their lands until a treaty was signed."[68] Plains nations regularly threatened to interrupt geological surveys and telegraph lines for similar reasons. The First Nations population across the North West was still vastly superior in numbers to the rest of the population, and Morris speculated that they "could place 5000 mounted armed warriors in the field" — far more than the government of Canada could muster on short notice.[69] With the defeat of the Macdonald government and a new Liberal administration in power, Morris communicated the urgency of the situation to David Laird, the new Minister of the Interior, in December 1873:

Prompt steps necessary when season permits for enforcement of law in North West; we have Police Force and small Battalion; Privy Council have not yet fully realized the magnitude of the task; force now here is inadequate; steps have not been taken hitherto with a view to enforcement . . . last summer [at Cypress Hills] a party of Americans shot 30 Indians; American outlaws have fortified posts in our territory and carry on illicit trade; there are no less than six forts of United States traders; have already recommended treaties; I could not leave my duties here; measures should be taken to punish perpetrators of the Indian massacre, suppression of liquor traffic and reinforcement of law and order; the difficulties Canada has assumed have never been fully appreciated by Government or People.[70]

The new prime minister, Alexander Mackenzie, responded personally to Morris's communication, indicating a shift in policy and a mandate to treat with the First Nations: "Quite appreciate difficulties of your position; have discussed Indian question; never doubted our true policy was to make friends of them even at a

Negotiating the Numbered Treaties

considerable cost; hope new administration may realize expectations."[71] Having finally convinced his government of the urgency of the situation, Morris travelled to Fort Qu'Appelle in September 1874 to negotiate a treaty with the Plains Cree and Ojibwa.

Treaty 4 differed from its predecessor in many respects. At the Angle, Morris had dealt with a single cultural-linguistic group and a representative leadership that had, for the most part, the support of their people. At Qu'Appelle, there were two disparate groups, the Plains Cree and the Ojibwa. Divisions arose both between the nations and among the Ojibwa, and the chiefs were reluctant to negotiate on behalf of bands that were not present. The greatest concerns and controversies, which occupied the bulk of the discussions, centred on the Hudson's Bay Company. The Indians, and especially the Ojibwa from the Fort Qu'Appelle area, refused to discuss terms before resolving these issues. On this matter, and in negotiating specific provisions, Morris proved, for the most part, unyielding. Not wanting to mislead his counterparts, he was reluctant to promise anything he knew the government could not or would not deliver. Instead, he built on his experience by focussing on establishing trust and an open and frank dialogue among the parties. Elaborating on his understanding of the treaty relationship, Morris once again used concepts of kinship, reciprocity, and equality in an attempt to convince the First Nations of the Crown's benevolence and sense of justice.

As at Treaty 3, Morris was joined by two other commissioners, David Laird and W. J. Christie. Morris had suggested that a member of the Cabinet be present at the negotiations, likely with a view to "enable the [Privy] council better to appreciate the character of the difficulties that have to be encountered in negotiating with the Indians,"[72] but the new Minister of the Interior appears to have played a limited role in the negotiations; a Prince Edward Islander, Laird had little experience with Indian Affairs or the North West, although he would prove, in the coming years, more sympathetic than many of his colleagues in Ottawa and more helpful to Morris's lobbying for treaty implementation.[73] The other commissioner, W. J. Christie, was a retired Hudson's Bay Company officer who had spent decades in the field, dealt personally with numerous Aboriginal groups, and had become fluent in a number of Indigenous languages. Christie doubtless brought to the Canadian negotiating team some grasp of the centuries-old diplomatic relationship that had formed between the Company and its trading partners.[74] Morris initially opposed Christie's appointment on the grounds that "it was important to emphasize the distinction between the Government and the Company."[75] In time, Morris and Christie developed a positive working relationship as they both pressed the government for treaty implementation. The three men decided that Morris should act as principal negotiator, owing to his "previous experience with the Indian Tribes" and his "official position as Lieutenant-Governor of the North West Territories."[76] He and his colleagues had come to appreciate the symbolic significance of his office.

The negotiations began badly, with disagreements over protocol. Morris did not receive the type of reception he had come to expect after Treaty 3. Initially, the Ojibwa chiefs refused even to meet with the commissioners, sending messengers instead. The significance of the snub was not lost on Morris, as he complained to Otakaonan (The Gambler), a spokesman for the Fort Qu'Appelle-area Ojibwa: "I held out my hand but you did not do as your nation did at the Angle. When I arrived there the Chief and his men came and gave me the pipe of peace and paid me every honour. Why? Because I was the servant of the Queen."[77]

The Fort Qu'Appelle Ojibwa refused to begin negotiations until certain outstanding issues with the Hudson's Bay Company had been resolved. They had been upset by the Company's survey of land in and around its post. They

W. J. CHRISTIE. *A long-time employee of the Hudson's Bay Company, Christie served as Treaty Commissioner at Treaties 4 and 6. His knowledge of Indigenous languages proved highly useful throughout Morris's tenure.* "Inspecting Chief Factor William Joseph Christie, ca. 1860" (HBCA 1987/363-E-700-C/94).

also disputed the legitimacy of the Company's £300,000 sale of the North West Territories to Canada. For their part, the other Ojibwa bands and the Cree were reluctant to enter negotiations until their colleagues from Fort Qu'Appelle were prepared to do so.

Discussions with Otakaonan finally opened when the negotiating tent, originally placed on disputed Company-claimed lands, was moved to more neutral ground, but Otakaonan's differences with the Company continued to inhibit negotiations.

"The Company have stolen our land," he declared.[78]

Morris asserted that the land belonged to the Queen under the Great Spirit, and to her predecessors, one of whom had given the Hudson's Bay Company special trading rights — an assertion not fully accepted by the Aboriginal negotiators. The Queen, Morris tried to explain, had determined that the Company's dominance in the North West was "not just, neither to the white nor the red man," and decided to "govern the country herself." To compensate the Company for the rights that were being removed, the Queen had granted them the land in and around their posts. "They had their forts, their places of trade where they raised cattle and grain, and she told them they could keep them, and she will no more break with them than she will with you."[79]

Otakaonan complained that the rationale behind the Company's survey around its post had never been explained to his band, and that the Company had ignored their protests when the survey was conducted. Morris promised to investigate the matter, promising that the Company would receive no more and no less land than the Queen had promised. Otakaonan suggested that the land had not been the Queen's to give in the first place, and implored Morris to use his authority to resolve the matter: "I know that you will have power and good rules and this is why I am glad to tell you what is troubling me."[80] Morris, careful to distinguish the government from the company, would promise only to verify that the surveys did not exceed the permitted amount. Chief Pasqua then stated that his people wanted the £300,000 that had been paid to the Hudson's Bay Company. This Morris flatly refused.

The negotiators reconvened two days later, at which point Morris hoped to move on to discussing the treaty terms. Otakaonan said that he wanted a provision in the treaty that would oblige the Company to continue trading, but limit it exclusively to the posts. Morris replied that the Company had the same right to sell goods anywhere that Otakaonan had. When the Ojibwa spokesman continued to insist on this point, negotiations nearly broke down. The Cree Chief Kakuishmay expressed a desire to discuss terms, but Chief Côté of the Fort Pelly Ojibwa, sensing an impasse, threatened to leave. "I do not think anything will go right," he said.[81] He was unprepared to discuss any land cession without further consultation with his band. Frustrated and physically exhausted — he had fallen ill before or during the proceedings[82] — Morris tried to pressure the bands into negotiating by threatening to leave and by repeatedly reminding them that, in light of the impending disappearance of the buffalo, if they failed to make a treaty and adopt agriculture as a new means of economic self-sufficiency, they would be jeopardizing their own future and that of their descendants. Any blame for failed negotiations, he warned, would be laid squarely at their feet.[83]

In the event, discussions over the precise terms of the treaty were brief. The chiefs wanted the same terms as those reached at the Angle. After conferring among themselves, Morris and the commissioners accepted, even though it would mean conceding a $12 gratuity per person, as opposed to the $8 they had originally offered. Chief Kamooses, a Fort Qu'Appelle Ojibwa, asked for larger annuities and the removal of all debts to the Hudson's Bay Company. This Morris refused. Despite disagreements, the chiefs signed the treaty "after having been assured that they would never be made ashamed of what they then did."[84] The Treaty ended as it had begun, with neither celebration nor ceremony.

For all the disagreement, the treaty contained elements that suggested the entering into of a relationship of reciprocity and the suggestion that, at heart, this was the desired outcome for all. For his part, Morris made a greater use of kinship terms and the discourse of reciprocity and equality than he had at Treaty 3. His opening comments explained the treaty in these terms:

> The Queen has chosen me to be one of her Councillors, and has sent me here to represent her and has made me Governor of all her Territories in the North West. . . . The Queen loves her Red children; she has always been friends with them; she knows that it is hard for them to live, and she has always tried to help them in the other parts of the Dominion. Last year she sent me to see her children at the Lake of the Woods. I took her children there by the hand, and the white man and the red man made friends forever.[85]

Morris evoked the presence of the Great Spirit — a practice he had doubtless learned from the Aboriginal negotiators — to lend legitimacy and solemnity to the process, and to emphasize the openness with which the parties were expected to speak. "I wanted you to meet me here today because I wanted to speak to you before the Great Spirit and before the world."[86] Chief Cheekuk, although anxious about the question of representation, later expressed a similar sentiment: "My ears are open to what you say. Just now the Great Spirit is watching over us; it is good, He who has strength and power is overlooking our doings. I want very much to be good in what we are going to talk about, and our Chiefs will take you by the hand just now."[87]

Morris repeatedly tried to gain the negotiators' trust, promising not to deceive them or to pledge anything the government could not deliver: "I would like to give you pleasure but I cannot do wrong; we won't deceive you with smooth words. We will tell you the simple truth what we can do and what we cannot do."[88] He implored the Aboriginal negotiators to speak of their concerns, and insisted on dealing with the legitimate representatives of the people. He was particularly interested in hearing from the elders.

Whereas at Treaty 3 Morris had threatened to deal separately with other chiefs when talks broke down, at Treaty 4 he insisted on dealing with all the chiefs present. He tried to convince them of the Queen's good will and kindness, and assure them that she had their best interest in mind. She "would like you to learn something of the cunning of the white man," he said. "When fish are scarce and the buffalo are not plentiful she would like to help you to put something in the land; she would like that you should have some money every year to buy things that you need."[89] He spoke of the equality that would exist among the Queen's subjects, or "children": "You are the subjects of the Queen, you are her children, and you are only a little band to all her other children. She has children all over the world, and she does right with them all. She cares as much for you as she cares for her white children."[90] Morris insisted that the Queen wanted her red children not to disappear, but to flourish and increase in number. The treaty relationship, he promised, was to last forever, and benefit future generations. Reminding them of the efforts that had been made to prosecute the Americans responsible for the Cypress Hills Massacre the previous year, Morris promised that, unlike in the United States, they would have the Queen's protection against alcohol and criminals, and justice would be done equally to both whites and Indians:

> In this country, now, no man need be afraid. If a white man does wrong to an Indian, the Queen will punish them. . . . if the Indians prove he did wrong, he will be punished . . . and it will be the same if the Indian does wrong to the white man. The red and white man must live together, and be good friends, and the Indians must live together like brothers with each other and the white man.[91]

The First Nations shared a similar desire for a reciprocal coexistence. Despite recurring disagreements, Otakaonan (The Gambler) responded to Morris's overtures by expressing the good will and larger objectives of his own people:

> There are different kinds of grass growing here that is just like those sitting around here. There is no difference. Even from the American land they are here, but we love them all the same, and when the white skin comes here

from far away I love him all the same. I am telling you what our love and kindness is. This is what I did when the white man came, but when he came back he paid no regard to me how he carried on.[92]

Otakaonan insisted that his band was not rejecting a treaty, but they wanted outside matters that were "in the way" to be dealt with first, and assurances that justice would be done with respect to the Hudson's Bay Company.

On behalf of the Cree, Kakuishmay expressed his desire that a treaty be made:

I would not be at a loss, but I am, because we are not united — the Crees and the Saulteaux [Ojibwa] — this is troubling me. I am trying to bring all together in one mind, and this is delaying us. If we could put that in order, if we were all joined together and everything was right I would like it. I would like to part well satisfied and pleased. I hear that His Excellency [Morris] is unwell, and I wish that everything would be easy in his mind. It is this that annoys me, that things do not come together.[93]

OTAKAONAN (THE GAMBLER) *acted as a spokesperson for the Ojibwa during Treaty 4 negotiations* (Provincial Archives of Saskatchewan, R-11962).

When the negotiations were on the verge of collapse, Morris reminded the Indians of the personal sacrifice he had made in order to secure a treaty, and of his desire to see it completed:

> The Chief said I was not very well, yet I am here. Why? Because the duty was laid upon me. I was afraid of the journey; but when a Chief has a duty to do he tries to do it, and I felt that if I could do you any good, as I believed I could, I ought to be here. I tell you this, trust my words, they come from the heart of one who loves the Indian people, and who is charged by his Queen to tell them the words of truth.[94]

The following day, the chiefs expressed a willingness to treat. Kakuishmay reiterated his openness to the proceedings, and implored his colleagues to do the same.[95] Chief Kamooses, a Fort Qu'Appelle Ojibwa, asked Morris for assurances that all would receive the benefits of the treaty, including those not present. He also sought assurances that the agreement would entail a reciprocal existence with their white cousins, the most important element of treaty. Only on receiving the assurance that "The Queen's power will be around him" did Kamooses and the other negotiators move on to the specific provisions of the treaty.[96]

Despite the lack of celebration, Treaty 4 was not without some symbolic exchange. Each session began with "the formal handshaking, which ceremony they repeat at the beginning and close of every interview."[97] At the end of the treaty, the commissioners presented the chiefs and councillors with official suits and silver treaty medals. Morris also promised to provide each chief with a flag, having come to appreciate the symbolic authority that these items bestowed on those who carried them.

Having seen the significance Mawedopenais had attributed to the treaty text the previous year, Morris and the commissioners had resolved to provide each chief with a copy. It would stand not only as a symbol of the compact being made, but also as a means of ensuring that future generations on both sides would be held accountable to the promises made.[98]

The text of Treaty 4 included elements of the principles of reciprocity, equality, and trust that had been communicated during the proceedings, consistent with the treaty relationship as understood by the elders. Under certain interpretations, the treaty text is consistent with the three elements of self-government found in the Aboriginal perspective.[99] First, "the authority to make decisions that determine the conditions of our lives" can be linked to the treaty text:

> [The chiefs promise] that they will maintain peace and good order between each other, and between themselves and other tribes of Indians and between themselves and others of Her Majesty's subjects . . . and that they

will assist the officers of Her Majesty in bringing to justice and punishment any Indian offending against the stipulations of this treaty, or infringing the laws in force in the country. . . .[100]

Like the Canadian elected officials who represent their own people under the Crown, so do First Nations chiefs become, through treaty, "officers of the Crown," continuing to represent and make laws on behalf of their constituents, and ensuring the shared values of peace, order, and good government flourish in their respective, semi-autonomous communities.

Second, "economic self-reliance" is evident in the promise of the continuation of traditional hunting, trapping, and fishing activities, and in the new economic opportunities detailed in the treaty text, such as education and agriculture.

Finally, the text is replete with language suggesting the intended "new relationship" that Aboriginal groups continue to lobby for:

it is the desire of Her Majesty to open up for settlement, immigration, trade . . . a tract of country . . . and to obtain the consent thereto of Her Indian subjects inhabiting the said tract, and to make a treaty and arrange with them, so that there may be peace and good will between them and Her Majesty and between them and Her Majesty's other subjects, and that Her Indian people may know and be assured of what allowance they are to count upon and receive from Her Majesty's bounty and benevolence.[101]

Their authority now flowing from the Crown (mandated by the Creator), the First Nations now have a duty toward the equally autonomous Euro-Canadian peoples — now partners under the Crown, or "Queen Mother" — to ensure a reciprocal, positive inter-community relationship. The text refers to the First Nations and the Queen as two "contracting parties," suggesting a formalized equality,[102] and Christie referred to the treaty as "a covenant between them and the Government."[103] Similar terms were written into the other treaties Morris negotiated.

Treaty 5

Treaty 5 differed in some respects from its predecessors. To begin with, there were only two commissioners, Morris and James McKay, leaving Morris with greater leeway in negotiations and writing the treaty. Instead of meeting the First Nations of the region at one location, as in previous treaties, Morris travelled to four different communities on a two-week, thousand-mile journey around and beyond Lake Winnipeg. "Every arrangement was made to secure the utmost economy in effecting the treaty," he recalled, "and yet to give satisfaction to the Indians concerned."[104]

The terms of Treaty 5 were less generous than previous treaties, reflecting the government's perception that much of the land was unsuitable for cultivation, and therefore of less value. Laird, accordingly, instructed Morris to offer a $5 gratuity, and 160 acres per family, as opposed to the $12 and one square mile that had been granted at Treaties 3 and 4. He also instructed Morris to identify the reserves during his trip.[105]

No transcription of the proceedings was made for Treaty 5. The only written record is Morris's official report and subsequent correspondence. Important information can be gleaned from this text, nonetheless, and, as Morris's reports for Treaties 3, 4, and 6 were consistent with written transcriptions of the proceedings — proceedings that were transcribed by someone other than Morris — there is no reason to believe that his information was inaccurate. Indeed, much of the sequence of events recorded in these reports and correspondence are corroborated by the diary of Captain Hackland of the *Colville*, the paddle-wheeled vessel that ferried Morris and his party around Lake Winnipeg.[106]

JAMES McKay. *An advisor to Morris on several key issues, McKay was an interpreter and facilitator at Treaties 1, 2 and 3, and a Commissioner at Treaties 5 and 6* (Glenbow Archives, NA-3242-2).

The Ojibwa and Swampy Cree of the region generally welcomed the prospect of a treaty, and trusted the promised benevolence of the government. Their hunting and fishing grounds had not been as adversely affected as those of their plains kinsmen, and the threat of mass immigration was not immediately present, but the decline of the Hudson's Bay Company and the fur trade left many looking for alternative employment and means of survival. One band from Norway House desired a treaty so as "to escape from starvation and cannibalism and to adopt the means employed by the white man to preserve life, by disturbing the soil and raising food out of the ground."[107] Others were likely encouraged by influential missionaries.[198]

Morris believed, as before, that there was some urgency for a treaty. Not only were portions of the region suitable for settlement — Icelandic communities were already being established — but, as Morris explained, "until the construction of the Pacific Railway west of the city of Winnipeg, the lake and Saskatchewan River are destined to become the principal thoroughfare of communication between Manitoba and the fertile prairies in the west."[109] Morris had lobbied Ottawa for a treaty, having himself received reports and delegations of First Nations requesting one. Laird had initially proposed an adhesion to Treaty 1, but Morris insisted that a new treaty was necessary. Despite mounting costs in all areas of government, the Department of the Interior gave its approval. Morris "expected that fewer than 200 families would be included in this new accord."[110]

Morris appears to have thoroughly enjoyed his trip aboard the *Colville*, perhaps especially because he had brought his two eldest daughters, Christine and Elizabeth, along for the journey.[111] The expedition was in some respects a voyage of discovery, as government knowledge of the region was limited. Despite the land's limited cultivability, Morris reported on its promise with the eye of an optimistic land speculator, remarking, in terminology reminiscent of his "Canada and Her Resources" essay, on its mining, navigation, and forestry potential, even going so far as to anticipate large settlements along the south-western shore. Once again, Morris negotiated with what he believed to be the government's best interests in mind. Nevertheless, he was accommodating on certain points, and for the most part the treaty was completed amicably, with the corresponding ceremony and celebration.

Morris's strategy for negotiations was to entice the Aboriginal negotiators by discussing the proposed terms of the treaty first, then to broach the more difficult question of reserves. In each case, this strategy brought "satisfactory results." Berens River was the first stop on the voyage, and the commissioners received a warm welcome, being greeted with volleys of firearms. Negotiations were held in a Wesleyan Mission schoolhouse operated by one Rev. Young, and lasted seven hours, going late into the night. "The question of reserves was one of some difficulty," Morris wrote, "but eventually this was arranged, and the Indians agreed

Negotiating the Numbered Treaties

to accept our offer, and the indenture of treaty was signed by the Chiefs and head-men."[112] James McKay and the Hon. Thomas Howard, acting as a secretary and paymaster, respectively, closed the meeting by paying out the $5 dollars per head, as provided in the treaty. At Norway House, where the arrival of the *Colville* was similarly greeted with a *feu de joie*, Morris and McKay met a Christian band and a band of "Pagan Indians" from Cross Lake. "I made an explanation of the object of our visit in English, and the Hon. James McKay in the Indian dialect. . . . The Indians gratefully accepted the offered terms, and we adjourned the conference to enable them to consult as to reserves." The Christian chief returned to Morris and expressed the desire of some of his followers to relocate south to Grassy Narrows on Lake Winnipeg, so as to "obtain a livelihood by farming and fishing," in light of their having lost employment from the Hudson's Bay Company. Mindful of the "proposed Icelandic settlement there," Morris and McKay suggested Fisher River instead — forty miles north of Grassy Narrows, which the band accepted. Morris recommended that those who remained should, in lieu of a reserve, "retain their present houses and gardens." The Cross Lake band desired a reserve at their present location, and the commissioners agreed. After these agreements were made, the treaty appears to have been concluded with due ceremony and celebration: [113]

> The treaty was then signed and the medals and uniforms presented. The Chiefs, on behalf of their people, thanked Her Majesty and her officers for their kindness to the Indian people, which I suitably acknowledged, and the payment of the presents was commenced. . . . We left that day at half-past three amidst cheering by the Indians and a salute of fire-arms.[114]

Negotiations at Grand Rapids a few days later were more difficult, and Morris was forced to compromise. In a situation not unlike that put forward by the Fort Qu'Appelle Ojibwa a year earlier, the band insisted that much of the land claimed by the Hudson's Bay Company post be included in their reserve. Morris's position was essentially unchanged: promises to the company would be honoured, just as promises to the First Nations were. When the band persisted, Morris promised to look into the matter to ensure that the company lands had been allocated lawfully.

The people wanted their reserve to include both the south and north shores of the river, the latter being where they had made their homes. Morris normally favoured allocating reserve lands where the people wished, especially if they had already begun to build or cultivate. In this instance, however, he kept the government's best interests in mind. The north shore being more strategically important for controlling transportation and communications along the river, and better suited for a town site, Morris suggested that the band relocate to the south shore. Initially they objected, but eventually they acceded to the request on the grounds of good faith, and "if a small sum was given them to assist in removing their houses, or building others." Recognizing the band's benevolence, Morris and McKay agreed to the compromise offer, "believing it to be alike in the interests of the Government to have the control of so important a point as the mouth of the great internal river of the Saskatchewan, and yet only just to the Indians, who were making what was to them so large a concession to the wishes of the Commissioners."[115]

Morris and McKay extended the people and the territory covered by the treaty beyond what had been approved by the Minister of the Interior. This was done in part to ensure that the treaty area corresponded with the lands claimed by the Ojibwa and the Swampy Cree. The new boundaries incorporated the bands who had signed at Norway House, whose traditional territory, Morris learned, extended beyond the originally proposed area. Additionally, the commissioners had been persuaded to meet the request of bands that demonstrated a desire to enter the treaty.

On their journey home, the *Colville* encountered yet another group at Dog Head Point, where they were again greeted with a *feu de joie*. The band, led by Thickfoot, had caught wind of the commissioners' mission and had been waiting for them. "Thickfoot said he had cattle and would like to have a place assigned to his people on the main shore, where they could live by farming and fishing," Morris wrote. "We suggested Fisher River to them, which they approved of. Eventually we decided on paying these Indians — took Thickfoot's adhesion to the treaty." The meeting ended cordially, Thickfoot expressing "gratitude for the kindness of the Government, and his belief that Indians of the various Islands and of Jack Head Point would cheerfully accept the Queen's benevolence and settle on a reserve."[116]

Given the *ad hoc* extension of the treaty area, Morris and McKay agreed that extensive work would have to be done in the next year to secure the necessary adhesions to the treaty.

Despite the lack of a transcription of the proceedings, Treaty 5 appears to have been completed with all the symbolism of reciprocity and equality of its predecessors. Ceremony played a role in the negotiations, including the customary distribution of clothing and medals among the chiefs and headmen, to be presented on the implementation of the treaty. The text of the treaty, which Morris reported he had fully explained through McKay, contained the same symbolic language of reciprocity and equality as that of earlier treaties.

Negotiations were difficult at times, but the atmosphere was amicable. The Grand Rapids band, for instance, must have been impressed by Morris's words, for they agreed to relocate to the south side of the Saskatchewan River in part because "the Queen's Government were treating them so kindly."[117] During his journey, Morris took every opportunity to leave the *Colville* and confer with the Indians,

Negotiating the Numbered Treaties

and they remembered him well when Thomas Howard and J. Lestock Reid arrived to secure adhesions and make treaty payments the following year.

Howard had come to the North West with the Red River Expeditionary Force in 1869, and remained in Manitoba to engage in the public life of the new province, holding various positions in the provincial administration until 1878. Reid was a surveyor and government official who had come to Winnipeg in 1870 after a brief career as a coffee and cotton planter in Australia and Fiji.

At Norway House, Reid reported that "there was a very hearty and apparently sincere expression of gratitude, on the part of all the Indians present, for the liberality extended to them, and a general and spoken wish that their thanks be conveyed to the Queen's Representative in this Province for his kind interest in their welfare."[118]

Morris advocated a speedy implementation of the treaty promises, including adhesions, the laying out of reserves, and the procurement of agricultural implements. He took noticeable pride in the accomplishment the following year when Howard and Reid secured the adhesions to the treaty, reporting to Laird that "having obtained the assent of the whole of the Indians within the region treated for so far, is a most satisfactory feature of the year's operations."[119]

Morris had evidently developed a personal commitment to the treaties and the fulfillment of the government's promises.

Treaty 6

Treaty 6 was a milestone for Alexander Morris. He knew it would likely be his last, and he was determined not to leave the task to anyone else:

> I undertook [the] arduous and responsible duty, knowing that my connection with the North West was about to cease, because I believed that, from my relations with the Indians, I was more likely to succeed than a stranger and because further, I was of opinion from my own experience that it was very undesirable that the new Lieutenant-Governor, whoever he might be, should take part in the negotiation of a Treaty which he would be called upon to administer.[120]

Whereas in Treaties 3 and 4, it was uncertain who would negotiate for the government, there was no question that Morris would take on the role for Treaty 6. "Your large experience and past success in conducting Indian negotiations," wrote Minister Laird, "relieves me from the necessity of giving you any detailed instructions in reference to your present mission."[121]

The negotiations for Treaty 6 marked the highest level of the development and articulation of Morris's understanding of the treaty relationship. They also revealed the level of anxiety he had developed over First Nations' future and survival.

The sources documenting these negotiations are more extensive than for any of the preceding treaties. They include the lengthiest transcription of proceedings to date, and the most detailed report of treaty negotiations ever prepared by Morris — a sign of his growing appreciation of the significance of the treaties and of the proceedings themselves. Peter Erasmus, the interpreter selected by the Cree, had his version of the proceedings recorded, providing another perspective as well as a means of verifying Morris's version. With a few notable exceptions, Erasmus's recollection of the proceedings was consistent with that reported by Morris and recorded by his secretary, Dr. A.G. Jackes.

Treaty 6 is significant in and of itself because of the terms of the agreement. Morris's strategy was to deal firmly with those who opposed the treaty, and accommodate as far as possible the more moderate elements of First Nations leadership. Laird would have presumed that Morris would negotiate terms similar, if not identical, to those of Treaty 4, and to the best advantage of the government's shrinking coffers, but Treaty 6 included the most generous terms yet offered by the government. This was a result of the tactics employed by the Cree, the general circumstances of the country, and the perceived value of this section of the "fertile belt." They also speak both to the increasingly accommodating attitude Morris took in his approach to Aboriginal demands, and to his evolving understanding of the broader implications and commitments that the treaty relationship entailed.

FORT CARLTON, 1876. *Treaty negotiations were often a grand affair, bringing together dozens of chiefs and councillors, and hundreds of their followers. Morris's tent was located on a hill overlooking the encampment* (Library and Archives Canada, C-064741).

The people of the region, primarily Cree — with some Assiniboines, Chi-pewyans, and Ojibwa — had been calling for a treaty since 1871. W. J. Christie, working for the Hudson's Bay Company at the time, warned that if a treaty was not promised the result might be violence and a protracted "Indian war," spelling disaster for the company, for any current or future settlement, and for the First Nations themselves. Disaster was averted only when Christie pro-vided the Aboriginal leadership with some "little presents" and provisions, and when he agreed to write a letter to "His Excellency Governor Archibald, our Great Mother's representative at Fort Garry." Sweetgrass, listed as the "Chief of the Country," stated his demand for a treaty to the Lieutenant-Governor. He disputed the legitimacy of the Hudson's Bay Company's sale of Rupert's Land to Canada, and called for agricultural assistance and "provision for us against years of starvation" in light of the impending disappearance of the buffalo. Sweetgrass also wanted the Crown to protect his people against illicit American traders, and to act as an arbiter among First Nations. "We made a peace this winter with the Blackfeet," he said. "Our young men are foolish, it may not last long."[122]

Sweetgrass's colleagues expressed a similar desire for treaty. Kihewin expressed the good will of the people and the desired relationship of reciprocity: "Let us be friendly. We never shed any white man's blood, and have always been friendly with the whites. . . . I want all my brother, Sweetgrass, asks." The Little Hunter wanted recognition of his authority: "You, my brother, the Great Chief in Red River, treat me as a brother, that is, as a Great Chief."[123] The Cree were concerned about smallpox in addition to the disappearance of the buffalo, and were equally apprehensive about Canadian and Métis encroachments on their land.

Apprised of the situation when he took office, Morris had been lobbying for a treaty in the region since December 1872, but the government insisted on a gradual policy of treaty making, "as the territory was required."[124] In March 1874, Morris forwarded an alarming report by one Charles N. Bell, warning that the Cree, many of whom were on the verge of starvation, were beginning to believe that no treaty would be made and that settlers would simply "come and occupy their country." Like the Ojibwa and the Swampy Cree, they were also upset by the Hudson's Bay Company surveys taking place around the trad-ing posts. Bell warned that sending telegraph construction and surveying par-ties "into Indian country before any treaties had been concluded was doing a great deal of harm."[125] Métis disaffection added to the tension. They, too, were worried about the possibility of starvation and the prospect of being driven from their lands.[126]

Without a mandate, Morris recommended that, at the very least, a force be sent to ensure the safety of the Hudson's Bay Company post at Fort Carlton. In 1875, the government ordered Colonel French of the North West Mounted Police to take a small force of 50 men, but upon his arrival, he, too, resolved that a treaty was necessary. Fellow officer Selby Smyth provided a poignant explanation of the situation:

> The question of the Indian action regarding their prohibition against any Government works geological or telegraphic being carried on until their Treaty is made, requires neither the interference of Military or Civil power — but merely the presence of someone armed with authority to conclude a satisfactory treaty which they say has been so long promised they can no longer rely on promises only — but decline permitting their country to be made use of by Government officials until the treaty becomes a fact. I am sure it is a subject to be regretted that this was not effected before government operatives appeared in their country, which would have prevented any misunderstanding, as I am informed the Indians are perfectly civil in their conduct towards the persons they have stopped.[127]

"After a great deal of telegraphing to Laird," Morris finally obtained approval to send Rev. George McDougall, a resident missionary, to inform the First Nations of the region that a treaty would indeed be negotiated at Forts Carlton and Pitt the following summer.[128]

Morris relished the opportunity of making one more treaty. He insisted on assuming the responsibility, both because he considered it his personal duty, and because he did not trust the task to anyone of less experience — this in spite of the difficulty of the journey and his ever-uncertain health. Nonetheless, the journey to Forts Carlton and Pitt proved rewarding to a man with a love for the open air and nature. As they travelled, Morris took note of the beauty of the countryside and its potential for agriculture. He described the view on arriving: "The view was very beautiful: the hills and the trees in the distance, and in the foreground, the meadow land being dotted with clumps of wood, with the Indian tents clustered here and there to the number of two hundred."[129]

Morris must have considered it important to educate his children about treaty making. He had taken his daughters Christine and Elizabeth to the negotiations of Treaties 3 and 5.[130] It was now the turn of his twin daughters, Eva and Margaret, "then young girls," to witness the proceedings at Treaty 6. "At the Indian Treaty made by my father," recalled Edmund Morris years later, "the Crees named them (Eva) Tabis Roo Amikook — Equal to the Earth, [and Margaret] Tabis Roo Kiyick — Equal to the Sky. They called my father Kitchiokimow — the Great Chief." The Cree gave the girls "each an elk tooth which was good medicine & was to bring them good luck."[131] In later years, Edmund, a painter, took inspiration from his father's experiences and developed a deep sympathy for the Aboriginal peoples of the North West.

The journey was also disconcerting, providing Morris with a firsthand view of the devastating effects wrought by the disappearance of the buffalo. "As I came here I saw tracks leading to the lakes and water-courses, once well beaten, now grown over with grass," he told the Aboriginal negotiators. "I saw bones bleaching by the wayside; I saw the places where the buffalo had been, and I thought what will become of the Indian."[132]

The negotiations were protracted and difficult. Morris arrived at Fort Carlton on August 15, 1876, where the terms would eventually be decided. After a few days delay, while Aboriginal leaders conferred among themselves, and following the preliminary introductions and ceremony, Morris took several hours to explain the terms, which were essentially the same as Treaty 4. They were not well received. While a number of the negotiators expressed their desire to reach an understanding, they considered Morris's initial proposal parsimonious. They knew that better terms had been offered in the United States. Moreover, they were doubtless aware of the difficulties other bands had experienced in attempting the transition to agriculture, and anticipated that the greatly diminished buffalo hunt would not be sufficient to sustain them during that process. They wanted reassurances of assistance as they attempted to take up the new way of life. Chief Poundmaker expressed this concern to Morris, hoping that he would guarantee a permanent fiduciary relationship between the Crown and his people:

We were glad to hear what you had to say, and have gathered together in council and thought the words over amongst us, we were glad to hear you tell us how we might live by our own work. When I commence to settle on the lands to make a living for myself and my children, I beg of you to assist me in every way possible — when I am at a loss how to proceed I want the advice and assistance of the Government; the children yet unborn, I wish you to treat them in like manner as they advance in civilization like the white man.[133]

Morris was concerned that the chiefs were requesting daily rations, which would be logistically impossible, aside from the expense, and would lead, in his opinion, to "idleness." For the moment, he also appeared to believe that ongoing hunting would supplement the transition to agriculture. Seeing that Morris had misunderstood, the Aboriginal negotiators clarified that what they wanted was assistance only in case of famine, disease, and pestilence, or in case their initial efforts at farming failed or took longer than expected to succeed.[134]

Morris began to understand his counterparts. Consistent with Poundmaker's wish for a long-lasting fiduciary relationship, Morris explained that this was an unwritten part of the treaty relationship, and, in any case, a simple policy of good government that should be demonstrated to all peoples:

I have told you that the money I have offered you would be paid to you and to your children's children. I know that the sympathy of the Queen, and her assistance, would be given you in any unforeseen circumstances. You must trust to her generosity. Last winter when some of the Indians wanted food because the crops had been destroyed by grasshoppers, although it was not promised in the treaty, nevertheless the Government sent money to buy them food, and in the spring when many of them were sick a man was sent to try and help them. We cannot foresee these things, and all I can promise is that you will be treated kindly, and in that extraordinary circumstances you must trust to the generosity of the Queen.[135]

Cree Chief Mistawâsis welcomed Morris's words, but remained concerned: "We were glad to hear what the Governor was saying to us and we understood it, but we are not understood, we do not mean to ask for food for every day but only when we commence and in case of famine or calamity."[136]

POUNDMAKER, 1885. *A nephew of Mistawâsis and a Cree chief at the negotiation of Treaty 6, Poundmaker was sceptical of Morris's promises, and signed the treaty with reluctance* (Library and Archives Canada, C-001875).

The chiefs were wary, too, of not having a more explicit promise of fiduciary responsibility written into the treaty text itself. Peter Erasmus, the interpreter, later revealed that Mistawâsis had instructed him to ensure that all that was promised during negotiations was written into the treaty text.[137]

The chiefs presented a counter-proposal on August 23, 1876. Chief Tee-teequaysay reminded Morris of the good will they had always shown the white population, and trusted that this would be reciprocated:

> When we look back to the past we do not see where the Cree nation has ever watered the ground with the white man's blood, he has always been our friend and we his; trusting to the Giver of all good, to the generosity of the Queen, and to the Governor and his councillors, we hope you will grant us this request.[138]

The counter-proposal included an increase in cattle and other animals, and an increase in agricultural implements and other supplies, "provisions for the poor, unfortunate, blind and lame," schoolteachers and missionaries, timber rights, "liberty to change the site of the reserves before the survey," exemption from military service, and "a free supply of medicines."[139] Morris did not begrudge the new demands, but he was apprehensive about the implications that such favourable terms would have on previous treaties. Despite this, he was sympathetic to the case the negotiators had made. "Often when I thought of the future of the Indian my heart was sad within me," he told the chiefs.[140] He reported to Ottawa:

> They saw the buffalo, the only means of their support, passing away. They were anxious to learn to support themselves by agriculture, but felt too ignorant to do so, and they dreaded that during the transition period they would be swept off by disease or famine — already they have suffered terribly from the ravages of measles, scarlet fever and smallpox. It was impossible to listen to them without interest, they were not exacting, but they were very apprehensive of their future, and thankful, as one of them put it, "a new life was dawning upon them."[141]

He had been particularly struck by the story of the Cree chief at White Fish Lake, James Senum. His people had already attempted farming, using hand-made hoes and going so far as to pull the plough by their own strength. At a time when many observers assumed that the plains peoples were fated to disappear, the tenacity and determination of such bands made Morris optimistic that they could have a future, if provided with the means. Like the chiefs, Morris believed that agriculture and education, along with hunting rights, would provide the means for both immediate sustenance and long-term stability.

It was in this context that Morris explained the purpose and utility of the reserves. He assured the negotiators that they would have a say in selecting their reserves, which would be protected from the settlers and squatters who were sure to flood the country in the coming years. The chiefs who accepted the treaty recognized the importance of identifying reserve lands early on because they did not want to be "cramped up by settlers."[142] Morris did not envision the reserves as a place of forced confinement: "The Government will not interfere with the Indian's daily life, they will not bind him. They will only help him to make a living on the reserves, by giving him the means of growing from the soil, his food."[143] While using the reserve as a location for permanent residence and agricultural purposes, he assured the chiefs and councillors that they would be at liberty to leave their reserves and continue hunting and fishing on Crown lands.[144]

After consulting with Christie and McKay, Morris presented a compromise — the most expansive offer that had ever been put forward by the government. Morris had come to accept the view that anything less would be unjust, but he was aware that the new terms might prove a hard sell in Ottawa. "I must do it on my own responsibility," he wrote, "and trust to the other Queen's councillors to ratify it."[145] The new offer included an increase in both agricultural implements and livestock, as well as a promise of $1,000 worth of provisions per year for three years as the bands made the transition to agriculture. The offer included provisions for medical supplies and assistance in times of pestilence and famine. The treaty text reads:

It is further agreed between Her Majesty and the said Indians. . .

That in the event hereafter of the Indians comprised within this treaty being overtaken by any pestilence, or by a general famine, the Queen, on being satisfied and certified thereof by Her Indian Agent or Agents, will grant to the Indians assistance of such character and to such extent as Her Chief Superintendent of Indian Affairs shall deem necessary and sufficient to relieve the Indians from the calamity that shall have befallen them.

That during the next three years, after two or more of the reserves hereby agreed to be set apart to the Indians shall have been agreed upon and surveyed, there shall be granted to the Indians included under the Chiefs adhering to the treaty at Carlton, each spring, the sum of one thousand dollars, to be expended for them by Her Majesty's Indian Agents, in the purchase of provisions for the use of such of the Band as are actually settled on the reserves and are engaged in cultivating the soil, to assist them in such cultivation.

That a medicine chest shall be kept at the house of each Indian Agent for the use and benefit of the Indians at the direction of such agent.[146]

These items proved to be the turning point, and the principle Chiefs Atâhkakohp and Mistawâsis agreed to sign the treaty. The terms were eventually accepted by the Willow Cree band of Chief Beardy and by the influential Cree Chief Sweetgrass at Fort Pitt.

Despite their display of solidarity in demanding better terms, First Nations leadership had been seriously divided. A significant minority continued to distrust the government and maintained that the terms were unfair. Some rejected agriculture outright, preferring to hold to their current mode of life. Rev. George McDougall, the missionary Morris had sent to reassure the Indians the previous year, suggested that younger and aspiring chiefs and councillors may have hoped

SWEETGRASS, ST. BONIFACE, JUNE 1872. *Anxious that his people have protection from whisky traders and the means to make the transition to an agricultural way of life, Sweetgrass signed Treaty 6 at Fort Pitt in August 1876* (Glenbow Archives, NA-1677-10).

to build their own profiles by opposing the treaty.[147] Morris hoped that the older, more pragmatic leaders would persuade the young, ambitious leaders to accept the treaty. "The main body of the Crees were honestly disposed to treat," he recalled, "and their head chiefs, Mistowasis [sic] and Ahtukuhkoop [sic], shewed sound judgment, and an earnest desire to come to an understanding."[148] Morris developed a tremendous respect for these "men of intelligence" during the negotiations. They were "anxious that the people should act unitedly and reasonably."[149] Throughout the negotiations he implored the bands to listen to these wise and respected leaders — a tactic he had applied at Treaty 4. Whenever the chiefs asked for more time to deliberate among themselves, Morris was willing to accede in the hope that the extra time would help the moderates persuade their colleagues.

Church and Métis officials also played a role in informal discussions outside the negotiations. The interpreter Peter Erasmus, a Métis, was invited into the councils, and though ostensibly neutral, his explanations and clarifications of the treaty terms did much to reassure council members and the senior chiefs.[150]

Even so, some were not appeased. At one point Poundmaker declared, "This is our land! It isn't a piece of pemmican to be cut off and given in little pieces back to us. It is ours and we will take what we want." Morris was visibly shaken by this statement, and the concurrence of a number of other leaders.[151] Poundmaker argued that the terms remained inadequate, and insisted that his people would need instruction in agriculture if they were to succeed. In the same vein, Joseph Thoma of the Battle River Cree asserted that the terms did not reflect the immense value of the land being surrendered. Nuswasoowahtum, the leader of a small delegation of Ojibwa from Quill Lake, had the harshest words for Morris:

> All along the prices have been to one side, and we have had no say. He that made us provided everything for our mode of living; I have seen this all along, it has brought me up and I am not tired of it, and for you, the white man, everything has been made for your maintenance, and now that you come and stand on this our earth (ground) I do not understand; I see dimly today what you are doing, and I find fault with a portion of it; that is why I stand back; I would have been glad if every white man of every denomination were now present to hear what I say; through what you have done you have cheated my kinsmen.[152]

Morris's response was equally biting. "I will not sit here and hear such words from the Chippewas. Who are you?" He was indignant that this group of Ojibwa, whose ancestors were believed to have migrated from Ontario into the North West within the last few hundred years, asserted that other newcomers had no right to the land.

"You come from my country [Ontario] and you tell me the Queen has cheated you; it is not so. You say we have the best of the bargains; you know it is not so."[153] The delegation did not sign the treaty. Fortunately for Morris, Poundmaker and the Quill Lake band represented a minority. Poundmaker ultimately did sign the treaty, but with reluctance and, according to Erasmus, resentment.[154]

While hard negotiations were central to the treaty's successful outcome, ceremony and symbolism also played a crucial role. Morris, bedecked in his blue Lieutenant-Governor's uniform, presented himself as the Queen's symbolic representative and messenger, as at previous treaties. He noted that his escort of 100 red-coated North West Mounted Police also played an important function — as Morris put it, "emblem and evidence of the establishment of authority in the North West."[155] Erasmus also recalled that the government's use of pomp and pageantry, especially with the reputation and display of the NWMP, did much to "establish in the minds of the tribes the fairness and justice of government for all the people regardless of colour or creed."[156]

RED PHEASANT *was a representative of the Battle River Cree at Treaty 6. His brother Wuttunee, the band's chief, asked Red Pheasant to sign in his place as he had misgivings about the treaty* (Provincial Archives of Saskatchewan, RA-12911).

The bands observed their own ceremonies, and many chiefs greeted Morris with deference. At Fort Pitt, Sweetgrass put his arms around Morris's neck and gave him "a fraternal kiss on either cheek."[157] At both Carlton and Pitt, the Indians performed a number of ceremonies, which, according to Erasmus,

> had a deep significance to the tribes and can only be explained as a solemn approach to a vital and serious issue for discussion. . . . Few people realize that those so-called savages were far more deeply affected and influenced by their religious beliefs and convictions than any comparable group of white people, whose lip service to their religion goes no deeper than that.[158]

The most important of these ceremonies was the pipe. According to tradition,

> religious formalities are as important and as significant as the subject of the matter at hand, whatever that subject may be. It is an Indian custom to conduct those formalities before undertaking any matters of importance. The purpose of this tradition is that the Indians have utmost and absolute belief in the sacredness of the pipe. In the presence of the pipe, only the truth must be used and any commitment made in its presence must be kept. In that sense, then, the only means used by the Indians to finalize an agreement or to ensure a final commitment was by use of the pipe.[159]

Some historians have suggested that Morris did not fully grasp the importance of the pipe ceremony, but this is unlikely. Similar ceremonies had been performed for centuries during the fur trade, and Morris was familiar with the traditions that existed between the Hudson's Bay Company and the First Nations.[160] He was familiar with his own role in the ceremony, having gone through the process at Treaty 3, and likely on other occasions as well. He viewed it as an important part of First Nations' treaty-making practices. His recording secretary, Dr. A. G. Jackes, described the event at Treaty 6:

> As they approached his tent, the Governor, accompanied by the Hon. W. J. Christie and Hon. Jas. McKay, Commissioners, went forward to meet them and to receive the stem carried by its bearer. It was presented first to the Governor, who in accordance with their customs, stroked it several times, then passed it to the Commissioners who repeated the ceremony. The significance of this ceremony is that the Governor and Commissioners accepted the friendship of the tribe.[161]

Morris knew that anything spoken of in the slightest way as a promise would be taken as writ by the chiefs. Throughout the proceedings, from Treaties 3 through 6, he was careful to avoid promises he knew he could not fulfill.

Treaty 6 was replete with symbolic language and imagery. Morris, appreciating both the utility and the significance of the language of kinship and reciprocity, used it to establish trust and to explain the treaty relationship as he understood it:

PETER ERASMUS, 1890S. *Erasmus, a Métis, had been called upon to act as the Crees' interpreter at Treaty 6. Initially sceptical, Erasmus was gradually won over by Morris's sincerity. His account of the negotiations, including a private meeting between the chiefs, provides a crucial source against which Morris's version of events can be measured* (Glenbow Archives, NA-3148-1).

I had ascertained that the Indian mind was oppressed with vague fears, they dreaded the treaty; they had been made to believe that they would be compelled to live on the reserves wholly, and abandon their hunting, and that in time of war, they would be placed in the front and made to fight. I accordingly shaped my address, so as to give them confidence in the intentions of the Government, and to quiet their apprehensions.[162]

After the pipe ceremony at Fort Carlton, Morris opened the negotiations by describing the equality that existed among all the participants:

> I shake hands with all of you in my heart. . . . What I say and what you say, and what we do, is done openly before the whole people. You are, like me and my friends who are with me, children of the Queen. We are of the same blood, the same God made us and the same Queen rules over us. . . . As the Queen's chief servant here, I always keep my promises.[163]

The treaty was to last forever, he promised, and be to the benefit of future generations:

> What I trust and hope we will do is not for today or tomorrow only; what I will promise, and what I believe and hope you will take, is to last as long as that sun shines and yonder river flows. You have to think of those who will come after you, and it will be a remembrance for me as long as I live, if I can go away feeling that I have done well for you.[164]

Following the pipe ceremony at Fort Pitt, Morris offered an optimistic view of the future in language that evoked the imagery of the coexistence of Canadians and First Nations. He described his understanding of the treaty relationship in his official report to Ottawa:

> After the conclusion of these proceedings I addressed them, telling them we had come at their own request, and that there was now a trail leading from Lake Superior to Red River, that I saw it stretching on thence to Fort Ellice, and there branching off, the one track going to Qu'Appelle and Cyprus [sic] Hills, and the other by Fort Pelly to Carlton, and thence I expected to see it extended, by way of Fort Pitt to the Rocky Mountains; on that road I saw all the Chippewas and Crees walking, and I saw along it gardens being planted and houses built. I invited them to join their brother Indians and walk with the white men on this road.[165]

Negotiating the Numbered Treaties

From Morris's perspective, one purpose of the treaties was to bring the First Nations of the North West under the Queen's governance. Morris was already referring to them as subjects of the Queen, but the treaties were a means of legitimating their position under the Crown.

Some authors have dismissed the negotiators' symbolism as "flowery language," used to avoid the "hard" issues.[166] But over the course of the negotiations, Morris appears to have been understood by the Aboriginal leaders, and to have won their confidence. "I was told the Governor was a good man," said Atâhkakohp, "and now that I see him I believe he is; in coming to see us, and what he has spoken, he has removed almost all obstacles and misunderstandings, and I hope he may remove them all."[167] Sweetgrass, on signing the treaty, expressed his trust in Morris's promises and a desire to establish a relationship of reciprocity among Indians and whites: "I am thankful that the white man and red man can stand together. When I hold your hand and touch your heart, let us be as one; use your utmost to help me and help my children so that they may prosper." [168] For Chief Seekahskootch, Morris's words effected a change of perspective: "I am glad of the goodness of the great Queen. I recognize now that this that I once dreaded most is coming to my aid and doing for me what I could not do for myself."[169] Similar examples can be found throughout the reports and transcripts of the negotiations.

Peter Erasmus was initially suspicious of the government party, but he was won over by Lieutenant-Governor Morris. Between the demands and resistance of the Aboriginal negotiators on the one hand and Ottawa's insistence that the terms be kept as inexpensive as possible on the other, Erasmus came to appreciate Morris's position, and thought of him as "a boxer sent into the ring with his hands tied."[170] Erasmus described the moment that he and the First Nations leaders came to trust Morris and his message, on the second day of the negotiations:

> The Governor went on to explain that unless certain lands were set aside for the sole use of the Indians, the country would be flooded with white settlers who would not give the Indians any consideration whatever. He made references to other areas where settlement was growing very fast. . . . His manner held a sincerity that was most effective in impressing his audience. Knowing the Indians as I did, I could see that they were receiving the message with a growing understanding of its purpose.
>
> Standing at the Governor's table I was able to observe the reactions of some of the listeners. I felt that Big Child [Mistawâsis] and Star Blanket [Atâhkakohp] were both convinced of the fairness and justice of the terms explained to them by the speaker. I had an increased confidence in my interpretations, my sympathies transferred to the Governor's side, and my early animosity to the party was completely gone. The translations came to my tongue without effort.[171]

Morris's manner of speaking had proved easy to translate for the experienced interpreter.

In private council among First Nations leaders, Atâhkakohp and Mistawâsis made the case for pragmatism, repeating a number of points that Morris had made in his opening remarks and demonstrating a trust in his words. "Indian eloquence had full play that day," Erasmus recalled. [172] Like Poundmaker, the Badger, and others opposed to the treaty, Mistawâsis lamented the passing of the buffalo and "the loss of the ancient glory of our forefathers." But he appealed to the council to consider the future:

> I speak directly to Poundmaker and the Badger and those others who ob-
> ject to signing the treaty. Have you anything better to offer our people? I
> ask, again, can you suggest anything that will bring these things back for
> tomorrow and all the tomorrows that face our people? I for one think that
> the Great White Queen Mother has offered us a way of life when the buf-
> falo are no more. [173]

Mistawâsis was especially concerned about the future of the Cree if they left themselves open to the attacks and illicit trade of the American traders who had devastated the once-powerful Blackfoot. He welcomed the protection being of-fered by the Crown, saying that, when the Queen sent out the Red Coats (the North West Mounted Police),

> the cutthroats and criminals . . . immediately abandoned their forts. . . .
> It was the power that stands behind those few Red Coats that those men
> feared and wasted no time in getting out when they could; the power that
> is represented in all the Queen's people, and we the children are counted as
> important as even the Governor who is her personal speaker.
>
> The Police are the Queen Mother's agents and have the same laws for
> whites as they have for the Indians. I have seen these things done and now
> the Blackfoot welcome these servants of the Queen Mother and invite her
> Governor for a treaty with them next year.
>
> I for one look to the Queen's law and her Red Coat servants to protect
> our people against the evils of the white man's firewater and to stop the
> senseless wars among our people. [174]

Mistawâsis implored his colleagues to renounce violence, and compared their situation with that of the First Nations in the United States, as Morris had often done: "There is no law or justice for the Indians in Long Knives' country." [175]

Atâhkakohp also renounced violence, emphasizing the disappearance of the buffalo and the inevitable arrival of settlers. Like Morris, he believed that his people would need to identify protected reserves before mass immigration could create conflict and leave them without any means of self-sufficiency. He repudiated those who sought to delay the inevitable only to weaken their position:

> There are men among you who are trying to blind our eyes, and refuse to see the things that have brought us to this pass. Let us not think of ourselves but of our children's children. We hold our place among the tribes as chiefs and councillors because our people think we have wisdom above others amongst us. . . . Let us show our wisdom by choosing the right path now while we yet have a choice. . . .
>
> For my part, I think that the Queen Mother has offered us a new way and I have faith in the things my brother Mistawâsis has told you. The mother earth has always given us plenty with the grass that fed the buffalo. Surely we Indians can learn the ways of living that made the white man strong. . . . I will accept the Queen's hand for my people.[176]

The words of Mistawâsis and Atâhkakohp persuaded most of those present. "After I had retired to our tent," Erasmus recalled, "I lay awake thinking of the things spoken by the two chiefs, and marvelled at the confidence they both felt in the fairness of the justice carried out by this slender arm of the Queen Mother." Many of the Indians, he went on, had been impressed by the promises of protection and justice, as exemplified by the government's attempts at bringing two American traders to justice for their part in the Cypress Hills Massacre of 1873.[177]

Morris was always careful to distinguish between American and Canadian policy. He believed in the superiority of British justice, and insisted that the principle of "friendship between the British, and the Indians" was a longstanding tradition. He took inspiration from the example of Isaac Brock and Tecumseh who, during the War of 1812, "fought side by side as brothers." He asserted that good relations between the Six Nations and the Queen persisted, as the Crown had assisted the Iroquois Confederacy in "old Canada" to take up agriculture and schooling.[178]

The comparison between US and Canadian policies clearly placed Canadian justice in a favourable light. Morris was well aware that the First Nations had been greatly impressed by the actions of the North West Mounted Police in establishing security and discouraging illicit trade, and by the tenacity of the Canadian government in its attempts to bring the perpetrators of the Cypress Hills Massacre to justice. He repeatedly reminded the Aboriginal leaders of this record. The NWMP, he said, would be friends, or colleagues, of the chiefs under the Crown: "Our Indian Chiefs wear red coats, and wherever they meet the police they will know they meet friends."[179] The NWMP were there to maintain order and justice: "The good Indian need never be afraid; their lives will be safer than ever before. Look at the condition of the Blackfeet. Before the red-coats went, the Americans were taking their furs and robes and giving them whiskey — we stopped it. . . ."[180]

After the signings of Treaty 6 at Forts Carlton and Pitt, Morris gave the chiefs medals, uniforms, and flags, recognizing them as officers of the Crown: "The chiefs and headmen are not to be lightly put aside. When a treaty is made they become servants of the Queen; they are to try and keep order amongst their people. We will try to keep order in the whole country. . . ."[181] He also gave them copies of the treaty, so that the promises could not be "rubbed out."[182]

Morris's understanding of the chiefs as officers of the Crown, and of the relative autonomy of Aboriginal communities, was consistent with his long-held belief in local self-government. For their part, many chiefs welcomed the recognition of their offices by the Crown, as it provided stability of leadership in otherwise turbulent times.[183] The medals and uniforms held great significance for them, and they wore them to Morris's farewell at Fort Carlton:

> The whole band, headed by their Chiefs and Councillors, dressed in their uniforms, came to Carlton House to pay their farewell visit to me. The chiefs came forward in order, each addressing me a few remarks, and I replied briefly. They then gave three cheers for the Queen, the Governor, one for the Mounted Police, and for Mr. Lawrence Clarke, of Carlton House, and then departed, firing guns as they went.[184]

Morris took pride in the final agreement, and his parting words were not without self-congratulation: "We have done a good work; we will never all of us meet again face to face, but I go on to my other work, feeling that I have, in the Queen's hands, been instrumental to your good."[185] At Fort Pitt, his farewell seemed more a lament: "Indians of the plains, I bid you farewell. . . . I rejoice that you listened to me, and when I go back to my home beyond the great lakes, I will often think of you and will rejoice to hear of your prosperity. I ask God to bless you and your children. Farewell."[186]

Morris had obviously developed a personal connection with the treaties and the chiefs and councillors who signed them. He had smoked the pipe with them. Again and again, he had put his own reputation on the line. Negotiations had often been emotionally and physically exhausting, but he did not question that it had been worth the effort: "I rise with a glad heart; we have come together and understood each other. . . . I feel that we have done today a good work; the years will pass away and we with them, but the work we have done today will stand as the hills."[187]

In his report to the government, Morris urged the speedy implementation of treaty promises, and offered suggestions as to how they could be carried out. "It is important," he wrote, "that the cattle and agricultural implements should be

Negotiating the Numbered Treaties

given them without delay. . . . I think it probable that cattle and some implements could be purchased at Prince Albert and thus avoid transportation." He recommended that the government immediately meet the "universal demand for teachers," and hoped that the churches would meet the request for missionaries.[188] He recommended that immediate action be taken to implement laws for the preservation of the buffalo. The North West Council had already developed a plan of action, he pointed out to the Minister of the Interior: "had our regime continued we would have passed a statute for their preservation. I commend the matter to the attention of our successors as one of urgent importance."[189]

Significantly, Morris urged the Department of the Interior to meet a number of demands he had been unable to promise during the negotiations:

> Though I did not grant the request, I thought the desire of the Indians, to be instructed in farming and building, most reasonable, and I would therefore recommend that measures be adopted to provide such instruction for them. Their present mode of living is passing away; the Indians are tractable, docile and willing to learn. I think that advantage should be taken of this disposition to teach them to become self-supporting, which can best be accomplished with the aid of a few practical farmers and carpenters to instruct them in farming and house building.[190]

At various points during the Treaty 6 negotiations, some chiefs had asked for assurances that lands occupied by the Métis would also be recognized. Morris had no mandate to make such guarantees, so he could do no more than say that he would report the request to the government. This he did, with a recommendation that measures be taken not only to protect Métis lands, but to assist them in agricultural practice, as they were equally affected by the devastation of the buffalo, and maintained a strong influence among the local Indian population.[191] This was not the first nor the last time that Morris lobbied in private for the interests of Aboriginal peoples.

J. B. No 6694 - ...

Articles of a Treaty made and concluded at near Carlton on the 23rd day of August and on the 28th day of said month respectively and near Fort Pitt on the 9th day of September in the year of Our Lord one thousand eight hundred and seventy six between **Her Most Gracious Majesty the Queen of Great Britain and Ireland** by Her Commissioners, the Honorable Alexander Morris, Lieutenant Governor of the Province of Manitoba and the North West Territories, and the Honorable James McKay and the Honorable William Joseph Christie of the one part and the Plain and Wood Cree and the other Tribes of Indians, inhabitants of the country within the limits hereinafter defined and described by their Chiefs, chosen and named as hereinafter mentioned, of the other part: ——

Whereas the Indians inhabiting the said country have, pursuant to an appointment made by the said Commissioners, been convened at meetings at Fort Carlton, Fort Pitt and Battle River to deliberate upon certain matters of interest to Her Most Gracious Majesty, of the one part, and the said Indians of the other;

And Whereas the said Indians have been notified and informed by Her Majesty's said Commissioners, that it is the desire of Her Majesty to open up for settlement, immigration and such other purposes as to Her Majesty may seem meet, a tract of country bounded and described as hereinafter mentioned, and to obtain the consent thereto of Her Indian subjects inhabiting the said tract, and to make a treaty and arrange with them, so that there may be peace and good will between them and Her Majesty, and that they may know and be assured of what allowance they are to count upon and receive from Her Majesty's bounty and benevolence;

And Whereas, the Indians of the said tract, duly convened in Council, as aforesaid, and being requested by Her Majesty's said Commissioners to name certain Chiefs and headmen, who should be authorized on their behalf to conduct such negotiations and sign any treaty to be founded thereon, and to become responsible to Her Majesty for their faithful performance by their respective Bands of such obligations as shall be assumed by them, the said Indians have thereupon named the following persons for that purpose, that is to say: — representing the Indians who make the Treaty at Carlton, the several chiefs and councillors who have subscribed hereto, and representing the Indians who make the treaty at Fort Pitt, the several chiefs and councillors who have subscribed hereto.

TREATY 6, PAGE 1, AUGUST 1876. *Following the practice of the time, most of the text was prepared before the negotiations actually took place* (Library and Archives Canada, E-004156541).

therefor by the said Government;

It is further agreed between Her Majesty and Her said Indians, that such sections of the Reserves above indicated as may at any time be required for public works or buildings, of what nature soever, may be appropriated for that purpose by Her Majesty's Government of the Dominion of Canada, due compensation being made for the value of any improvements thereon, _____

And further, that Her Majesty's Commissioners shall, as soon as possible after the execution of this treaty, cause to be taken an accurate census of all the Indians inhabiting the tract above described, distributing them in families, and shall, in every year ensuing the date hereof, at some period in each year, to be duly notified to the Indians, and at a place or places to be appointed for that purpose within the Territory ceded, pay to each Indian person, the sum of five dollars per head yearly.

It is further agreed between Her Majesty and the said Indians that the sum of $1500 per annum shall be yearly and every year expended by Her Majesty in the purchase of ammunition, and twine for nets for the use of the said Indians, in manner following, that is to say:— In the reasonable discretion as regards the distribution thereof among the Indians inhabiting the several Reserves or otherwise included herein, of Her Majesty's Indian Agent having the supervision of this treaty;

It is further agreed between Her Majesty and the said Indians, that the following articles shall be supplied to any Band of the said Indians who are now cultivating the soil, or who shall hereafter commence to cultivate the land, that is to say:— Four hoes for every family actually cultivating; also two spades per family as aforesaid; one plough for every three families as aforesaid; one harrow for every three families as aforesaid; two scythes for every family as aforesaid, and also two axes, and also one cross-cut saw, one hand saw, one pit saw, the necessary files, one grindstone and one auger for each Band; and also for each Chief for the use of his Band, one chest of ordinary carpenter's tools; also, for each Band, enough of wheat, barley, potatoes and oats to plant the land actually broken up for cultivation by such Band; also, for each Band, four oxen, one bull, and six cows; all the aforesaid articles to be given once for all for the encouragement of the practice of agriculture among the Indians.

It is further agreed between Her Majesty and the said Indians, that each Chief duly recognized as such, shall receive an annual salary of twenty-five dollars per annum; and each subordinate officer, not exceeding four for each band, shall receive fifteen dollars per annum, and each such Chief and subordinate officer as aforesaid shall also receive, once every three years, a suitable suit of clothing; and each Chief shall receive, in recognition of the closing of the treaty, a suitable flag and medal

Treaty 6, Page 5, August 1876. *The number of changes visible on this page, including additional provisions, implements, and moneys for the bands, speaks both to the negotiating skills of the chiefs and Morris's growing flexibility in such matters* (Library and Archives Canada, E-004156545).

6

That in the event hereafter of the Indians comprised within this treaty being overtaken by any pestilence or by a general famine, the Queen on being satisfied and certified thereof by her Indian Agent or agents will grant to the Indians assistance of such character and to such extent as her chief Superintendent of Indian affairs shall deem necessary and sufficient to relieve the Indians from the calamity that shall have befallen them.

That during the next three years after two or more of the reserves hereby agreed to be set apart to the Indians shall have been agreed upon and surveyed, there shall be granted to the Indians included under the Chiefs adhering to the treaty at Carlton, each Spring, the sum of one thousand dollars to be expended for them by Her Majesty's Indian agents in the purchase of provisions for the use of such of the band as are actually settled on the reserves and are engaged in cultivating the soil, to assist them in such cultivation.

That a medicine chest shall be kept at the house of each Indian agent for the use and benefit of the Indians at the discretion of such agent.

That with regard to the Indians included under the Chiefs adhering to the treaty at Fort Pitt and to those under chiefs within the treaty limits who may hereafter give their adhesion hereto (exclusively however of the Indians of the Carlton region) there shall during three years, after two or more reserves shall have been agreed upon and surveyed, be distributed each Spring among the bands cultivating the soil on such reserves, by Her Majesty's chief Indian Agent for this treaty, in his discretion a sum not exceeding one thousand dollars in the purchase of provisions for the use of such members of the band as are actually settled on the reserves and engaged in the cultivation of the soil, to assist and encourage them in such cultivation.

That in lieu of wagons, if they desire it and declare their option to that effect, there shall be given to each of the chiefs adhering hereto at Fort Pitt or elsewhere hereafter (exclusively of those in the Carlton district) in recognition of this treaty so soon as the same can be conveniently transported, two carts with iron bushings and tires. —

TREATY 6, PAGE 6, AUGUST 1876. *Page 6 is entirely new, containing the "famine and pestilence" and "medicine chest" clauses* (Library and Archives Canada, E-004156546).

TREATY 6, PAGE 8, AUGUST 1876. *Morris's signature (middle right) and those of a number of chiefs and councillors are visible on this page* (Library and Archives Canada, E-004156548).

LIEUTENANT-GOVERNOR ALEXANDER MORRIS *in the formal regalia of his office, including a ceremonial sword. He would have been similarly attired during treaty negotiations* (Library and Archives Canada, C-052090).

PART IV

§

Indian Affairs

9

Alexander Morris and Indian Affairs

Taking on the Role

Alexander Morris remained Lieutenant-Governor of Manitoba and the North West Territories until the implementation of the *Northwest Territories Act* of 1876, and he remained Lieutenant-Governor of Manitoba until 1877. As Lieutenant-Governor, he was inevitably implicated in the administration of Indian Affairs. This flowed from a combination of historical precedent and the symbolic importance attached to the office. First Nations leaders consistently preferred dealing with the highest-ranking government official available, and with someone who could claim a direct link to the Queen. Morris's efforts toward meaningful treaty implementation in the bureaucracy and behind the scenes were consistent with the promises he had made at the negotiations, and spoke to his understanding of the broader significance of the treaties, his respect for the First Nations of Canada, and his personal desire to see the treaties succeed. Dealing with chiefs and councillors, he had always walked a delicate path between what they wanted and what the government would give. Similarly, when it came to treaty implementation, he was careful not to promise anything that he knew could not be provided.

By late 1872, Morris had already set out his recommended policy for the administration of Treaties 1 and 2. This was the foundation on which he would advocate for the rest of his tenure. The Government "should maintain constant communication with these Tribes," he wrote Secretary of State Joseph Howe, "and see that all the provisions of the Treaty are rigidly carried out. . . . [I]t is of the first importance to retain the Confidence and maintain the friendliest relations with the Indians."[1] All promised farming and other implements should be promptly delivered, reserves identified, and schools provided. Even more, it was crucial that the parties understand each other and maintain contact.

As to future treaties, Morris was anxious that they be negotiated, both for strategic reasons and to maintain the credibility of the government. He had heard that the Sioux in the US had delivered tobacco to the Cree and Ojibwa in Canada, and understood its significance. He was concerned that if Canada did not secure an alliance with her own First Nations, the American Sioux certainly would. In December 1872 he recommended that Canada act quickly to ally itself with the peoples north of the medicine line, the Canadian-American border. Open communications and sound diplomacy were in order:

> The Indians in the plains were, as I am informed, told that they would receive a visit last Summer from the Commissioner, to prepare the way for a Treaty, but this was not carried out, and as the Indians look for the rigid performance of promises, they should be complied with as speedily as possible. I believe that they can be retained in close alliance and friendship, by treating them fairly, kindly, and justly. They should be advised by men they trust, of the real meaning of the Boundary Survey, and explanations should be given them as to the intended Railway Surveys, and all stipulations of the Treaties should be scrupulously carried out. To attain these ends I would propose that there should be a resident Indian Commissioner here, who should be a good business man . . . competent to draw up Treaties, attend to matters of account, etc., etc.[2]

Having developed an appreciation for the significance of gift-giving, Morris recommended that the government provide a sum of cash to the commissioner annually to visit the bands and provide them with presents to maintain their alliance. The commissioner, he continued, should have two assistants, French and English Métis familiar with the dialects of the region and trusted by the Indians.

Morris recommended James McKay, an English "half-breed" who spoke Ojibwa, Siouan, and Cree. He was, Morris assured Howe, a man "who has great influence with the Indian Tribes, and who gives largely to them of his own means."[3] Morris ultimately had to settle for a political appointment, in the person of J. A. N. Provencher, but McKay nonetheless proved to be one of Morris's closest advisors and confidants in the years to come.

Morris's approach to the administration of Indian Affairs, including the negotiation of the numbered treaties and their subsequent implementation, had always been determined by two factors: first, by the interests of the Canadian state, which included his own personal sense of patriotism and responsibility as a public servant; second, and increasingly over time, by his understanding of First Nations' concerns.

From the beginning, Morris understood the political climate of the North West, and he had a growing appreciation and understanding of First Nations diplomacy. As an administrator, he listened to his advisors and reported all the news he deemed important, both good and bad, to Ottawa. He was no "yes man"; he did not shield department officials from what others might have seen as trifling or inconvenient. As he became acquainted with the First Nations of the plain, he developed a rapport that was certainly unmatched by any official in distant Ottawa, and even many in the North West.

As Morris's sympathies with the Aboriginal point of view grew, so, too, did his frustration with the Ottawa bureaucracy. Morris advocated a faithful implementation of the treaties, arguing that the government should, at the least, uphold its written promises. He knew from his legal background and experience with land titles that any breach of the treaties would threaten the legitimacy of Canada's claim over the territory. The Indians themselves saw the failure to implement treaty promises as a breach of the agreement. More important, to Morris, was

J. A. N. PROVENCHER, *described by a colleague as a "tall, bulky fellow, with an odd-looking head, hands of a Hercules, sloppy-garb, heavy gait, and enormous bushy mop of hair," was one of the government's more parsimonious Indian Affairs administrators in the North West* (Glenbow Archives, NA-47-40).

that his reputation was at stake: he was determined to fulfill the promises he had made, personally, to the First Nations of the North West.

Morris also advocated for the faithful implementation of the *spirit* of the treaties, arguing that oral promises, from specific agricultural implements to general principles of reciprocity and mutual assistance, should be honoured as a matter of simple justice. The "outside promises" of Treaties 1 and 2 had a significant impact on Morris's understanding of the Indian view of treaty promises. The reluctance of officials in Ottawa and Manitoba to honour their treaty obligations was a major source of frustration to Morris in the 1870s. His attitude can be measured over time in the tone of his correspondence. He responded by intervening in treaty implementation more frequently and personally. His approach was increasingly at odds with Ottawa, and by 1876 the Department had begun to take steps to diminish Morris's role in Indian Affairs administration.

Problems with Provencher

J. A. N. Provencher was appointed Indian Commissioner in February 1873. His duties included overseeing the survey of reserves and the distribution of annuities, agricultural implements, cattle, and other items promised under Treaties 1 and 2. Morris soon found fault with the setup of Indian Affairs in general and with the commissioner in particular. He wrote to Minister of the Interior Alexander Campbell to express his concerns: "The Indian question is, I am sorry to say, a very large one, and one that will tax the best skill of the Government to solve satisfactorily."[4] The government could ill afford to leave it to a mediocre administrator. Normally a man of calm words, Morris voiced extreme frustration with Provencher. The Indian Commissioner was difficult to get hold of, did not consult Morris on issues of importance, and repeatedly failed to reply to Morris's queries. Morris had no control over Provencher, and didn't know what he was saying or doing about issues of Aboriginal concern.

Morris was particularly agitated by Provencher's mishandling of a band of Sioux who had moved from the United States to the vicinity of Portage la Prairie. As many as 600 Sioux refugees from Minnesota had made their way into Manitoba and the surrounding area after the outbreak of hostilities with the American government in 1862. By 1869 some 500 had settled near Portage La Prairie.[5] Intermittent violence had continued between the Sioux in the United States and the American military, and Morris was concerned that the Americans might pursue those who had retreated across the border into Canadian territory. He had cause for concern. "General Green in St. Paul asked if Americans would be allowed to pursue Sioux across line," Morris warned Minister Campbell in August 1873. "[I] am not an alarmist but impress upon government the magnitude of the question."[6]

Aware of the state of war between the Sioux and the Americans, and fearful that the Sioux in the United States might attempt to persuade their brethren in British territory to similar violent effect, Morris was adamant that the Sioux who had recently moved to Canada should be treated with sensitivity and tact. While acknowledging that they had no territorial claims in Manitoba, he still believed they should be given a reserve, for both compassionate and strategic reasons. When Provencher failed to attend a meeting with McKay and the Sioux at Portage la Prairie to identify land for a reserve, Morris was understandably frustrated. "I need not point out how improper it is to break such an appointment as this, especially with such a tribe," he complained to Ottawa.[7]

Provencher had been on the job only a couple of months when Morris began receiving complaints about him. Chief Henry Prince, from a band of Ojibwa north of Winnipeg, appealed to the Lieutenant-Governor as the representative of the Queen, with whom his people had signed their treaty. He complained that Provencher had failed to provide agricultural implements for his band, who were anxious to begin farming. Prince was insulted by Provencher's conduct and insensitivity. He suggested that the Indian Commissioner had irritated the Sioux in a similar manner.[8] Prince's remarks were corroborated by Archdeacon Abraham Cowley, who knew the Christianized band intimately. Cowley appealed to Morris: "Possibly Mr. Provencher thinks of our Indians as savages to whom time is of small value. If so, then all the more serious the error of his plan. . . ."[9]

Morris sided with the Ojibwa, and wrote to Minister Campbell: "I feel my position very embarrassing. Provencher has avoided me ever since he came here, and I have no right to direct him, though I see things going wrong, and yet am held responsible by the Indians."[10] It was an impossible situation, with Provencher's word against that of the Ojibwa. Understanding that he had no option but to work with Provencher, Morris insisted to Campbell that he should sit on any board that might oversee Indian Affairs management. Further, he requested that Campbell instruct Provencher "to act with me and under my advice."[11] It was a sign of things to come; Morris, in consideration of the shortcomings of his colleague, increasingly took it upon himself to intervene in the administration of Indian Affairs and help bring about the implementation of the treaty obligations.

The Structure of Administration

Provencher was not the only source of difficulty for treaty implementation. During 1873-1878, the country suffered one of the most severe economic recessions in its history, and throughout Morris's tenure Ottawa's policy was one of fiscal restraint. Among other things, the Department of the Interior encouraged its officials in the North West to deliver as few implements and provisions as possible — often without regard to the amounts promised in the treaties — and to supplement small amounts of cash for more costly treaty implements. Senior departmental staff often chided officials on the ground for being too generous in distributing agricultural implements and annuities, and demonstrated reluctance in approving reserve lands selected by the First Nations.

There were also logistical difficulties. The huge expanse of the territory made transportation costly and time-consuming. Getting the promised annuities and agricultural implements to the many scattered bands, or sending officials to help identify reserve lands, was no simple task. It was compounded by the fact that Indian Affairs in Manitoba and the North West Territories was grossly understaffed. It was equally difficult for the Indians to travel hundreds, or even thousands of kilometres to see Provencher or Morris, especially when they were hunting, trapping, or seeding. The ultimate decision-making authority lay with the Minister of the Interior in distant Ottawa, and issues requiring immediate action were often delayed by a months-long approval process.

Morris lobbied throughout his tenure for a more efficient structure to the administration of Indian Affairs in the North West. His recommendations were shaped by a combination of practical considerations, past experience in managing his own land interests, and a desire to place the incompetent Provencher under his authority. He wanted to centralize decision-making authority in Manitoba, and thus bypass the delays caused by referral to the bureaucracy in Ottawa. He became increasingly convinced that Department officials simply did not appreciate the reality of the situation in the North West, nor the need for more liberal spending. As he became more personally attached to the treaties through the negotiation process and his constant interactions with First Nations leaders, he grew less inclined to leave the direction of treaty implementation to anyone else.

The "eminently unsatisfactory" system Morris had inherited on his appointment as Lieutenant-Governor consisted of a "Board of Indian Commissioners for Manitoba and the North West Territories" which set policy and oversaw administration. In 1874 the Board was made up of Morris, Provencher, and the Chief Lands Officer of Manitoba.[12] Morris wanted the Board abolished, and the North West Council — "a body comprised of intelligent and representative men" who understood the local circumstances — to set policy and run the administration of Indian Affairs. This arrangement would put Morris in charge of major decision-making as the top executive of the Council, and place the troublesome Provencher officially under his authority, if not under his direct supervision.[13] A feature of Morris's plan was to increase staff on the ground and separate the implementation of existing treaties from the negotiation of new ones. The practice of having a single Indian Agent and an officer make treaty payments over the whole territory was simply unrealistic.[14] Morris advocated the "employment of the Métis as Indian agents"[15] — an idea supported by the Manitoba government.

Such a move would have been seen as a meaningful diplomatic gesture by both the First Nations and the Métis.

Morris gave specific recommendations as to how treaty implementation was to be managed efficiently. "I regard it as of vital importance that the existing Treaties should be carried out to the letter," he wrote. The Chief Indian Agent, assisted by a good accountant, would have the sole responsibility of overseeing treaty imple-

EDMUND ALLEN MEREDITH, OTTAWA, NOVEMBER 1868. *A career public servant who increasingly resisted the honouring of treaty promises, Meredith served as Deputy Minister of the Interior from mid-1873* (Library and Archives Canada, PA-033231).

mentation. Drawing from his experience managing his own land speculation, in which he paid local individuals to oversee his interests in the far-flung reaches of Ontario, Morris recommended that the chief agent have sub-agents; these would be appointed *to* him, not *by* him, to ensure a check on the process and on the power of the chief agent. The sub-agents would each carry out the treaty provisions in a given district. They would be responsible for visiting each reserve — or a location predetermined in agreement with the band — once a year, and "make the payments to them, report as to the state of the schools where established, see to the distribution of grain, agricultural implements, ammunition, twine, and any other articles promised in the Treaties." The chief agent would supervise the sub-agents, and, with his accountant, "have charge of the receipt of all monies, and the distribution of these through the sub-agent to the Indians."[16]

Morris's instructions would have the funds kept out of the hands of the sub-agents as far as possible. Nor would the sub-agents be able to act independently with the given bands; there would be a mechanism for accountability, allowing the bands recourse if they had any grievances regarding a sub-agent. The chief agent would be obliged to visit each sub-agent semi-annually, and "from time to time, to visit any Indian Band who might bring any grievance before him, or whose condition he might desire to ascertain."[17] This last recommendation was likely inspired by Morris's experience at the North West Angle, where he had promised Mawedopenais that those responsible for treaty implementation would be held to account. Morris did not envision the much more invasive system, developed after his tenure, in which each band would have a resident agent appointed to it, effectively to run its affairs and screen decisions made by the band council.

Morris urged that the delicate task of negotiating new treaties should be given only to the most competent individuals, and be completed by 1875. This guaranteed that the Chief Indian Agent (i.e., Provencher) would play no role in negotiating new treaties, but be restricted to implementing existing ones. Rather than making the Board responsible, Morris recommended that "three special Commissioners . . . be appointed from time to time, as occasion may arise, for negotiating each Treaty." Morris believed the responsibility could only be entrusted to individuals who understood the Aboriginal peoples and the local context: "Fitting men for such a duty could be found among the members of the North West Council or elsewhere in the country here; men of good business habits, familiar with the Indian character, and some of them with the languages."[18]

Morris's recommendations received approval from the Privy Council in March 1874,[19] but problems persisted. Identifying agents was a lengthy process, and Morris's recommendations occasionally met with resistance from officials who were more concerned with railway development and the interests of settlers.[20] The board was not immediately abolished, and Morris's structure of administration failed to address the problem of spending authority having to be approved in distant Ottawa. In April 1874, for instance, he and the Indian Board requested that authority be given for the early payment of annuities for Treaty 2 — in May rather than July — to give the bands an opportunity to purchase seed in time for cultivation. Morris and Provencher waited over a month for a reply from Deputy Minister Edmund Allen Meredith. Meredith agreed to the early payment, but refused Morris's request for an additional $2,500 for purchasing "seed grain or potatoes to be made to the other Bands of Treaty No. 1."[21]

Authorities in Ottawa insisted that spending lay strictly within the written terms of the treaty, but Ottawa was not cognizant of the practical difficulties facing administrators in Winnipeg, and often refused expenditures that local officials deemed necessary. When the Department of the Interior did approve spending, it was often too late for officials in Manitoba to act. Arranging meeting times with the various bands, and handing out the annuities took considerable time and planning. By the time the bands received their money from the procrastinating Provencher, they might find themselves well into June, or even July, well past seeding time.[22]

By May 1874, Provencher had received spending authority. Until then he had been under instructions from Ottawa not to spend more than the money at hand, and he was obliged to return any funds left over at the end of the year. Had he been allowed to carry over the funding to the following year, he could have avoided delay in paying the next year's annuities.[23] It was a moot point, in any case. In early 1875, Meredith sent one of the Department's officials, Rob Sinclair, to report on Provencher's management of Indian Affairs expenditures. According to Sinclair, Provencher was grossly mismanaging the funds, miscalculating purchases for treaty implements, and often spending more than Sinclair deemed necessary. He went so far as to suggest that Provencher might be embezzling money. Sinclair recommended tightening the spending controls on Provencher.[24] It was on these grounds that in April 1875 Meredith cancelled Provencher's access to a $100,000 credit that had been made available for making rapid purchases for Indian Affairs administration.[25]

In June, Morris requested that full authority for Indian Affairs management be transferred to Manitoba, with an expanded role for the Lieutenant-Governor. The treaties had become too important to Morris to leave their implementation to officials who were either less competent, like Provencher, or, like Meredith and others in Ottawa, ignorant of First Nations diplomatic traditions and the realities on the ground. Morris's years in Manitoba had convinced him that the First Nations of the North West would settle for nothing less than a direct relationship with an official representing the Crown:

My experience during the past two and a half years has been that the Indians will invariably pass by the subordinate officers of the Indian Department and come with their requests or grievances to the Lieut. Governor. . . . It will be impossible to prevent their doing this, nor would it be wise to attempt to do so, as the position of Lieut. Governor gives that officer greater influence with them, than any other can elicit, and a courteous reception and kindly hearing from him always gratifies them.[26]

Once reluctant to implicate himself directly in Indian Affairs management, Morris by mid-1875 wanted to be placed in a position of direct authority over treaty negotiation and implementation. If approved, this would allow him in many cases to bypass Ottawa and its conservative fiscal policies and address issues that the Department of the Interior had long neglected. At the same time, he was urging action on the "outside promises" of Treaties 1 and 2, "which the Indians allege with so much persistency . . . and which have led to so much dissatisfaction amongst them." Referring to a despatch of March 16, 1874, Morris remarked with some impatience that "I have frequently called attention to this subject."[27]

Morris's new recommendations would effectively place him at the top of the administrative pyramid:

I would propose that the Board should be composed of the Lieut. Governor, the Chief Indian Agent, and one other person to be selected on my recommendation, and to possess familiarity with the character of the Indian Tribes, influence with them, and other necessary business qualifications. . . . The Board should be clothed with power of supervision over the Agents and should also fix the times and places of payment of the several Bands of Indians and assign to the Chief Agent and sub agents, the Bands whom they should respectively visit from time to time. . . .

All questions relating to the carrying out of the Treaties with regard to which any difficulty might arise should come before the Board. Tenders for supplies to the Indians should be referred to the Board for approval before acceptance.

I think that if such a plan was adopted, that the delays arising from a reference to Ottawa of matters of detail would be avoided and a firm and prompt administration of Indian Affairs would be obtained.[28]

Whereas the first Indian Board had been purely advisory, the new board would assume an executive role. It would also place Morris in direct authority over Provencher. Morris waited eight months for a decision on his recommendations. In the meantime, he informally took on an ever-increasing role in Indian Affairs administration.

Morris and the Sioux

One of Morris's most pressing concerns with regard to Indian Affairs was with the Sioux bands now living in Canada. The status of the Sioux in Manitoba was uncertain, as they had only recently begun moving into the province as refugees from the United States. Some of them had been living on the British side for a decade or so, but they had no territorial claim on which to base a treaty. Nonetheless, Morris urged that they be granted a modest reserve, and, later, that the government provide assistance for farming and temporary sustenance.

His reasons were both strategic and humanistic. As early as 1872, he and the North West Council had called for a reserve for the Sioux refugees at the junction of the Assiniboine and Little Saskatchewan Rivers, at a safe distance from the United States, Canadian settlers, and the Ojibwa — occasional enemies of the Sioux.[29] Strategically, Morris was concerned that the Sioux, if not treated generously in their desperate state, might resort to violence, attacking settlers newly arrived from Ontario, or threatening the Hudson's Bay Company post of Fort Ellice.[30] Morris suggested that some kind of force be created, possibly made up of a local militia, including Métis volunteers.[31] It was an early conceptualization of what would eventually become the NWMP. Morris was equally concerned that the Sioux on the American side might destabilize the entire region, from Manitoba to the Cypress Hills, persuading not only their Sioux brethren in Canada to ally with them in war against the Americans, but also agitating among the Ojibwa and the Cree. Some of the reports Morris was receiving from officials on the ground were cause for alarm.[32]

Morris was careful to follow a cordial diplomacy with the Sioux. In one of his many reports to Ottawa, he told of a meeting at Qu'Appelle with a party of Sioux residing at Wood Mountain. "The Queen wishes to be good to you though you are not her children," he told them.[33] He readily received the "recognised chiefs of the Sioux nation" at Government House when they visited Fort Garry, and observed the practice of gift-giving on each occasion.[34] James McKay, who could speak the Siouan language and was on good terms with the Portage la Prairie band, was normally present as an interpreter. Morris and McKay managed to reach an understanding of sorts with the band. Morris promised them a reserve, and forwarded their requests for agricultural implements to Ottawa. In exchange, he "impressed upon them the necessity for their being orderly and quiet, told them that they must on no account trouble the settlers or the other Indians, and must go at once on to their reserve lands — all which they promised." Morris sealed the exchange with gifts for the chiefs and councillors. Impressed by the band's work ethic and their cordial relations with the settlers at Portage la Prairie, Morris was optimistic that, if properly assisted, "the Band will settle down and become useful."[35]

Such matters normally would have fallen to the inept Provencher, but Morris took it upon himself as Lieutenant-Governor. After some additional persistence, Morris got approval from Ottawa for the reserve and the farm implements. The reserve, however, was to be located on the western shore of Lake Manitoba, not at the junction of the Little Saskatchewan and Assiniboine Rivers as Morris and the North West Council had recommended.[36] Additionally, the promised implements were late in arriving. By January 1874, Morris found himself once again being visited by the Sioux, anxious to have their reserve and the means to begin cultivation, and having to persuade a new government in Ottawa to meet the commitments that had been made the previous year.[37] Morris met with the Portage Sioux in mid-1875 to finalize the location of their reserve — at the river junction, as they had requested.

Morris's report of this meeting reveals his understanding of how the reserve system was to function, and the security he hoped the First Nations might one day enjoy.[38] The reserves would be the subject of much controversy after Morris's departure. Unlike the officials who succeeded him, Morris never envisioned a system in which the First Nations would be forcibly confined to their reserves. The Sioux, he reported to the Minister of the Interior, had come to believe that

> they would be confined on it and would not be able to hunt. . . . I suc-
> ceeded in removing the erroneous impression, and caused them to be as-
> sured that while the Reserve was to be their home, they would be at liberty
> to hunt and fish, and their men could in the ploughing and harvest season,
> hire out their labour, taking care to plant and harvest their own crops.[39]

The reserve would give them a safe place to live, but it would be only one means of making a living.

While it has been argued that the ultimate objective of Canadian Indian policy was assimilation, Morris did not envision any scenario in which the First Nations would disappear into the larger society. His reference to hunting and fishing indicates that he believed they would be allowed to continue their traditional practices as they adopted new ones. His understanding of the reserve system, in which bands would continue to exist as distinct communities, with a measure of self-government, ran counter to assimilationist objectives.

Morris came increasingly to empathize with the plight of the Sioux, and he was sympathetic when they expressed their intent not to move immediately to the reserve:

> They said as they had no means of living there this winter and no farm
> produce, they would remain in the settlement for the winter, earning what
> little money they could by cutting hay and working for the farmers and

eking out a living by catching fish at Lake Manitoba. . . . I thought their views reasonable and could not in the circumstances urge them to go to the Reserve this autumn.[40]

Morris recommended that Ottawa provide funding for an agriculturalist to assist the Sioux during their first years of cultivation. He believed this would be temporary, and would terminate when the Sioux no longer needed direction. He was confident that, given the tools and the knowledge, they would become self-sufficient.

By this stage in his tenure, Morris had developed a generally accommodating approach to the negotiation of reserve locations, provisions, implements, and other forms of assistance. He was impressed by the character and resilience of the Sioux leadership.[41] Perhaps not surprisingly, his views increasingly diverged from those of government officials in Ottawa. When, in early 1876, Deputy Minister Meredith expressed his anxiety at the Lieutenant-Governor's handing out of provisions and presents to the Sioux in Canada — Meredith was concerned that the Sioux should not become dependent on the provisions Morris had given them[42] — an exasperated Morris found himself having to explain and defend the time-honoured practise of gift-giving. He reminded Meredith that Ottawa would do well to avoid the folly of American Indian policy when it came to the Sioux:

> Their importance is magnified far beyond their number, by their relation to the Sioux in the United States, who cost the American Government so much in the maintenance of troops, and with whom a constant warfare is waged. The Sioux in Canada can be made valuable subjects, but when times of poverty such as now visit the Province, it will be necessary to aid them. I adhere to my policy of settling them on Reserves, and by a small aid, enabling them to become settlers of the soil, and that policy will be the cheapest and best for the Dominion. With regard to the small presents I give them, I did so, in conformity with a custom prevailing here, descending from the Hudson's Bay Company's rule, and apart from that, as a matter of simple humanity.[43]

Some officials were more helpful than others. While many criticized Morris's generosity, David Laird, Minister of the Department of the Interior and one of the commissioners who had negotiated Treaty 4, eventually approved of a number of Morris's recommendations with regard to the Sioux. Laird also consented to the terms Morris negotiated with the Sioux to entice them to "remove as early as possible this year to the new Reserve," including $800 worth of additional cattle and farm implements. Morris personally made arrangements to procure implements and oxen for the Sioux.[44]

Negotiating the Numbered Treaties

Morris obviously appreciated the initiative shown by First Nations to take up agriculture. His approach to the Sioux had repeatedly put him at odds with Provencher and the keepers of the federal purse, but his generosity in dealing with the Sioux was demonstrative of his sympathies with the plight of Aboriginal peoples in general, and of his desire to see them succeed as independent communities, integrating — not assimilating — in the larger Canadian politic.

Treaties 1 and 2: The "Outside Promises"

The earliest treaty implementation challenge Morris had to face involved the "outside promises" of Treaties 1 and 2, signed in 1871. These were a series of items that the First Nations leadership insisted had been included in the negotiations with Archibald and Simpson, but had not been written down. The miscommunication lay partly with Adams Archibald and his interpreter, Molyneux St. John, the latter apparently having promised more than was said. Additionally, Lieutenant-Governor Archibald and Indian Commissioner Wemyss Simpson made different promises. By late 1872, the Aboriginal parties to the treaty had begun to voice strong complaints that the treaty as they understood it was not being fulfilled. Some refused their annuities to signal their rejection of it.[45]

The government was reluctant to acknowledge the outside promises. First, the new Dominion was in debt, faced a severe economic recession, and had few sources from taxation. Ottawa did not welcome the prospect of having to add a number of expensive provisions to treaties that had already been signed. Second, officials in Ottawa — and, to some extent, Fort Garry — were concerned that acknowledging the promises would only encourage more demands. Finally, the Euro-Canadian legal tradition on which the treaty text was based depended heavily on a literal interpretation of the written word of the law, not the context of the negotiations or the intent of the parties. Morris was himself a product of this tradition, but in time, the outside promises would go a long way toward informing his outlook on treaty making and implementation, and his perception of Aboriginal understanding. Ultimately, he came to believe the signatories had been short-changed, and he took it upon himself to personally renegotiate the two treaties and to ensure that the promises were carried out.

The precedent of the outside promises led Morris to appreciate the value of a full and mutual understanding among the parties during negotiations, and the importance of having a capable interpreter. As he came to realize that the government-Aboriginal relationship entailed a fiduciary responsibility that went beyond a literal reading of the treaty terms, he was forced to reconcile government financial considerations and his own letter-of-the-law worldview with his growing empathy for his Aboriginal colleagues.

Morris took up the cause of the outside promises slowly. Many of the difficulties facing the Treaty 1 and 2 signatories had been exacerbated by the unfortunate administration of Provencher. Morris first attempted to mitigate the problem by intervening on a more regular basis. In March 1874 he reported to Ottawa on the destitution of the Indians near Lower Fort Garry, owing to a plague of grasshoppers and the failure of their crops and fishery. Morris suggested that annuities be given early, and that additional flour, pemmican, and funds for seed be provided. The government approved $1,000 and early annuities,[46] but Provencher delayed. Over a month later, he was writing Ottawa to question whether the money to be spent had indeed been approved — something that a glance at his records or a brief talk with Morris would have confirmed. Provencher also applied an obstinately literal interpretation of the treaty to question whether the bands should be given seed for potatoes, as this was not explicit in the text, whereas grain was. He also delayed on the grounds that he did not know exactly what families living among the band were under the treaty. Provencher maintained that Ottawa's policy was to provide agricultural implements strictly to treaty Indians. The inevitable result of his constant referral to Ottawa was further delay and discouragement for the Indians, who had made honest efforts at cultivation. Oddly, the only discretionary action Provencher did take was to provide fewer implements than Ottawa had approved. "I curtailed, considerably, the number or rather ration of ploughs for which it was authorized to make requisition," he reported, perhaps with a sense of accomplishment.[47]

Morris's frustration was evident. "Their want is very great indeed," he telegraphed to Laird on April 25, 1874. A week later his tone betrayed even greater urgency: "Can no help be extended them — answer."[48] The Department stonewalled. Deputy Minister Meredith pointed out that the Indians had already received over $14,000 in annuity payments and challenged Morris to identify where in the text of Treaty 1 it was promised to provide extra seed. It was at this point that Morris invoked the outside promises for the first time, referring to a number of dispatches by Archibald and St. John in which the promises had been referred to. Morris also argued that, since the white population was being "aided by local govt," it would be hypocritical not to extend assistance to the Aboriginal population. The letter of the treaty may have been carried out, but with the destruction of the crops, the Indians required additional seed. Moreover, the spirit of the treaty relationship — of mutual assistance — should be carried out on the basis of good faith and compassion.

Morris learned firsthand of the many grievances of the Treaties 1 and 2 signatories through the constant visitation of chiefs and councillors to Fort Garry. The records of Morris's encounters with these leaders are significant in tracing his understanding of the First Nations of the plains, his capacity to communicate with them, and the extent of his sympathy. In July 1874, in the first of many encounters,

Morris spent four hours discussing the outside promises with Chief Yellow Quill and a number of band members from the vicinity of Portage La Prairie. Yellow Quill insisted that his reserve was not as large as had been promised. Despite the corroboration of James McKay and Molyneux St. John, Morris was unsympathetic, arguing that, according to the written terms of the treaty, the band had in fact received more than they were technically due on a per-family basis.[49]

He was more sympathetic when Yellow Quill brought up the "other things promised and not given to them." In his report to the Minister, Morris acknowledged the likelihood that certain promises had been made, and that they should be kept, regardless of whether they had been written down, in order to retain the trust of the Indians:

> These I found were what I have of late referred to as the outside promises made at Treaty 1 and 2 viz. seed grain, implements, etc. I found the Indians of all the Bands claim the fulfilment of these promises and you have already been furnished with corroborative testimony as to them. I would strongly urge a decision by the Government with regard to this question, as the harm that arises from the Indian mind being impressed with the belief that the white has broken his promises is very great, spreading as it will do through all the tribes.[50]

Yellow Quill also referred to the better terms of the North West Angle treaty, saying that "at the Treaty he was told that all the Indians were to be treated alike." The chief went on to complain that the provisions were meagre and it was increasingly difficult to keep his people fed, especially when they were assembling to collect their annuities. He also pointed out that those who periodically missed the annuity payments did not receive arrears. Morris promised only to report Yellow Quill's complaints to the Minister of the Interior, but in private correspondence with Laird, he admitted that it was unjust to penalize the Indians for their nomadic lifestyle and to break the annual practice of reaffirming the treaty relationship: "I think that there is no good reason why the arrearages of payment should not be paid. The Indians had a roving life and though they may be a couple of years absent in the plains, they always return, and naturally look upon the non-payment of the money as a breach of faith."[51]

Morris also came to appreciate the significance of the medals, flags, and suits worn by the chiefs and councillors. When Yellow Quill at first refused them, Morris understood it as the chief's rejection of the treaty and his own position as an official of the Crown:

> I asked him why, and he said because the promises were not kept. I told him he was under the flag and ought to have it and ought to take the coat

given by the Queen. He declined, however, until I told him he was acting very badly and thus throwing back my hand when I offered it to him. He immediately disclaimed any intention of shewing disrespect to the Queen's servant and then said he would accept the coats and flag and would take the medal, though he was ashamed to wear it as it was base metal.[52]

Morris promised to procure silver, as opposed to pewter, medals. He remarked that the chiefs at Treaty 3 had reacted in the same manner. "I hope that this small concession may be made," he wrote. "The Indians attach great importance to them and I am constantly shewn the King George medals, which have been handed down as objects of great value."[53]

While Morris disagreed with Yellow Quill on the land question, he was wholly impressed by him. He reported to the Department: "The result of the interview was to impress me with the absolute necessity of having a decision come to as to how the outside promises are to be dealt with."[54]

While not yet advocating a revision of Treaties 1 and 2, Morris believed that the problem lay with the administration of the treaties and the inefficiency of having one Indian Commissioner providing the annuities, farm implements, and reserves to all the treaty bands in the North West.

Morris demonstrated more flexibility when it came to other reserves. He was often persuaded by the dignity and intelligence of certain chiefs to accede to their demands. During Treaty 4 negotiations, for instance, Morris was visited by Chief Mekis, the leader of a band of Ojibwa from the Riding Mountain area and a party to Treaty 2. The band wanted to change the location of their reserve, "to where their grandfathers lived," in another area of Riding Mountain.[55] The band also raised the issue of the outside promises, and pointed out the many discrepancies between the terms of Treaty 2 and the new treaty being negotiated at Qu'Appelle. This was a shrewd move on Mekis's part, considering the presence of other bands who were about to sign a new treaty on the understanding that the government would act in good faith. "They trusted to the Queen's goodness to do this," Morris reported, "as the land they had given up was good land and they had always been orderly and well behaved. I would suggest that inquiry should be made as to the propriety of acceding to their request for a change of the location of the Reserve."[56] He repeated Mekis's concern over the outside promises.

Morris was more accommodating with regard to the outside promises than many of his colleagues, even those who had lived and worked in the North West. Both Laird and Provencher dismissed out of hand the complaints of Henry Prince, a chief Morris respected. When Prince reported that white men had begun cutting down trees on his reserve, Laird and Provencher responded that he had no proof. Morris would have at least insisted on verifying the claim. In their dealings with

Prince, Provencher and Laird proved unable or unwilling to use the language of kinship and reciprocity that Morris habitually used with First Nations.[57]

In mid-1874, members of the Brokenhead Reserve visited the Minister of the Interior, David Laird, to demand clothing, animals, tools, and other implements under the outside promises, and to complain that the land allotted them was of poor quality. Laird refused to acknowledge the outside promises, saying only that he could give them what was written in the treaty. He referred them to Provencher, virtually guaranteeing that they would have to appeal again over the head of the administrator to Morris, or back to Laird.[58] And so it proved. After the unsuccessful meeting with Laird, the Brokenhead band turned to Morris, sending emissaries to Fort Garry in January 1875.[59] As had become his practise, Morris wrote a detailed report of the complaints and issues raised by the First Nations with whom he held conference. Among other things, they were upset that a promised schoolhouse had not been provided, and that houses they had built and land they had cultivated before the treaty had not been included in their reserve. Morris could only promise them that he would bring their complaints before the minister. Privately, however, the local context of the outside promises had a profound impact on Morris's thinking. He had come to appreciate the fact that the Indians never forgot the pledges the Crown had made to them, and that the promises would have to be kept not only to maintain their good will, but the legitimacy of the treaties themselves and the willingness of the Aboriginal signatories to be bound by them.

In his correspondence with Laird, Morris betrayed a growing impatience with Ottawa. "I take the opportunity of again earnestly urging that a speedy decision may be arrived at," he wrote with regard to the outside promises. "I am of opinion that so fertile a source of discontent and complaint should be considered and steps taken to set the matter finally at rest."[60] Morris waited four months for a formal and altogether negative reply.[61] While the federal government seemed intent on dragging its feet on this potentially costly issue, Morris was equally intent on a speedy resolution. Indeed, officials in Ottawa were beginning to tire of the Lieutenant-Governor's persistence.[62] Nonetheless, he continued to report on each meeting he had with emissaries from Treaties 1 and 2, and to lobby for action on the outside promises. His reports grew in detail, and his language became increasingly impatient with Ottawa's inaction on the outside promises and the administration of Indian Affairs:

I was called upon on the 3rd inst by Kay ta-hi-gannass, chief of the Band of Indians beyond Lake Manitoba on the Waterken River. He came to complain that the promises made when Treaty No. 2 was entered into were not being kept though four years had passed . . . of which, you have, so often heard. . . . I heard him patiently, and told him I would report what he said to the Government. He then left after thanking me for listening to him. I earnestly trust, that this season will not be allowed to pass without steps being taken to settle this long difficulty, and to secure a more thorough administration of Indian Affairs, by the appointment of sub-agents under effective control, and the adoption of other measures.[63]

The following month, August 1875, Morris's lobbying finally paid off: the Privy Council approved a review of Treaties 1 and 2, and Morris set off to conduct the negotiations.[64] The interpreter James McKay once again accompanied him, and proved instrumental to the success of the renegotiation.

Most bands welcomed the new terms, whose provisions were similar to those of Treaty 4, including an annuity increase from $3 to $5. The Yellow Quill band, however, was still reticent. When Morris met with them at Round Plain on the Assiniboine River, they maintained that their reserve was neither the size nor the location promised. Morris was still reluctant to yield on the land question, and negotiations soon reached an impasse. Resolving to "deal firmly with them," Morris accused the band of insulting both himself and the Queen, and threatened to end the negotiations. Yellow Quill and his councillors returned to the table. "I accepted their apology and then proceeded to practical business," he reported with satisfaction, "the whole tone and demeanour of the Indians . . . having become cordial and friendly." For his part, Morris moderated his position on the location of the reserve after the band's claims were once again corroborated by McKay:

> They appealed to Mr. McKay whether the Reserve was not promised to be on both sides of the river, and he admitted that it was. . . . I promised to state their claims as to the [size of the] Reserve, but told them it would not be granted, but that I would change the location of the Reserve as it had been selected without their approval and would represent their views as to its locality and as to crossing the River, the navigation of which, however, could not be interfered with.[65]

While avoiding a public promise to enlarge the reserve, Morris privately recommended that it be extended at least to correspond with the written treaty. Having secured the first concession, the band tentatively accepted the new terms. Given the larger strategic considerations at play, Morris was satisfied with this result: "I left the band contented and you are aware of their intimate relations with the Plain Indians and the difficulties their messages to Qu'Appelle, that the White Man had not kept his promises, caused us, and it is very important that they should be satisfied."[66] Morris had learned how crucial it was to keep faith with these people he had come to respect and admire, lest he jeopardize his personal reputation and risk having them spread rumours among their peers that the government was not to be trusted.

Morris recommended concessions for other bands as well, reiterating that "the arrears due to Indians who have not yet received their annuities should be paid in full at once," although he qualified the demand, recommending "that a period of two years should be fixed for those bona fide members of the Band to come in and be paid and that after that they would only receive one year's payment."[67] Morris recommended that the White Mud band, a small group of Ojibwa without status, be recognized and given a reserve and assistance under the treaty. He also called for the recognition of a distinct group within the Yellow Quill band who chose to follow Young Chief, also known as Short Bear. Yellow Quill had been appointed by the Hudson's Bay Company long ago, but Young Chief retained the hereditary title of Chief.[68] It would have been more convenient simply to recognize Young Chief as chief of the entire band, Yellow Quill having proved difficult in negotiations — deposing troublesome chiefs would become a common practice among Indian Agents after Morris's tenure — but Morris had come to accept the Indians' right to select their own leaders, whether through the preferred method of elections, or, if necessary, through traditional hereditary practice.

Predictably, the approval of Morris's recommendations and the implementation of the new treaty terms met with delay in Ottawa. The only decision the Department made before 1876 was that Indians who failed to take up permanent residence on the reserve would not be paid the cash gratuity and the annuities.[69] This ran counter to the promises Morris had made during negotiations, and by October 1875 he was writing the Department once again to urge the fulfilment of the new promises "to the letter." Morris had given his own word and the word of the Privy Council, but some First Nations leaders were beginning to question whether they could be trusted. With the year almost out and promises not yet fulfilled, he was concerned that Ottawa was intent on making a liar out of him. He began writing orders directly to Provencher, instructing the commissioner to provide what had been promised under the new terms.[70]

Morris continued to lobby well into the next year for the fulfillment of the new terms, arguing both on the principle of good faith and out of consideration for the government's reputation in future negotiations. By April 1876, Deputy Minister Meredith had reluctantly approved Morris's recommendation that Yellow Quill be allowed to select a new reserve, but he refused to recognize the White Mud band or grant them a reserve, arguing that their numbers did not warrant it. "In no case . . . are Indians to . . . settle on any fresh lands in that neighbourhood," he told Morris, and curtly reiterated the Department's position on arrears: "I do not see any sufficient reason to depart from the rules already laid down on this subject which were fully explained to you in my letter of the 4th October last."[71] The following month, Meredith refused Morris's request to "have funds advanced on special warrant" to implement the new treaty terms in time for seeding.[72] Meredith's reply indicated that the funds would not be available until July, which of course was too late for planting. The bands would be delayed yet another year, and have further cause to doubt Morris's sincerity and the intentions of the government.

While waiting for authority to follow through on the promises made the previous year, Morris finalized agreements with the Yellow Quill, White Mud, and Short Bear bands in late June 1876 — a "very difficult negotiation" conducted under equally difficult conditions. It rained heavily, and "the roads were in so bad a condition, that I was four days on reaching the Long Plain" — a journey of some 150 km — "while we were also subjected to inconvenience and expense by the detention of the provisions owing to the same cause. Added to my other discomforts, was the presence of mosquitoes in incredible numbers, so that the journey and the sojourn at the Plain were anything but pleasurable."[73] He was greatly relieved when these various logistical difficulties were overcome, for when he reached the meeting location, he found the bands' food supply had begun to run out during the wait. Unlike later administrators, such as Edgar Dewdney, Morris never considered using starvation tactics to force recalcitrant bands to sign treaties. He did, however, apply a strategy of divide and conquer; once arrived at Long Plain, he asked each of the different groups to put forward their positions separately:

> I took this course as I had ascertained that the plan of Yellow Quill's headmen was to make no settlement this year, and that they had induced the other Indians to agree to act in that way. I accordingly so shaped my opening speech, and my dealing with the Indians, as to defeat this project, by securing the support of Short Bears [sic] and the White Mud Indians, which I succeeded in doing, though Yellow Quill's spokesmen taunted the others, with having broken their agreement.[74]

Contrary to Meredith's instructions of April 1876, Morris promised, "under the discretionary powers I possessed," to establish reserves at the behest of the White Mud and Short Bear bands, so as to secure their support for the new treaty terms. Yellow Quill and his councillors reluctantly signed the final agreement, but only after Morris agreed to their demand "to select a Reserve higher up the River Assiniboine." Morris also agreed to recommend that their councillors be paid as headmen, as per Treaties 3 - 5. "It will be difficult to explain why the difference is made," he told Laird, "and it will secure in every Band, men who will feel that they are officers of the Crown and remunerated as such." Given the history of miscommunication surrounding Treaties 1 and 2, it was important to Morris that the terms of the new agreement be clearly understood by both sides. As at Treaty

6, he had his own interpreters and interpreters selected by the Indians read out the written settlement of the outside promises.[75] He was careful to write up the new terms personally, in part to finalize the agreement but also to ensure that a record would be available to hold the government and future administrators to account.

Morris sealed the agreement by distributing medals and suits of clothing, and paying out the increased annuities. Yellow Quill reciprocated: "Yellow Quill then presented me with a skin coat, and said that he parted with the other Indians as friends, and that there would be no hard feelings." Morris observed that, for the first time, all the chiefs and councillors ended with him on friendly terms, and his departure was accompanied by a pomp and ceremony that Morris clearly enjoyed: "The Indians assembled near my waggon and gave three cheers for the Queen and three for the Governor, and I then drove off, amid a salute of fire arms from all sections of the encampment."[76]

Morris's first action on returning to Government House was to secure speedy approval for the new agreement and permission to identify new reserves for the White Mud, Short Bear, and Yellow Quill bands. He had grown increasingly sympathetic to these people, and was especially impressed by the trust the Short Bear and White Mud bands continued to place in him.[77] "I see no reason why their desire should not be complied with," he told the Minister of the Interior.[78] Persuaded, Laird approved Morris's recommendations and put them before the Privy Council in July 1876.[79] In the meantime, Morris instructed J. Lestock Reid to consult with the Yellow Quill, White Mud, and Short Bear bands to identify their reserves.[80] In October, Short Bear called on Morris to inquire why "the implements and cattle they are entitled to under the Treaty as revised" had not been provided. Not trusting Provencher's assurances that he had given the Short Bear band "what they were entitled to under the Treaty," Morris took matters into his own hands and instructed Reid "to report to me what implements and cattle he finds to be in the possession of the three Bands." Morris attempted to reassure Short Bear of his sincerity by presenting him with a medal.[81]

Morris also met with Yellow Quill and his councillors to resolve the dispute over their reserve size. Morris once again refused the band's request for a larger reserve. With McKay as interpreter, Morris negotiated an understanding. "After a protracted interview I succeeded in getting them to comprehend what extent of land they would receive," he reported. "The Chief and Councillors agree to point out the locality and assist Mr. Reid in its survey." Having been reassured that the councillors would be paid as headmen, "They left me satisfied and I hope may remain so, as it is important to have the difficulty finally settled."[82]

By mid-November 1876, Reid and the bands had succeeded in identifying the locations of all three reserves. Reid and Morris agreed that the reserves would be larger than the official entitlement, to make up for portions that were muskeg.[83]

Reid's report included a letter from Yellow Quill, thanking Morris for his persistence in seeing that he got his promised reserve. Morris, having finally established a relationship of mutual trust with this difficult band, was moved by the chief's letter. Morris wrote with some pride that it had been "dictated by [Yellow Quill] himself and expressed in his own words, tendering me the best wishes of himself and his people, intimating his intention to remain on the Reserve and asking for the articles promised by Treaty No. 1 as revised by me."[84] He forwarded Reid's report to the Department of the Interior for final approval.[85]

Resolving the outside promises had been one of Morris's greatest challenges and personal accomplishments in the North West. "The settling of this matter," he wrote, "is a source of much satisfaction to me, as it closes a very troublesome controversy, which has occupied much of my time and has been more difficult to deal with than the negotiations which resulted in Treaties with large bodies of the Indians."[86] He had come to understand the North West far beyond its potential for exploitation and settlement. By 1876, the interests of the First Nations and the fulfillment of the government's treaty promises were pre-eminent in his thinking.

Unfortunately, Morris's months of diplomacy and labour were not to bear fruit. In October 1876 a new Minister of the Interior, David Mills, replaced David Laird. Whereas Laird had at least a rudimentary understanding of the challenges of the North West, having accompanied Morris in the making of Treaty 4, Mills was not sympathetic. Earlier in the decade he had been a "key player" in winning the Ontario-Manitoba boundary dispute for the senior province. During his tenure as Minister of the Interior, he proved reluctant to relinquish self-government to the North West. He was especially sensitive to the country's financial position, having served as chair of the select committee established to investigate the depression since January 1876.[87] Mills had no experience or contextual knowledge of the affairs of the North West and of the various First Nations, and was unenthusiastic when faced with the financial demands of the expensive Indian Affairs portfolio. In December 1876, Deputy Minister Meredith advised Morris of the government's reversal of its approval of the Short Bear and Yellow Quill reserves. They had decided instead to set aside the lands for the use of the Hudson's Bay Company, the Public School Endowment, and future settlers.[88]

Morris was livid. He pointed out to the new minister that none of these concerns had been raised by Laird, who had authorized the surveys for the reserves. He referred Mills to a variety of correspondence, dating back to Adams Archibald's tenure as Lieutenant-Governor in 1871, to make Mills appreciate "the difficulties that I encountered," the complex history of the negotiations, and the protracted and delicate diplomacy by which a final agreement with the bands had been arrived at.[89] Morris clearly suspected that the government was attempting to plead ignorance of its previous commitments in order to shirk its treaty responsibilities once again: "The difficulties, as to the Reserves of these Bands have been reported to the Privy Council by my predecessor and myself, at various times during the past five years, and have been constantly kept under consideration," he reminded Mills. Deputy Minister Meredith, who had served in the department for years, should certainly have known better than to feign ignorance. Morris continued:

DAVID MILLS, JANUARY 1877. *Mills succeeded David Laird as Minister of the Interior and, like E. A. Meredith, showed little regard for the government's treaty promises and obligations. By the time this photograph was taken, his working relationship with Alexander Morris had deteriorated completely* (Library and Archives Canada, PA-026513).

When, under the instructions of your predecessor and in the public interests, undertaking a difficult and delicate negotiation, altogether without and beyond my functions of Lieutenant-Governor, I have succeeded in adjusting the difficulty, it is anything but satisfactory to be met with questions, which . . . should have been asked last April.[90]

There were larger issues at play than administrative incompetence. The matter was personal. Morris had made the commitment for the reserves on the understanding that he had the authority to do so, and was now being told that he had no such authority. Reneging once more on Treaties 1 and 2 would destroy First Nations' trust in both the government and himself — a trust he had worked hard to establish:

I must urgently urge that the Reserves should be confirmed. It will be impossible to satisfy the Indians that they have been justly dealt with, if they are set aside, and the dissatisfaction will spread through the whole Tribes and work trouble. At Qu'Appelle, this Reserve question of Yellow Quill's was a stumbling block, and this winter round the camp fires, I have no doubt the story is told, that the Whites have treated Yellow Quill justly.[91]

Acceding to the argument that the Hudson's Bay Company was entitled to a portion of the new reserves under the terms of the 1869 sale of Rupert's Land would only encourage it to lay claim to land in all reserves, Morris feared, and paint the picture of a government that favoured the interests of the Company over those of its Aboriginal allies. "I have to express my gravest apprehensions of the disturbing results that will follow throughout the entire Indian Treaties, if the claims of the Hudson's Bay Company to one twentieth of the land, within them, is raised," Morris warned, recalling his experiences at Treaty 4:

At Qu'Appelle, the position of the Company and the hostility of the Indians towards them, cost the Commissioners four days of discussion, before they were able to quiet the Indian mind. If this question is entertained with regard to the Reserves in question, it must arise with regard to the other Reserves, and will inevitably lead to trouble and difficulty.[92]

Morris argued that the treaties should take both legal and moral precedence over other claims:

The Privy Council are bound by Treaty, to give these Indians Reserves. As to the sales, homestead and pre-emption rights, I attach little importance to these. The Treaty of 1871 provides that "if there are any settlers within the bounds of any lands reserved by any Band, Her Majesty reserves the right to deal with such settlers as she shall deem just so as not to diminish the extent of Land allotted to the Indians."[93]

Morris knew that the agreement with the Hudson's Bay Company had preceded the numbered treaties, but in the absence of a legal argument he appealed to a moral one. It would only be right, he argued, that the Company "should be assigned other lands in lieu of that, to which they might be entitled within the Reserve . . . and I have no doubt, but that the Company would cheerfully accede to the assignment."[94] Morris knew that it would require parliamentary action to overrule the 1869 agreement with the Company in favour of the treaties if the Company were to refuse a compromise; he also knew it was a matter of political will — the old legal scholar's emotive appeal was something of a last resort.

Before moving to the North West, Morris had seen the region above all as a means of fulfilling his patriotic vision of settlement and development. The North West was Canada's birthright. Now he saw the Indians as having first claim to the land, and he was beginning to see the North West in terms of Aboriginal priorities, to the extent of asserting precedence over the interests of the settlers and the Euro-Canadian communities whose development he had once enthusiastically anticipated. Morris now viewed such communities as a potential threat to the future of the Aboriginal peoples. He was still keen on seeing the North West developed, but his focus now was on mitigating the collision of cultures that might ensue.

Morris's appeal to the Department fell on deaf ears. Mills's reply of February 6, 1877 restated his earlier position and refused the reserves that Morris had promised the previous year. The Lieutenant-Governor was appalled by the government's lack of respect for both the Indians and the treaties. He reminded Mills that his predecessor, David Laird, in approving Morris's earlier actions, "had when here, personal cognizance" of the local situation, which Mills did not. He was not surprised at the tenor of Mills's letter, he wrote,

> when you state, at the outset, that you do not deem it necessary "to enter into any inquiry, as to the origin of the negotiation with those Indians," such knowledge being, in my judgement, absolutely essential to a proper appreciation of the position, and a right adjudication of the matters in issue, between the Crown and the Indians.[95]

Morris had come to understand that there was more to the treaty than the document: it was a process involving complex negotiations and the establishment of a relationship of mutual trust and reciprocity. It was the solemn duty of administrators to live up to that relationship and to the commitments of their predecessors:

Now Sir, I protest against your thus ignoring the responsibility of the Minister of the Interior, with regard to these Reserves, and placing it upon me, because you had full information that these Reserves, were assigned and surveyed, under the direct authority of the Minister of the Interior. True, you were not then that officer, but you cannot avoid responsibility for the acts of your predecessor, as under our system of government, there is not only a continuity of office, but a *solidarity* of responsibility.[96]

Mills's argument that "the Reservation for Indians, should not include lands, which have been set out for settlement" and already surveyed, Morris refuted in no uncertain terms, pointing out that it had been unjust for the government to conduct the surveys before the treaties had been negotiated. In consequence of the Department's "disinclination to make any inquiry into the origin of the negotiations, which led to the Reserves in question," Morris continued,

> you fail to perceive that the action of the Government is the cause of the necessity, which has arisen for these Reserves being selected in surveyed lands. The Queen and Privy Council, entered . . . into Treaty obligations, to assign these Indians a Reserve, as an equivalent for the surrender, by them, of their title to the lands of the Province of Manitoba. At that period, the lands in the Western part of the Province, where these Indians had always lived, were not surveyed, and the difficulty you invoke has been directly caused by the action of the Government in surveying the lands, before having arrived at an adjustment of the dispute with the Indians, as to the locality of their Reserve.[97]

Morris's recognition of Aboriginal title emerges clearly here, as does his perception that laying claim to the land prior to reaching an agreement with its original inhabitants and legitimate claimants was inherently unjust, even illegal. It was a far cry from his previous assertions, only fifteen years earlier, that the North West belonged to Canada by right.

The Minister asserted that new reserves could be chosen out of the "ample" unsurveyed lands in the north, but Morris knew that such lands would be of poor quality and relatively uncultivable. While Mills and others preferred a policy of removing Indians to lands that would be of little attraction to potential settlers, Morris was of the opinion that they should be allowed to settle, insofar as possible, in places that best suited their interests, and advocated for lands that would be well wooded and with good cultivable land, but also accessible to hunting and trapping areas, so as to ease the transition to agricultural practice. Above all, Morris reminded Mills, it was their right to settle on such lands: "The extent of such lands in the Territories is aside from the question, and has no bearing on it

Negotiating the Numbered Treaties

whatever, as the Treaty obligation is to set off the Reserve within the Province of Manitoba." Changing reserve locations would be demoralizing for the Indians who were struggling to make the difficult transition from a nomadic, hunting lifestyle to a sedentary and agricultural one. Laying this moral issue at the Minister's feet, he informed Mills that the Indians had already started building houses and cultivating, and that "their eviction will be a necessary consequence of your present decision."[98] In closing, Morris warned Mills that, owing to his obstinacy, he had been forced to appeal over the Minister's head to the Privy Council:

> This matter is so important and your action will have so disturbing an effect on the Indian mind, regarding it, as they will do, as a breach of Treaty obligations, that I have deemed it my duty, to call the attention of the Privy Council thereto, being persuaded, that . . . the results will be disastrous and destructive of the confidence which the Indian tribes now repose in the Canadian Government. [99]

Morris did not shy away from expressing his anger to Cabinet. The officials of the Department had belittled a matter of deep significance. He regarded it "as no mere Departmental matter, but as seriously affecting the relations of the Government towards a large and influential Band of Saulteaux [Ojibwa] Indians, who maintain the closest and most intimate relations with the Indians of the Western Plains." He repeated a number of the legal and practical considerations contained in his appeals to the Minister, but his emphasis was clearly on the principle of justice: "when the question is one of carrying out the obligations of the Crown . . . no light difficulties ought to be allowed to prevent the fullest compliance with the provisions of the Treaty." Anything less would be considered a breach of faith by the Indians. [100]

This appeal, too, fell on deaf ears. The matter was left to the Department of the Interior, and neither Mills nor Meredith altered his position. Yellow Quill and two of his councillors met with Morris in June 1877, anxious to know whether their reserve had been confirmed, as they had begun to plant crops.[101] They requested additional timber lands for their reserve. Morris refused, threatening to have the councillors removed from their posts. It was an unusual tactic, but a sign of Morris's growing exhaustion and frustration, caught between the Indians and the government. He nonetheless forwarded Yellow Quill's demands to the Department, including demands for the implements promised under the new treaty terms, and he reiterated the larger strategic considerations. He did not press the issue much further, as he had often done in the past, for he had little faith that he would receive any constructive response.

Meredith had grown tired of Morris's insistent reports about unfulfilled treaty promises. "I need not again refer to the legal impediments to the confirmation of this Reserve," he wrote, restating his position on the Hudson's Bay Company, which was maintaining "that they have a right to one twentieth of the lands reserved for the use of the Indians wherever these lands come to be disposed."[102] The Department of the Interior, lacking political will, said the issue was beyond their control, and the problem was left unresolved.

Implementing Treaties 3 - 6

Implementing the other treaties Morris had negotiated proved equally difficult. The logistical problems facing the implementation of Treaties 3 - 6 mirrored those of Treaties 1 and 2, but were compounded by the even greater distance from the supply and management centre at Fort Garry. Similar disagreements arose between Morris and Ottawa as to how much should be spent on agricultural implements. Disagreement over Treaties 5 and 6, particularly, intensified as Morris took on an increased role in directing treaty implementation from late 1875 to early 1877.

Chiefs and councillors began to complain early on over unfulfilled treaty promises, including a lack of reserves, provisions, and agricultural implements.[103] They came to Morris in part because of his position as the principle negotiator and representative of the Crown, but also because of his personal reputation for fairness and sympathy. In June 1875, for instance, voicing the desire of the Fort Frances and Rainy River bands for agricultural instruction in their language, Rev. Robert Phair, an Anglican clergyman, appealed directly to Morris, "knowing the interest your Excellency takes in the Indians and believing the matter will have your consideration." While it had not been explicitly written into the treaty text, Morris forwarded the request to the Minister of the Interior, presenting it as wholly reasonable, and "Trusting you will give the matter your full consideration."[104]

Morris's personal relations with Aboriginal leaders grew ever closer during this period, emerging in his increasingly detailed reports of his meetings with chiefs and councillors. Around the time of Phair's plea, Morris was visited by Keetakapinais, the hereditary chief of the Ojibwa from Fort Frances. Keetakapinais, he wrote to the Minister of the Interior, "is the recognized principal chief of the Saulteaux [Ojibwa], and being struck by his apparent extreme age, I asked him his age, and he replied that he was ninety eight, or as he put it holding up two fingers — two years less than 100." [105]

Keetakapinais had come to reaffirm the treaty relationship that had been arrived at two years earlier, and to state his intention of establishing peaceful relations with the Sioux who had settled in Manitoba:

He stated, that he called to inform me, that his people had sent him, to see me; that we had been as brothers at the North West Angle, and they wished to know if it was true that there was peace in this country. He said

Negotiating the Numbered Treaties

that I had told them to live at peace with all the other Indians, and that they had obeyed me, and that in consequence of my wishes, in that regard, his people had sent him, to go and see the Sioux Indians, and smoke the pipe of peace with them. [106]

Morris was greatly pleased by the chief's intentions, and met his request for a flag and uniform, the symbols of authority that marked treaty chiefs and councillors as officers of the Crown. "The Chief asked me, for a uniform and flag, that the Sioux might see that he was a chief."[107]

Messengers from the Qu'Appelle region came to Morris requesting cattle and implements for the farms they had started under the promises of Treaty 4.[108] Morris began advising W. J. Christie, the retired Hudson's Bay Company officer who had been tasked with Treaty 4 implementation. Christie reported to Laird that he had consulted with Morris and received "every assistance from his Honour to enable me to carry out" the treaty promises.[109] Like Morris, Christie advocated delivering the promised agricultural assistance as soon as possible. Laird was not impressed. "You have far exceeded your own estimate of supplies," he complained to Christie. "Can you not do with less flour and oxen?"[110] Christie defended his estimates, stating that Morris had deemed them "as being far below" what was needed.[111]

By mid-1875, the Department of the Interior was beginning to adopt an even more stringent fiscal policy. Officials in the North West were pressured to spend less on food and other provisions at their meetings with the Indians, including at treaty time. The Department had also adopted a policy of giving agricultural implements and cattle only to those bands they believed intended to use them, regardless of what had been promised.[112] By mid-1876, Laird had gone even further, adopting a policy whereby certain implements promised under the treaties could only be given out by explicit permission of the Department,[113] assuring further delays and breaches of the treaty promises.

To ensure that its new policies would be followed, the Department began to limit Morris's power of appointment for implementation duties and treaty adhesions.[114] In June 1876, he was instructed that hiring was to follow new criteria established by Deputy Minister Meredith. Previously, Morris had hired men like W. J. Christie and Angus McKay, a Métis, to distribute provisions, implements, and annuities, and help the bands identify reserve lands. These were people who understood and sympathized with First Nations. It was McKay who pointed out the hypocrisy of demanding that the Indians prove their abilities in agricultural practice before being given the implements to do so.[115] Shortly after Mills's appointment in late 1876, McKay's contract with the Department of the Interior was terminated, despite Morris's best efforts to defend him. Christie, who had been replaced a year earlier, complained bitterly that Meredith, unlike Morris, had no grasp of the local situation.[116]

One of Christie's replacements, surveyor William Wagner, demonstrated impatience and a complete lack of understanding of First Nations' customs and culture in the Treaty 4 area. Where Morris reported every grievance, even when disagreeing with them, Wagner was dismissive. He complained of the "foolishness of the Chief," and spoke of some of their concerns as "too ridiculous to mention." He withheld provisions and implements that Christie had ordered, convinced that the Indians would not use them but sell them off. He also decided not to include in the reserve lands the homes the band had built. "The desire of the Indians, wherever I have surveyed, to get their Reserves located in the woods confirmed me in my belief that from this and the next generation no hope can be entertained that the red man will entirely devote himself to agriculture."[117]

Wagner's prejudice spoke to a larger problem. Bands that sold their cattle or implements likely did so to avoid starvation, not necessarily because they were unwilling to take up agriculture. By operating on the assumption that all Indians would rather sell what they received under the treaty than use it, and consequently withholding necessary and promised agricultural implements, officials

WAYWAYSEECAPPO, *an Ojibwa chief from the Fort Ellice area, in September 1874 signed an adhesion to Treaty 4 on behalf of his people when he met with Morris following the close of negotiations at Fort Qu'Appelle* (Provincial Archives of Saskatchewan, c-12926).

effectively inhibited bands that were anxious to begin cultivation. Reports such as Wagner's only contributed to the perspective in Ottawa that the Indians were given to idleness and would fail as farmers.

Readings of the treaties had become more literal and rigid when it suited government interests. Only the precise amount and type of seed, for instance, was to be provided.[118] At the same time, the Department was willing to interpret treaty provisions more broadly when it proved convenient. Promised wagons for certain chiefs, for instance, were supplemented with cash instead. By late 1876 the Department of the Interior had more or less abandoned the intent and spirit of the treaties, taking control of treaty implementation policy and paying no heed to the concerns of First Nations.[119]

Over the course of his last two years as Lieutenant-Governor, Morris increasingly protested against what he perceived to be a breaking of the treaties and the violation of the treaty relationship, especially the direct link between the First Nations and the Crown embodied in the office of the Lieutenant-Governor. At the very least, he argued, the Department should abide by a strict reading of its obligations. But the government hardly stood up to the commitments that even it had recognized, let alone the further commitments that Morris was lobbying for in encouraging a more generous interpretation of the treaties.

The new policies from Ottawa put a strain on Morris's relations with First Nations leaders. While urging the Department to greater generosity when dealing with chiefs and councillors, he could only act within the limits of his immediate resources and promise what he knew the government was willing to provide. In October 1875 he reported a meeting with Waywayseecappo, a Treaty 4 chief from the Fort Ellice Band of Ojibwa:

> He wanted a supply of provisions, for the winter and said that he could not live without. I replied, that he must live as he had done before, that he had the same right of hunting as before and had in addition a large sum of money paid to his Band, and that the Government did not intend to and could not support all the Indians, but that they must make a livelihood for themselves.[120]

Despite the firmness of his response, Morris gave Waywayseecappo "a small quantity of the surplus stock of provisions which remain from those provided for Treaty No. 5, and he left expressing himself satisfied." He also recommended accommodation on the question of Waywayseecappo's reserve location.[121]

In July 1876, Morris met with Jacob Berens, the Treaty 5 chief of the Berens River band. The band had already established a rapport with the Lieutenant-Governor, as Morris had acted on a complaint against Provencher in 1874 and supported the band's recommendation for a local Justice of the Peace the following year.[122] The chief was anxious about his agricultural implements and wanted confirmation of his reserve. The band also wanted to add hay-growing land to their reserve. Knowing that he was not authorized to give them more land, Morris told the chief that they would have to give up an equal portion of the existing reserve in order to secure the new lands. Privately, however, he told Laird, who was still in office at that time, that the request was reasonable, as "the region in which they live is a very uninviting one, with swamps, rocks and only patches of good soil."[123]

Morris responded to Berens's concerns about Hudson's Bay Company claims on their land by asserting that, if legitimate, they would have to be respected. He recommended to Laird, however, that the government settle privately with the Company so as to remove their claim from the band's preferred location.[124]

In June 1876 Morris took it upon himself to arrange for the completion of the adhesions to Treaty 5 and pay the annuities to those who had signed the previous year. It was a responsibility that would normally have fallen to Provencher, but Morris thought it required the sensitivity of a competent diplomat.[125] He instructed Thomas Howard and J. Lestock Reid to treat the adhesions as "new Treaties,"[126] believing that no necessary expense should be spared in securing treaty adhesions and the legitimacy of the treaty as a whole.[127]

Financing the adhesions and early implementation of Treaty 5 required something of a fiscal juggling act. The Department had originally delegated $14,660 to Provencher for Treaty 5 annuities, but Morris was not convinced that this would be enough. He scrounged from every corner, borrowing from traders and the Hudson's Bay Company to secure the additional $7,000 required by Howard and Reid to complete their task. This was not the only time he borrowed from individuals, banks, or even from his own pocket to see the treaties properly implemented.[128] Morris used money earmarked for the yet-to-be negotiated Treaty 7 to reimburse the traders and the Company.[129] It was a shrewd move, as Ottawa would have little choice but to replenish the funds if it wanted to secure a successful negotiation and settlement of one of the country's most volatile regions. Morris did get approval for the $7,000, but Department officials were not impressed. On Rob Sinclair's insistence, all future funds for the administration and implementation of Treaty 5 — and, subsequently, Treaty 6 — would be placed under the explicit authority of Provencher, who was more likely to follow the Department's policies.[130] Sinclair was apparently more content with the inept, embezzling Provencher handing out annuities than the generous Morris. The Department seemed to prefer losing money to inefficiency than to meeting its treaty promises.

By mid-November, Howard and Reid had completed their work, at a final cost of $21,576. Morris had reason to be pleased, for it vindicated his efforts to secure greater funding.[131] More importantly, the pair had successfully secured "the adhesion of the Indians who had not been met with when Treaty No. 5 was concluded," and paid annuities to those who had signed the previous year.[132] Howard and Reid had also gathered details of the Indians' preferred reserve locations. Morris recommended a speedy laying out of these lands by someone the Indians trusted — an individual who had been involved in treaty negotiations and discussions with them. The Department accepted Morris's recommendation that Reid fulfill this task.

While Morris's intervention in Treaty 5 implementation sparked some controversy, the Treaty 6 terms created yet another point of contention between Morris and the Department. When they read the treaty text, officials in Ottawa were unpleasantly surprised by several items that had been added beyond the terms of previous treaties. A Department memorandum, likely authored by Deputy Superintendent General of Indian Affairs Lawrence Vankoughnet, detailed the "onerous provisions" contained in the terms,[133] including the additional farm implements and monies meant to assist in the early years of transition to agriculture. Vankoughnet was especially livid over the famine and pestilence clause, "a provision which is wholly new":

> This stipulation the undersigned regards as extremely objectionable, tending, as it will, to predispose the Indians to idleness, since they will regard the provision as guaranteeing them protection against want, and they will not be inclined to make proper exertions to supply themselves with food and clothing, thereby largely increasing the expenditure imposed upon the country in the management of its Indian affairs.[134]

The Department promptly sent Morris a letter through his superior, the Governor General, demanding an explanation. "It cannot be doubted that this stipulation as understood by the Indians, will have a tendency to predispose them to idleness," it read. The Department confronted Morris with the larger implications the Treaty 6 terms would have in relation to the other existing treaties, saying it would lead to dissatisfaction among First Nations who had already taken treaty and raise false expectations among those that had not, making them "more exacting in their demands than they otherwise would have been."[135]

The treaty document had not arrived in Ottawa until January 1877, as Morris had sent it by post, for safety. He could easily have informed officials of the terms earlier — via telegraph, for instance — but it seems likely that he delayed in order to force the government's hand. "I must do it on my own responsibility," he told the chiefs at Treaty 6, "and trust to the other Queen's councillors to ratify it,"[136] but it is unlikely he would have assumed the Department would quickly acquiesce had they known of the terms, given the difficulties he had experienced in securing funding for other treaty matters. In the end, despite "some of the provisions being exceedingly objectionable and such as ought not to have been made with any race of savages,"[137] the Department had little choice but to recommend ratification: "the Mischiefs which might result from refusing to ratify it might produce discontent and dissatisfaction, which . . . would prove more detrimental to the Country than the ratification of the objectionable provisions referred to."[138]

As an official independent of the Department, Morris defended the treaty in strong and unapologetic language — language that revealed both his understanding of the treaty relationship and his exasperation with those who had no such understanding. There was a world of difference between the point of view of a local official like himself, and someone unfamiliar with the region and its people:

> I undertook an arduous and responsible duty, knowing that my connection with the North West was about to cease, because I believed that, from my relations with the Indians, I was more likely to succeed than a stranger and because further, I was of opinion from my own experience that it was very undesirable that the new Lieutenant-Governor, whoever he might be, should take part in the negotiation. . . .[139]

The increase in agricultural implements, he wrote to the Minister of the Interior, "was not only justified by the circumstances, but was right and proper." He reminded Mills of the moral obligations involved in negotiating fair terms — "We were seeking to acquire their country to make way for settlement, and thus deprive them of their hunting grounds, and their means of livelihood" — and it followed that the Crown should be prepared to make substantial financial sacrifices of its own. He explained the First Nations' apprehensions over making the transition from hunting to agriculture, citing the example of James Senum's band "dragging the plough through the ground by their own strength."[140]

If they were going to overcome these challenges, the government would have to be much more generous in distributing implements. From the Aboriginal point of view, it made little sense to take up agriculture without a reasonable expectation of success. The onus was on the Crown to convince them it was worthwhile. "I have been convinced for some time," Morris revealed, "that if we are to succeed in inducing the Indians to cultivate the soil, the provisions of the former Treaties are not sufficiently liberal with regard to implements and cattle to accomplish the desired end."[141] He didn't seem bothered by the fact that the First Nations who had signed previous treaties now had grounds for demanding better terms, in light of the superior terms of Treaty 6. Given his tactics in implementing Treaty 5 and his view that the old treaty provisions were inadequate, it is likely that Morris was attempting once again to force the government's hand.

Morris had learned long ago that terms could not be imposed, but that commissioners had to make decisions and compromises to meet the needs and demands of the diverse nations of the North West:

> I would call your attention to the fact that in dealing with the Indian people, the Commissioners, away from all opportunity of obtaining advice, must act at times largely on their own responsibility and deal with the emergencies which arise. There is, moreover, no cast iron form of Treaty which can be imposed on these people. I have taken the leading part in negotiating Treaties Nos. 3, 4, 5 and 6, and in revising Treaties Nos. 1 and 2 and have encountered on all these occasions difficulties which the Commissioners overcame but which they were able to deal with only by assuming responsibility and at the moment without hesitation making stipulations to obviate the failure of the Treaties.[142]

Morris maintained that he had always done his utmost to negotiate terms that both sides could accept. He understood far better than his colleagues in Ottawa that the Indians were under no obligation to make treaties. They might have demanded better terms, or even walked away from the table, but for a combination of self-interest, pragmatism, and good faith. His only wonder was "that the Indians made the Treaty at all."[143]

He pointed out that the government had been urgently in need of securing the good will of the Aboriginal peoples, and that they would not have signed the treaty but for the promise of general assistance during times of famine and pestilence. He cited "the uneasiness of the Indians and the danger of collisions between them and the surveying, telegraph and other parties," and the need to avoid the type of violence that had occurred "between the Americans and the Sioux . . . not far distant from our frontier." He argued that it was the government that should be returning the good will that had been shown to it, not the reverse. The inclusion of the famine and pestilence provision in the treaty was a part of this reciprocity. The food question, Morris explained, "was the turning point of the Treaty." The commissioners made their promise "with the full conviction, that if not given, the Treaty would not be made, and that a failure would lead to consequences of a serious character, with regard to the Indian Tribes and entail heavy expenses on the Government."[144]

Morris took offence at the assertion that the promise of general assistance in times of disaster would engender idleness among the plains nations. He had often praised the various bands' work ethic and their desire to farm in order to regain the self-sufficiency they had lost with the disappearance of the buffalo. The famine and pestilence provision was insurance against unforeseen disaster while the bands made the difficult transition to agriculture. Morris argued that it could only "prove a stimulus to exertion."[145]

The promise of mutual assistance in times of need was part of the larger spirit of the treaties, a product of the diplomatic traditions that had existed for generations among Aboriginal groups, and later with the Hudson's Bay Company. Officials in distant Ottawa, Morris told the Minister, did not understand the nature of the famine and pestilence provision because they were "without full consideration or knowledge" of the local situation and context. It was entirely consistent with the principles of Christian humanism, British justice, and good government, and it was "as old in practice as the history of civilized government."[146]

The promise of assistance in times of need had been inspired by the unwritten spirit of the treaties that preceded Treaty 6, and by 1876 Morris had good reason to include the provision in the text; he had learned that Ottawa would not live up to the spirit of the treaties unless it was explicitly written in the document itself. In this sense, the famine and pestilence provision, along with other "new" articles promised in Treaty 6, was an attempt by Morris and the other commissioners to frame the relationship of reciprocity in the familiar language of Euro-Canadian legalese. By incorporating the provisions into the treaty text, Morris was attempting to force the government to recognize *de facto* that these terms were also part of the previous treaties. The government had always promised that the different First Nations groups would be treated equally, and he knew by now that, hearing of these terms, bands in other treaty areas would insist on their having been part of the earlier treaties. It was important that future governments and their officials recognize their obligation to provide assistance in times of disaster.[147]

Morris's defence of Treaty 6 appears to have brought the debate to a close, at least officially. His views were whole-heartedly supported by James McKay.[148] The Privy Council ratified the treaty as it was written, but it was the last one that Morris would negotiate. He served as Lieutenant-Governor of Manitoba for the remainder of 1877, but the task of completing Treaty 7 went to David Laird, now Lieutenant-Governor of the North West Territories and Superintendent General of Indian Affairs.

Removed from Power

During the final year of his tenure, Morris's many disagreements with Ottawa finally came to a head. Since at least early 1876, officials in the Department had been working to diminish his role in Indian Affairs. Despite their best efforts, however, Morris was able to use his rapport with David Laird to ensure his political survival. In fact, his level of involvement increased in 1876 with the resolution of the outside promises, the negotiation of Treaty 6, and the implementation of Treaties 3-5. Under the new minister, David Mills, however, Morris's influence finally diminished, as Edmund Allen Meredith and Rob Sinclair had hoped.

Officials of the Department had become increasingly annoyed at the amount of money being spent on treaty implementation. In February 1876, Sinclair was once again tasked with investigating the internal workings of Indian Affairs management in the North West. Part of the problem, he reported, was misman-agement. While he applauded Provencher's fiscally conservative approach in dis-bursing implements, annuities, and provisions, he abhorred his bookkeeping and money management. A particularly troublesome issue to Sinclair was the amount being spent on annuities. Provencher had failed to mention that there were more Indians in the territory than the government had initially thought. Sinclair rec-ommended a less liberal spending policy, handing out implements only when the Department judged that they would be required or actually used. He called for a census of each band, forcing the chiefs to commit to a list of named members. His recommendations contained the seeds of the policy of restricting Indian status by legislation. "No doubt the appointment of local agents will do much to rectify this irregularity," he wrote, "as they will be able to become personally acquainted with the Indians under their charge."[149]

Sinclair attributed cost overruns in treaty implementation to Morris, who was much too generous, and far more generous than Provencher. The problem was that Morris did not answer to the Department:

> I believe, that both gentlemen look at the Indian question from different points of view. Gov. Morris has no financial responsibility resting on him as regards the Indians and is disposed to be very conciliatory. Mr. Provencher on the other hand is responsible to the Department for his expenditure and is obliged to be very firm and decided in meeting with a negative, many demands pressed on him by the Indians. On this account, I think His Honour is disposed to think that the Supt. is given to harshness in his treatment of the Indians.[150]

Morris had entered into Indian Affairs administration through his own initiative, and Sinclair wanted him removed. Morris wanted Provencher removed. It was Provencher who kept his position.

Shortly after Sinclair issued his confidential report to the minister, the De-partment moved to consolidate absolute control over Indian Affairs in the North West. Instead of placing the Lieutenant-Governor at the head of a Board of Commissioners setting Indian Affairs policy and managing treaty implementa-tion, as Morris had recommended, the new plan called for the creation of two superintendents who were answerable directly to the Department. These officers would oversee the sub-agents for all of Manitoba and the North West Territories. The Lieutenant-Governor, who answered not to the Department but to the Gov-ernor General, would effectively be left out of the process.

Morris warned that the new arrangement would cut off the First Nations from the direct relationship with the Crown that they valued so highly, and that it was completely out of step with the diplomatic and practical context of the North West:

> From long use and want, under the regime of the Hudson's Bay Company, and in conformity with the natural bent of the Indian mind, they will come, whenever they have a grievance to represent or a request to make, to the Lieutenant-Governor, as being the Chief representative of the Crown, and they will not rest satisfied with meeting any subordinate officer.[151]

Morris was deeply concerned that the new regime would eliminate the reciprocal relationship he had developed with his Aboriginal counterparts, and he warned that giving the superintendents "all authority to deal with Indian matters . . . irrespective and independent of the Lieutenant-Governors, will . . . create difficulties and embarrassments of a serious character."[152]

He was not prepared to brush aside the chiefs and councillors who were certain to continue to visit him. "I have been notified that a chief from 300 miles North is coming in to see me," he wrote. "That he will not be satisfied unless he interviews me, is beyond doubt, and yet under your system, I have no right to receive him."[153]

A system in which the Indian Commissioner and various Indian Agents exercised administrative independence, with little recourse for the Indians, was abhorrent to Morris. Reminding the Department that his views were drawn from "nearly four years of experience, and . . . constant contact with the Indian Tribes in this region," he argued that the Lieutenant-Governor must have authority to look into any grievances and requests the Indians might bring forward, "otherwise, there will be constant jarring and difficulty and the dissatisfaction, which has prevailed in the past amongst the Indian Tribes, and which I have done my utmost to allay and mitigate, will continue and be intensified."[154]

Morris managed to secure some concessions. In April, he travelled to Ottawa to lobby for assurances that he would retain some level of meaningful authority. At first, his efforts appeared successful. "His Honour represented very strongly the necessity of his having some recognized official position in connection with the Administration of Indian Affairs," Laird told the Privy Council, so he was given "the honorary title of Chief Superintendent of Indian Affairs in the Manitoba Superintendency."[155]

The title was purely honorary. As the chief representative of the Crown, Morris could continue to meet with the Indians "to set forth any grievance or complaints," and he retained his "authority to call upon the Local Superintendent . . . to give explanations upon any Indian matters that may be brought under his notice," but he would have no authority over financial matters, which were left in the hands of the parsimonious Provencher. The Department evidently hoped that the Lieutenant-Governor would continue to placate the First Nations by granting them audiences, but his capacity to act would be severely limited.

Morris, to his credit, managed to turn his symbolic authority to practical use in the administration of Treaties 3, 4, and 5. He was not supposed to intervene in financial matters, but he did anyway, advising and assisting treaty implemen-

PIAPOT, REGINA, 1885. *An influential Cree chief from the Qu'Appelle Valley, Piapot signed an adhesion to Treaty 4 on the understanding that the terms would be improved. He stayed true to his treaty promises, but spent the rest of his life trying to get the government to fulfil theirs. He died in 1908* (Glenbow Archives, NA-1296-4).

tation officers and lobbying for more funding. It was for this persistent intervention that Deputy Minister Meredith, perhaps the true authority on Indian Affairs administration and policy in Ottawa, blasted Morris almost a year after the Department's attempt to reign him in. Morris was interfering in the implementation process "with the Indians, especially in connection with Treaty No. 5 — business which under ordinary circumstances should have been performed by the Indian Superintendent." Morris's involvement in Indian Affairs created a variety of logistical inconveniences from the viewpoint of "Headquarters" in Ottawa. "Where the Lieut. Governor as well as the Superintendent is engaged in the administration of Indian Affairs," it led to "conflicting action." Morris's popularity and interaction with the Indians tended "to weaken the authority of the Indian Superintendent proper and to lower his influence with and authority over the Indians." Particularly annoying were Morris's continuous reports of Indian grievances, and the fact that "large sums of money have been disbursed." Meredith warned that if such spending were to continue, Morris's actions would soon "subject him to suspicion of favouritism" for the Indians over the rest of the population.[156]

The heart of the problem was the Lieutenant-Governor's immunity to departmental authority. It was "impossible to call him to account or to subject him to the same rigid rules as an ordinary subordinate of the Department." In order "to secure an efficient and economical administration of the Indian Affairs in any Superintendency, the sole and undivided responsibility . . . should rest with the Superintendent" — in this case, Provencher — "a subordinate officer of the Department." Morris could keep his title, but he should "be strictly limited" from interfering "in the execution or administration of Indian Affairs, especially in financial matters."[157]

Meredith's policy would shape the administration of Indian Affairs to come. Morris was the last truly independent Lieutenant-Governor to play a significant role in treaty negotiation and implementation.

Meredith's scathing assessment of Morris points to the clear differences between the Lieutenant-Governor and his colleagues in Ottawa. While Morris had begun his tenure in the North West with the firm hand of financial conservatism, he had, through years of interaction with the people of the country, come to believe that Ottawa was not doing enough to meet their needs and its lawful obligations toward them. Taking his own measures to remedy the situation, he overcame the barriers of his own social formation and came to empathize with their plight and, to a significant extent, understand their world view. The officials he dealt with in Ottawa had little opportunity for such an intellectual transformation.

Morris continued to intervene in Indian Affairs as much as his diminished position would allow. He instructed agents on making annuity payments. Chiefs and counsellors continued to come to him to maintain diplomatic relations, and to voice their concerns. Many continued to hold Morris and his office in much higher esteem than they did Provencher. "They . . . wished to see me as I had made the Treaty with them and was the Governor," Morris reported in April 1877 to the Minister of the Interior on meeting with Treaty 3 Chiefs Powhassan and She-she-gence.[158]

Morris may have been diminished in influence, but he continued to act on the grievances that were brought to him. He reminded Ottawa that the Indians were upholding their treaty promises by making sincere efforts at farming, and that the government should reciprocate by providing the promised assistance. Chief Constant of the Pas Reserve, in the remote Treaty 5 area, for instance, appealed directly to Morris to secure the delivery of provisions, implements, and schools promised under treaty. He assured Morris of his band's agricultural activities. Taking Constant at his word, Morris forwarded the request to the Minister of the Interior.[159]

The Department was not so trusting, and referred the matter back to Provencher, who put off the schools question and denied the band's request for more seed. He had embraced the stringent new policies, regardless of what had been promised in the treaties:

> It has been the constant practice of the Indians to say that they were ready to receive every article, cattle, implements, that they may be entitled to, in certain conditions, according to the Treaties. But I would strongly recommend that no such engagements should be fulfilled before the Indians have really showed that whatever article is given to them shall not be wasted or traded.[160]

The tragedy of history does not lie in the treaties, but in Canada's failure to honour its promises. The Crown's negotiators — Alexander Morris, James McKay, W. J. Christie — were personally committed to the treaty relationship, but they lacked the support of the government on whose behalf they had negotiated.

First Nations leaders proved early on their commitment to the treaty relationship. Shortly after signing Treaty 4, Ojibwa Chief Côté wrote a "thanks [to] Morris for coming," reminding him that he "intends to keep the treaty made."[161] According to Saskatchewan treaty elders today, the provisions were to be closely observed, and the inheritors of the treaties were "not to change anything."[162] After taking treaty, the plains nations no longer disrupted telegraph lines and settlement, and at times assisted immigrants in their search for suitable land. Many of "the new settlers who flooded in over the next couple of decades, principally from Ontario," Jean Friesen explains, "survived their pioneer years because the Indians permitted them access to the fish and game resources."[163]

The Crown's negotiators lobbied tirelessly for the proper implementation of the treaty promises, but their advice often went unheeded by those who controlled the purse strings in Ottawa. Requests for increased staffing were only half met. There were times when agricultural implements were readily available in storage, but there was no one to distribute them.[164] At other times there were fewer implements than promised, and they were frequently of poor quality.[165] Christie was soon echoing Morris's demands that the "terms and conditions of treaty [be] attended to at once."[166] David Laird, on moving to the North West after Morris's departure, noted that "many of the Cree leaders were complaining that the government was not providing the farming assistance promised," and called on the government to establish reserves and honour the treaties.[167]

The situation deteriorated further when the Macdonald government, returned to power in 1878, appointed Edgar Dewdney to the newly created and all-powerful position of Commissioner of Indian Affairs for the North West Territory in 1879. With the explicit support of the Macdonald government, Dewdney abandoned the treaties and set in motion a policy that he called "sheer compulsion."[168] He confronted an increasingly agitated Aboriginal leadership with starvation tactics, withholding rations and farm implements from those bands who protested the government's behaviour. He undercut First Nations autonomy by incarcerating chiefs; he impoverished bands by confiscating horses and carts; he increased the size of the Mounted Police to station officers on reserves; and he prohibited people from leaving their reserves.[169]

Disillusioned treaty Indians came to conclude that Alexander Morris had made "sweet promises," and nothing more.

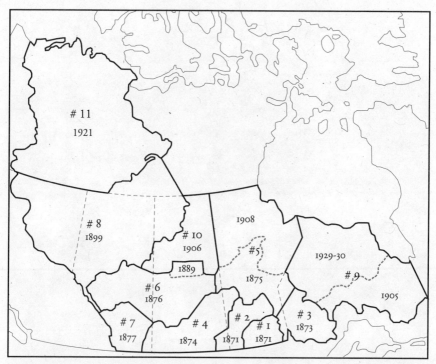

THE NUMBERED TREATIES. *Alexander Morris negotiated Treaties 3 – 6 and renegotiated Treaties 1 and 2 with the First Nations of Western Canada.*

FOUR CHIEFS, ONTARIO, OCTOBER 1886. *Ojibwa Chief Louis O'Soup and interpreter Peter Hourie stand behind (from the left) Cree Chiefs Atâhkakohp, Kahkiwistahaw, and Mistawâsis* (Library and Archives Canada, C-019258).

10

Pride and Satisfaction

DESPITE THE MANY DISAPPOINTMENTS AND DIFFICULTIES he had experienced with Ottawa, Morris left the North West with a sense of accomplishment. His objectives had been, first, to secure Canada's future and economic prosperity by way of a peaceful annexation of the territory, and second, to ensure the survival of the Aboriginal peoples. He had reconciled his dream of expanding the Canadian state with his desire to see its original peoples prosper alongside their new neighbours. In his view, he had achieved both goals. "I cannot help saying that my residence, my position in this province, has been a pride and satisfaction to me," he told a Winnipeg gathering in 1877. "I leave this Province as one who feels that five years of his life have been worked into its history, and that it is his good fortune to carry away with him the friendship of the community."[1]

Morris had become deeply attached to the peoples of the North West. He celebrated the diversity of the people, and championed the principle of peaceful coexistence they had upheld. Any language about the "fusion of races" or rendering the population thoroughly British — a notion of Morris's earlier years — was absent from this speech:

[H]ere in this province there dwells a community of the most mixed character that can be found in any country under the sun, and . . . here, thanks to Providence, thanks to the good sense of the community, to the spirit of conciliation and adaptation to each other which has been developed among us, there is peace, harmony and concord.[2]

Morris promised that, after his departure, he would do his utmost to uphold the interests of the people he had come to respect and admire: "Next to my duty to my Queen, let my hereafter be short or long in it, will be found devotion to the interests of Canada, Manitoba and the North West."[3]

Morris's term as Lieutenant-Governor of Manitoba came to an official close on 2 December 1877, but he was not yet finished with public life. In 1878, he ran in the federal election to represent Selkirk, Manitoba, but lost by nine votes to his opponent, Donald A. Smith, "the most unscrupulous liar I ever met."[4] By the end of the same year he had won a seat in the Ontario Legislative Assembly, representing the constituents of Toronto East. He took a prominent role among the opposition Conservatives, preaching against American annexation and championing the cause of federal rights against the ruling Liberal administration of his erstwhile legal colleague, Oliver Mowat. Morris also spoke out against Mowat's claim that "Indians possess no title in the unceded lands of the Crown." Mowat's comments came at a time when the province was looking increasingly to exploit the forestry and mineral resources of north-western Ontario, including those on reserves. Morris argued vigorously that the First Nations retained both a legal and a moral claim to the land, "a title which had been recognized not only by England but by several European nations, by the American Colonies before and since Independence, and by old and new Canada." He rejected the pretension that the mere "right of discovery gave [Europeans] the right of ownership." Morris pointed out that the Indians "maintained their claim to be sovereign proprietors of the soil, and acknowledged no obedience to any foreign sovereign. They have always asserted this right, and yielded it up only when lost by conquest or given up by a voluntary cession."[5]

Morris's financial circumstances had suffered somewhat by the end of his tenure as Lieutenant-Governor, but he retained land interests in the North West, including lots in Winnipeg and Edmonton, and farmland in Manitoba.[6] In mid-1881 he helped the Presbyterian Mission at Prince Albert acquire land on the North Saskatchewan River, in part to support a high school "in which," he advised, "provision should be made for the free education of Indian children."[7]

He became something of an unofficial advisor on Indian Affairs to the prime minister, Sir John A. Macdonald, especially when the North West Rebellion broke out in 1885. Morris blamed the situation on the failure of treaty implementation derived from Liberal policies during his time as Lieutenant-Governor. "Had my advice in 1876 been followed this would have been long since settled," he told Macdonald in March 1885. "For all the work I did I never had a word of thanks," he later wrote:

On the contrary, my Indian career was closed with the highest censure.
The Government gave us little or no direction or instructions to aid them

[Indians] in pestilence and famine of a national character. If we had not done as we did there would be no treaty and no order as we had from '76 to '85. . . . I warned Mills as to breach of faith concerning Indian Treaties. I had two years of fighting with Mills and would have resigned but for Lord Dufferin who stood by me and advised me not to do so.[8]

The general mismanagement of Indians Affairs, and of Treaty 6 in particular, remained a bitter memory. Still, Morris's reputation as Lieutenant-Governor and his role in Indian Affairs had left a positive impression among many Aboriginal people, and among those who knew them. "The treaties already made here have been for the satisfaction of all," wrote Father Lacombe in his report to Morris from the Saskatchewan in February 1875:

Everyone knows very well the justice of your actions when it comes to the poor Indian. . . . I am certain that you want the best for the Indians, given that since the first years of your public life you have been advocating so well for the cause of the poor children of the forests and the plains. . . .[9]

Lacombe was well respected by the Cree and Blackfoot, having learned their languages and lived among both peoples. Morris forwarded Lacombe's report to the Secretary of State and Governor General, underlining passages that he felt were particularly significant:

Allow me to confess to your Excellency that for my own part, I think that the arrival of the Whites among the Indians, with all the gentleness of civilization that it has brought them, has still been a great ill for the Indian tribes. . . . [T]he Indians who have never encountered the White man are better off in terms of the corporal life than those to whom we have taught needs and wants that they hadn't known before.[10]

During his tenure, First Nations leaders had come directly to Morris in the knowledge that he would give them a more sympathetic hearing than Provencher or other officials. In their countless encounters with him, at treaty negotiations or in less formal meetings at Fort Garry, they expressed their respect and friendship toward him, and Morris amassed a sizeable collection of gifts and artefacts during this time.

Long after leaving the North West, Morris was remembered well. In 1886, chiefs travelling east called on Morris in Toronto. The group included Mistawâsis and Atâhkakohp, the principle negotiators at Treaty 6. After Morris's death in 1889, a number of chiefs from Manitoba and the North West made the long journey to his funeral to pay him a final honour. Among them was Chief John Prince of Clandeboye, Manitoba, who famously stated that "the Great Spirit called me here to be by the side of my friend."[11]

Well into the next century, First Nations leaders evoked Morris's name to remind the government of its promises.[12]

The Treaties of Canada. . . .

Shortly after his departure from the North West, Morris decided to write a book on the history of treaty making in Western Canada, with a focus on the numbered treaties. The book was published in 1880 under the descriptive and typically Victorian title, *The Treaties of Canada with the Indians of Manitoba and the North West Territories, Including the Negotiations on Which They Were Based, and Other Information Relating Thereto*. Morris compiled his own recollections, transcriptions of the proceedings, reports submitted to the government by himself and others, and the texts of the treaties and adhesions. It remains the most important single source of written information on Treaties 1 through 7.

Morris had his reasons for publishing the book. He believed that, in order to understand the treaties properly, one had to be familiar with the people and the historical and contemporary contexts under which they had been negotiated. In the twilight of his career and in uncertain health, having faced the criticism of his colleagues, he was anxious to validate his term as Lieutenant-Governor. It was a means, also, of shoring up his personal legacy as a nation-builder. He did not shy from boasting in the preface that he "had considerable part" in the negotiating and signing of the treaties and Canada's subsequent territorial expansion westward. In other speeches and publications throughout his career, Morris had not scrupled about pointing out his contributions to the making of Canadian history.

Morris's book has been criticized as "wholly self-serving . . . written to justify Morris's work in the negotiation and his British Imperial vision of Canada's future, a vision which was quite at odds with the objectives of the Aboriginal Nations."[13] But there are sound reasons for believing that the work is reliable. The transcripts and correspondence in the book essentially match the original copies now housed in archival records. The bulk of the book is made up of documents written during the period, not recollections made in hindsight. Morris insisted on the accuracy of the accounts of the spoken proceedings, and his reports to the Department corroborated the spoken record. Historian John Taylor, generally critical of Morris, acknowledges that the transcribed proceedings provide a crucial source in understanding the treaties.[14] In recent years, too, Aboriginal groups have turned to Morris to build their legal arguments in favour of treaty rights. "The primary source is Morris," the National Indian Brotherhood announced in 1980, at the height of the constitutional renewal process in Canada.[15]

Many events, places, and personalities in the book have been confirmed in other written sources. Morris's son, Edmund, met some thirty years later with a number of figures, both government and Aboriginal, and his conversations with them are recorded in his diaries,[16] and events described in Alexander Morris's chapter on Treaty 5 are corroborated by the diary of the captain of the vessel that took Morris and McKay on their journey across Lake Winnipeg.[17] Peter Erasmus's recollections of Treaty 6 negotiations are, with a few exceptions, also consistent with Morris's version, though from a different perspective. Much has been made of Morris's omission of one of Poundmaker's criticisms of the treaty, contained in Erasmus's record,[18] but equally striking examples of opposition or suspicion were included in Morris's book.[19]

That Morris saw fit to publish transcripts of the negotiations, and not just the treaty texts, suggests that he had come to see the spoken exchange as part of the larger agreement. Interestingly, much of Morris's book, according to the National Indian Brotherhood, "confirms the oral tradition of Aboriginal elders."[20] Had he wished to limit the perception of the treaties or certain promises that were made but not recorded in the text, he could have doctored the transcripts or omitted the record altogether. Morris's understanding of the significance of the treaties may be more conservative than that of First Nations in the last half of the 20th century and the first part of the 21st, but it was certainly more liberal than that of the federal government of the late 19th century.

The treaties occupy an important place in Canadian history, and it was Morris's desire that they be remembered:

> It is the design of the present work to tell the story of these treaties, to preserve, as far as practicable, a record of the negotiations on which they were based, and to present to the many in the Dominion and elsewhere, who take a deep interest in these sons of the forest and the plain, a view of their habits of thought and speech, as thereby presented, and to suggest the possibility, nay, the certainty, of a hopeful future for them.[21]

The book was marketed to a general audience, but also to set the record straight for government administrators. It had been compiled as a record of the treaty-making, but also as "an aid to the . . . equally important duty . . . of carrying out, in their integrity, the obligations of these treaties." Morris had developed a personal and emotional stake in the fulfillment of the treaties and in the future success of the First Nations. He described treaty implementation as "the completion of a work, in which I had considerable part, that, of, by treaties, securing the good will of the Indian tribes, and by the helpful hand of the Dominion, opening up to them, a future of promise, based upon the foundations of instruction and the many other advantages of civilized life."[22]

Morris's gradual acceptance of the oral proceedings as an integral part of the treaty nevertheless had begun as early as 1874. Shortly after the conclusion of Treaty 4, he remarked:

> It is obvious that such a record will prove valuable, as it enables any misunderstanding on the part of the Indians, as to what was said at the conference, to be corrected, and it, moreover, will enable the [Privy] council better to appreciate the character of the difficulties that have to be encountered in negotiating with the Indians.[23]

By late 1876, Morris was less interested in clearing up "misunderstanding on the part of the Indians" than in influencing government thinking on treaty making and implementation. To this end, he presented the minister with a transcript of the Treaty 6 negotiations, "which I think ought to be published, as it will be of great value to those who will be called on to administer the treaty, showing as it does what was said by the negotiators and by the Indians, and preventing misrepresentations in the future."[24] Morris hoped that future policy makers and officials responsible for treaty implementation would refer to his book in the execution of their duties.

The book gave a favourable reading of the treaties, and downplayed the divisions between Morris and his colleagues. In no place did Morris mention his frustration with Provencher, or the inability of Ottawa to understand the nature of events in the North West. Neither did he mention his frustration at never being granted the centralized authority he believed necessary for the proper administration of the treaties. His belief in the "solidarity of the public service" rendered any such public disclosure inconsistent with his sense of professionalism.[25]

If anything, Morris painted a picture in which the Department of the Interior appeared to approve of the sometimes controversial measures he took to negotiate the treaties and implement the government's promises. In the chapter on the renegotiation of Treaties 1 and 2, for instance, the correspondence ends with his report of June 8, 1876, in which he recommended approval of the Yellow Quill reserve, immediately before major differences arose with the Department. "Thus was so far closed, a controversy which had lasted for some years," Morris cheerfully concluded.[26] But this was hardly the end of it; the Department did not approve the Yellow Quill reserve, and disputes between the band and incoming settlers persisted into the 1880s. With regard to Treaties 1 and 2, Morris appeared to believe that only the correspondence from June 8, 1876 and earlier were legitimate — before Mills became minister. By including only his own recommendations, and not the refusal of the Department to approve the reserve, Morris was effectively writing the opinions of officials that he had found objectionable *out* of the history. "The despatches of the Lieutenant-Governor to the Minister of the

Interior [Laird], giving an account in full of the negotiations for the revision of the Treaties Numbers One and Two, will complete this record," Morris wrote, "and will be found to give a clear narrative of them."[27] In a similar vein, the chapter on Treaty 5 included various correspondence relating to its implementation, but none of the subsequent correspondence in which the Department objected to Morris's expensive interventions.[28]

In the Treaty 6 chapter, Morris's selective citation of Mills might have led the reader to believe that the Minister wholeheartedly endorsed the additional treaty provisions,[29] whereas a reading of the private correspondence clearly shows that Mills and the Department had chastised Morris for his excesses. As with the chapters on Treaties 1, 2, and 5, Morris stopped including correspondence at the point at which government officials became critical of the treaties. The book promoted Morris's version of events over that of his colleagues in Ottawa. It was designed to counter the perspective of his more parsimonious counterparts, including Mills, Meredith, and Vankoughnet. If his book became a reference for public officials in determining policy, he thought, then future policies might be changed accordingly.

The Treaties of Canada took a few parting shots at treaty administration in general. In the final chapter, Morris alluded to Ottawa's departure from its treaty obligations, and repeated a number of his own recommendations for proper administration. He insisted that the government not break faith with the First Nations and the treaties they entered into:

> I remark in the first place that the provisions of these treaties must be carried out with the utmost good faith and the nicest exactness. The Indians of Canada have, owing to the manner in which they were dealt with for generations by the Hudson's Bay Company, the former rulers of these vast territories, an abiding confidence in the Government of the Queen, or the Great Mother, as they style her. This must not, at all hazards, be shaken. It can be easily and fully maintained.[30]

Careful observation of the treaties provided the best assurance for peace and stability in the region, he advised.[31] Morris reiterated the terms of the treaties, trying to convince readers that it remained well within the means of government to uphold the bare minimum of its promises. He explained the significance of the flags, medals, clothing, and salaries given to the chiefs and headmen, and warned against some of the policies that had been adopted since his departure:

> The power of the Chiefs has been much broken of late, and I am of opinion that it is of importance to strengthen the hands of the Chiefs and Councillors by a due recognition of their offices and respect being shewn them. . . .

It is . . . of the utmost importance to retain their confidence and cause their office to be recognized and respected by both whites and Indians.[32]

Morris argued that the government needed the chiefs to maintain law and order in the country, among newcomers as well as First Nations. He cited the example of a chief who had helped bring a murderer to justice:

This case affords an illustration of the value of the recognition of the Chiefs of the various bands, and shews of how much advantage, it is to the Crown to possess so large a number of Indian officials, duly recognized as such, and who can be inspired with a proper sense of their responsibility to the Government and to their bands, as well as to others. In all the negotiations for treaties, the chiefs took a controlling part, and generally exhibited great common sense and excellent judgement.[33]

Morris urged that the reserve lands be upheld and respected. The reserves were to provide permanent homes for the original inhabitants of the country, and "cannot be interfered with, by the rush of immigration." Moreover, they would provide a means to "learn the arts of agriculture." He reminded settlers and policy makers alike that the reserves "cannot be sold or alienated without their [the Indians'] consent, and then only for their benefit." At a time when reserve lands were either being denied or moved for the benefit of the government and settlers, Morris maintained that it was up to the Indians themselves to determine the location of their reserves: "The Indians, have a strong attachment to the localities, in which they and their fathers have been accustomed to dwell, and it is desirable to cultivate this home feeling of attachment to the soil." He warned that a system such as that in the United States, in which peoples were relegated to non-ancestral, remote, inferior lands, away from urban markets, would lead to "Indian wars and great discontent." [34]

Morris refuted the assumption of Social Darwinists that, as a people, the First Nations were "unconscious of their destiny" and doomed to disappear. He insisted that they were fully capable and willing to learn agriculture so as to survive and maintain their economic independence: "They are tractable, docile, and willing to learn. They recognize the fact that they must seek part of their living from 'the mother earth,' to use their own phraseology."[35]

Morris repeated his insistence that the agricultural implements promised in the treaties should be provided, and argued that the government should go beyond the treaty text in order to treat justly with those who had kept faith with them. The cattle assigned to each band, for instance, had been "comparatively limited," out of a bureaucratic concern that the Indians might not take up agriculture and properly care for the animals. Morris admitted that "the Government

Negotiating the Numbered Treaties

are not bound to extend the number," but insisted that "the Indians are turning their attention much more to cultivating the soil," and cited several examples from different treaty areas.[36] He wrote with admiration of the First Nations' work ethic, and their determination to survive and make a living.

He repeated an earlier recommendation he had made to Mills, perhaps hoping that it might be better received among the public. In 1876, he wrote, "I reported to the Minister of the Interior, the Hon. David Mills, after my return from the negotiation of the treaties at Forts Carlton and Pitt, that measures ought to be taken to instruct the Indians in farming and building." He noted that Laird had made a similar recommendation two years later, and "that the Government of Canada, decided to act on these suggestions, at least in part."[37] Morris saw the implementation of the schools promise as central to agricultural instruction.

The final chapter included a section on the Métis. "For my own part," he wrote, "I can frankly say, that I always had the confidence, support and active cooperation of the Half-breeds of all origins, in my negotiations with the Indian tribes, and I owed them this full acknowledgment thereof."[38] Quoting the former Governor General, Lord Dufferin, Morris praised the Métis for "preaching the Gospel of peace and good will, and mutual respect, with equally beneficent results to the Indian chieftain in his lodge and to the British settler in his shanty. They have been the ambassadors between the east and the west."[39] He implored the government to recognize the land holdings of those Métis who had settled and taken up agriculture, and to set aside lands and provide agricultural assistance for the "large class of Métis who live by the hunt of the buffalo, and have no settled homes."[40] This last recommendation, Morris pointed out, he had been making since 1876.

With praise for the missionary work of all denominations across the North West, Morris called on the clergy, appealing to the Christian sensibilities of his readership as well as his own religious beliefs. The churches "have their duties to fulfil," he wrote, in all sincerity. "There is a common ground between the Christian Churches and the Indians, as they all believe as we do, in a Great Spirit. The transition thence to the Christian's God is an easy one. . . ."[41]

Morris concluded *The Treaties of Canada* with an appeal for the government to uphold the treaties, on moral as well as legal grounds. Through the mutually beneficial treaty relationship, Canada could guarantee security and peaceful settlement in the North West, and the First Nations could secure their own survival and the means for economic independence:

> Let us have a wise and paternal Government faithfully carrying out the provisions of our treaties, and doing its utmost to help and elevate the Indian population, who have been cast upon our care, and we will have peace, progress, and concord among them in the North West; and instead

of the Indian melting away, as one of them in older Canada, tersely put it, "as snow before the sun," we will see our Indian population, loyal subjects of the Crown, happy, prosperous and self-sustaining, and Canada will be enabled to feel, that in a truly patriotic spirit, our country has done its duty by the red men of the North West, and thereby to herself.[42]

Conclusion

ALEXANDER MORRIS STANDS AS AN EXAMPLE of the intellectual exchange that could occur between First Nations and newcomers in the 19th-century North West. Despite his social formation and the convictions that informed his initial outlook on the region and its people, Morris demonstrated a significant degree of intellectual flexibility. Over time, he incorporated many Aboriginal concepts into his own understanding of the treaty relationship, particularly the principles of reciprocity and mutual assistance in times of need.

Morris's early interest in Indigenous peoples provided a basis for his developing sympathies later in life. This early awareness was informed by religious paternalism, Christian humanism, and a general concern for Indian survival as they came into contact with other cultures. He was throughout his life a supporter of Christian missions to Indigenous peoples in Canada and around the world.

For a time, his personal financial and career interests overshadowed his earlier concerns. Like his father, Morris made much of his fortune in land speculation. It was through his commercial interests that he honed his shrewd and often unforgiving negotiating skills — skills he would later apply at treaty negotiations. It was through his land speculation that Morris became aware of the impending land shortage that spelled disaster for the Canadian economy. When the economic and agricultural potential of the North West became known, Morris promptly called for annexation. He had been a Canadian nationalist since childhood, and the conservative ideology that he inherited helped determine that his nationalism would be of an economic and decidedly British variety. It was on this foundation that the ambitious young lawyer built his political platform. Before moving to the North West, then, Morris viewed the region in terms of its exploitative potential.

It was through his interactions with Aboriginal leaders, and at treaty negotiations in particular, that the interests of the region's original inhabitants took on a new and greater prominence in Morris's thinking. He came to know firsthand the hard realities that annexation and immigration presented to the Aboriginal peoples. The highly personalized and solemn practise of treaty making made an equal impression. Morris came to admire many Aboriginal leaders: for their skill with language and oratory, which he attempted to emulate; for their wisdom in opting for a pragmatic course that they believed would ensure their future; for their resilience in taking up agriculture despite the tremendous difficulties they endured; and for their integrity in upholding the promises they had made. Morris's mature admiration lacked the condescension that his former preoccupation with moralism had engendered.

Repeatedly, Morris put his own reputation with First Nations on the line, and he was determined that his integrity remain untarnished. He argued that it would be personally damaging, entirely illegal, and simply unjust for Canada to shirk the responsibilities the treaty relationship entailed, especially given the immense sacrifices and hardships the First Nations had endured. It was in these terms that he explained and defended the treaties to sceptical officials in Ottawa, and to the Canadian public.

Words were followed with action as Morris attempted to oversee the treaties' implementation. He continually met with Aboriginal leaders, observing the diplomatic traditions and paying them due respect. He did not shrink from reporting in detail the grievances of the chiefs, often lending his own support to their viewpoint, and successfully lobbied for the renegotiation of Treaties 1 and 2 in order to meet the outside promises that had long been ignored by the government. He helped identify agents who understood the peoples they dealt with, and oversaw the logistical arrangements for the delivery of provisions, annuities, and laying out the reserves. He repeatedly, and with occasional success, called on Ottawa for increased funding in all treaty areas. It is not unlikely that the disbursement of treaty implements and annuities would have been much less generous had Morris not intervened, frequently without Ottawa's sanction. As well, many of the reserves that did get approved could very well have been further delayed if not for Morris's insistent appeals to the Department of the Interior.

Throughout his tenure, Alexander Morris advocated for a more centralized system of Indian Affairs administration in which decision-making would be prompt and informed by individuals who were familiar with the context and the people of the North West. He was increasingly convinced that he should be at the head of any new administrative arrangement, in part because he had come to appreciate the value the Indians placed in the office of the Lieutenant-Governor as the representative of the Crown. Their reasons were as practical as they were symbolic. As an official independent from the Department of the Interior, Morris was more likely to achieve results. He was also more inclined to take the leading role in treaty implementation because he had developed a personal and emotional stake in the treaties. Indeed, he did not trust the task to anyone else. Ultimately, he would find himself removed from Indian Affairs administration because of his sympathetic and generous attitude toward the peoples he had come to admire.

Alexander Morris remains the subject of controversy in some circles to this day. Viewed from a 21st-century century perspective, the terms he negotiated with the First Nations of the North West seem parsimonious. At Treaty 3, for instance, he had permission to negotiate an annuity of $7, but managed to secure a $5 annuity instead. Critics argue that Morris should have been more accommodating when it came to reserve size, too; he should have anticipated that the population would outgrow their small reserves. As a matter of simple justice, the first inhabitants of the territory should have been left with more land.

While much of this criticism is understandable, it is misplaced. Morris's actions must be viewed in the context of his background and the pressures he faced from the government. As an officer of the Crown, his first obligation was to secure the most cost-effective terms possible. Naturally, he turned to the hard-nosed negotiating tactics of his earlier land speculation. He was under constant pressure from a cash-strapped federal government to keep costs to a minimum. Had he managed to negotiate more generous terms, it is more than likely that Ottawa would not have approved them. This proved to be the case when the Department refused to approve certain reserves Morris had promised under the renegotiation of Treaties 1 and 2. Morris was a professional who believed strongly in the solidarity of the public service. He was deeply disillusioned by the government's betrayal of faith, but that he had revolted at all was remarkable in itself.

By the end of his tenure, Morris had begun to believe that the terms of *all* the treaties might be inadequate. Despite his legal training, which emphasized a literal interpretation of legal documents and land cessions in particular, he continually lobbied the Department for monies and implements that had not been explicitly included in the treaty texts. He similarly proved flexible when it came to requests as to reserve location, and occasionally on the issue of reserve size. Morris often justified these requests by appealing to general principles of humanity, or reciprocity — principles that were consistent with the Aboriginal understanding of the treaty relationship.

The spirit in which the treaties were negotiated remains as relevant today as it was in the 19th century. Recent years have witnessed a renewed interest in the treaties as tools for fostering understanding and partnership among First Nations and non-Aboriginal Canadians. The latter, however, remain largely uninformed about the treaties. It has been far too easy to cast them aside as tragedies of history, absolving ourselves of responsibility for promises made by our ancestors. But we are all treaty people. We are all responsible for upholding the relationship to which our ancestors committed their descendents over 130 years ago. As Alexander Morris said, "You cannot avoid responsibility for the acts of your predecessor."[1]

He was right.

List of Abbreviations

USED IN THE REFERENCES AND BIBLIOGRAPHY

AO, F51	Archives of Ontario, Alexander Morris family fonds
HBC, HBCA	Hudson's Bay Company Archives
FSI	Federation of Saskatchewan Indians
INAC	Indian and Northern Affairs Canada library
LAC, MG26-A	Library and Archives Canada, John Alexander Macdonald papers
LAC, MG27-IC8	Library and Archives Canada, Alexander Morris fonds
LAC, RG10	Library and Archives Canada, Black Series, Indian Affairs files
LG	Lieutenant-Governor's Collection
MA, MG4166	McGill University Archives, Torrance and Morris files
MR, MS 837	McGill University Rare Books Collection, Alexander Morris files
NIB	National Indian Brotherhood

References

Note to Introduction

1   Alexander Morris, *The Treaties of Canada with the Indians of Manitoba and the North-West Territories, Including the Negotiations on Which They Were Based, and Other Information Related Thereto* (Saskatoon: Fifth House, 1991); reprint of the 1880 edition (Toronto: Belfords, Clark).

Notes to Chapter One

1   Jean Friesen, "Magnificent Gifts: The Treaties of Canada with the Indians of the Northwest, 1869-76," *Transactions of the Royal Society of Canada*, series V, vol. I (1986), p. 42.

2   John W. Chalmers, *Laird of the West* (Calgary: Detselig Enterprises Ltd., 1981), pp. 47, 40.

3   Jean Friesen, "Magnificent Gifts," p. 42.

4   John L. Tobias, "Canada's Subjugation of the Plains Cree, 1879-1885," *Canadian Historical Review* LXIV, 4 (1983), p. 520.

5   Jean Friesen, "Magnificent Gifts," p. 43.

6   *Ibid.*

7   Rob Innes, "'I Do Not Keep the Lands nor Do I Give Them Away:' Did Canada and the Plains Cree Come to a Meeting of the Minds in the Negotiations of Treaty Four and Six?" *Journal of Indigenous Thought*, no. 2 (1999), p. 3.

8   Jean Friesen, "Alexander Morris," *Dictionary of Canadian Biography Online.* John English and Réal Bélanger (Eds.). University of Toronto / Université Laval, 2000. Library and Archives Canada. www.biographi.ca/EN/ShowBio.asp?BioId=39842.

9   See, for instance, Helen Buckley, *From Wooden Ploughs to Welfare: Why Indian Policy Failed in the Prairie Provinces* (Montreal: McGill-Queen's University Press, 1992), pp. 32-36; and Treaty 7 Elders and Tribal Council, et al., *The True Spirit and Original Intent of Treaty 7* (Montreal: McGill-Queen's University Press, 1997), pp. 304-305.

10   See Kenneth S. Coates and William R. Morrison, *Treaty Research Report: Treaty 5 (1875)* (Treaties and Historical Research Centre, INAC, 1986), p. 19.

11 Geo. Maclean Rose (Ed.), *A Cyclopaedia of Canadian Biography: Being Chiefly Men of the Time. A Collection of Persons Distinguished in Professional and Political Life; Leaders in the Commerce and Industry of Canada, and Successful Pioneers* (Toronto: Rose Publishing, 1886), pp. 536-537.

12 Lila Staples, "The Honourable Alexander Morris: The Man; His Work," *Canadian Historical Association Report* (1928), 91-100.

13 R. G. Babion, "Alexander Morris: His Place in Canadian History" (M.A. thesis, Queen's University, Kingston, 1945).

14 Lila Staples, "The Honourable Alexander Morris," p. 91.

15 See Carl Berger, *The Sense of Power: Studies in the Ideas of Canadian Imperialism, 1867-1914* (Toronto: University of Toronto Press, 1970); Douglas Owram, *Promise of Eden: The Canadian Expansionist Movement and the Idea of the West, 1856-1900* (Toronto: University of Toronto Press, 1980); John C. Weaver, *The Great Land Rush and the Making of the Modern World, 1650-1900* (Montreal: McGill-Queen's University Press, 2003).

16 See Harold Cardinal and Walter Hildebrandt, *Treaty Elders of Saskatchewan: Our Dream Is that Our Peoples Will One Day Be Clearly Recognized as Nations* (Calgary: University of Calgary Press, 2000); Arthur J. Ray et al., *Bounty and Benevolence: A History of Saskatchewan Treaties* (Montreal: McGill-Queen's University Press, 2000); Frank Tough, "Aboriginal Rights versus the Deed of Surrender: The Legal Rights of Native Peoples and Canada's Acquisition of the Hudson's Bay Company Territory," *Prairie Forum* 17, no. 2 (1992); J. R. Miller, "'I will accept the Queen's hand': First Nations Leaders and the Image of the Crown in the Prairie Treaties," in J. R. Miller, *Reflections on Native-Newcomer Relation: Selected Essays* (Toronto: University of Toronto Press, 2004), pp. 242-268.

17 Mary Fitz-Gibbon (Ed.), *The Diaries of Edmund Montague Morris: Western Journeys, 1907-1910* (Toronto: Royal Ontario Museum, 1985), p. 1.

Notes to Chapter Two

1 H. J. Bridgman, "William Morris," *Dictionary of Canadian Biography Online* www.biographi.ca/EN/ShowBio.asp?BioId=38218&query=morris.

2 Archives of Ontario. Fonds F51, "Alexander Morris family fonds" (hereafter AO, F51), Reel 4, Memorandum by Edmund Morris regarding the Morris family, n.d.

3 *Ibid.*

4 R. G. Babion, "Alexander Morris," p. 9.

5 *Ibid.*, pp. 8-9.

6 AO, F51, Reel 4, Memorandum by Edmund Morris, regarding the Morris family, n.d.

7   See the "Editor's Introduction," in Alexander Morris, *Nova Britannia; or Our New Canadian Dominion Foreshadowed* (Toronto: Hunter, Rose & Co., 1884), p. vi. These comments would have been made by journalist John Charles Dent. As Dent was fifteen years younger than his subject, this was likely dictated to Dent by Morris himself. See G. H. Patterson, "John Charles Dent," *Dictionary of Canadian Biography Online*, www.biographi.ca/EN/ShowBio.asp?BioId=39595&query=dent.

8   Alexander Morris, "An Incident in the Rebellion in Canada in the Years 38-9," in the Goodwin-Haines Collection, William Lyon Mackenzie Papers, McLaughlin Library, University of Guelph. Submitted to one Rob Buchanan on April 14, 1843, during Morris's studies at Glasgow University.

9   See Carl Berger, *The Sense of Power*, pp. 90-93, for a discussion of the militia myth and the loyalist tradition in 19th-century historiography.

10   AO, F51, Reel 4, Memoranda by Edmund Morris, regarding the Morris family, n.d.

11   *Ibid.*

12   *Ibid.* See also R. G. Babion, "Alexander Morris," p. 10.

13   Macdonald became closely associated with the senior Tory politician, William Morris. See Library and Archives Canada (LAC), MG26-A. Prime Ministers' Fonds – John Alexander Macdonald papers, correspondence between William Morris and Macdonald, May 1847.

14   Jean Friesen, "Alexander Morris."

15   MR, MS 837, Obituary for Elizabeth Morris, newspaper clipping, n.d.

16   LAC, MG27-IC8, Alexander Morris fonds. See Reel M-68, Morris family genealogy.

17   AO, F51, Reel 4, J. Elliott to Alexander Morris, 21 June 1881.

18   See Jean Friesen, "Alexander Morris"; and MR, MS 837, newspaper clippings from the London *Daily Free Press*, n.d. and Obituary for Alexander Morris from *The Globe*, 29 Oct. 1889.

19   All quotations in this paragraph are from G. Blaine Baker, "Law Practice and Statecraft in Mid-Nineteenth-Century Montreal: The Torrance-Morris Firm, 1848 to 1868," in C. Wilton (Ed.), *Beyond the Law: Lawyers and Business in Canada, 1830 to 1930* (Toronto: Butterworth, 1990), pp. 51-53.

20   See British American League, "Minutes of the Proceedings of a Ponvention of Pelegates of the British American League" (Kingston: Chronicle and News, 1849). Copy held at Library and Archives Canada.

21   Alexander Mackenzie in Cephas D. Allin, "The British North American League, 1849." Paper read before the Ontario Historical Society (Toronto: 1915).

22   British American League, "Minutes of the Proceedings," p. 17.

23   H. E. Montgomerie and Alexander Morris, *The Question Answered: "Did the Ministry Intend to Pay Rebels?"* in *A Letter to His Excellency the Right Honourable the Earl of Elgin and Kincardine, K. T., Governor General of British North America, by a Canadian Loyalist* (Montreal: Armour & Ramsay, 1849), p. 16.

24   *Ibid.*

25   *Ibid.*, p. 17.

26   British American League, "Minutes of the Proceedings," p. 23.

27   See Alexander Morris, *Nova Britannia,* pp. vi-vii.

28   AO, F51, Reel 3, Draft of speech "On Industry and Perseverance viewed in connection with the progressive development of the mental faculties," n.d, p. 56.

29   *Ibid.*, p. 57.

30   See Mercantile Library Association of Montreal, *Annual Report of the Mercantile Library Association of Montreal, 1847-1848* (Montreal: Lovell and Gibson, 1848). Copy held at LAC.

31   Alexander Morris, "Nova Britannia; or, The Consolidation of the British North American Provinces into the Dominion of Canada," lecture given to the Mercantile Library Association of Montreal on March 18, 1858, in *Nova Britannia,* pp. 3-4.

32   AO, F51, Reel 3, "On Industry and Perseverance," pp. 49-50.

33   H. J. Bridgman, "William Morris."

34   R. G. Babion, "Alexander Morris," pp. 157-158.

35   AO, F51, Reel 1, Sale to the Hon. Wm. Morris of Pew #40 in the Gallery of St. Andrew's Church, Beaver Hall, 20 Jan. 1852.

36   R. G. Babion, "Alexander Morris," p. 13.

37   *The Juvenile Presbyterian* (Montreal: The Lay Association). Copies held at LAC include issues from 1856-1858 and 1861.

38   Alexander Morris, "Nova Britannia," p. 6. This is a reference to the 1857 Sepoy rebellions in India.

39   LAC, MG27-IC8, Alexander Morris fonds. See, for instance, Reel M-68, John Strachan to Alexander Morris, 18 Aug. 1857; George Weir to Alexander Morris, 28 Aug. 1857; and L. Bariden to the Editor of the "Presbyterien" (Alexander Morris), 25 Sept. 1857: *"Il ne sera pas sans intérêt pour les membres de votre église qui ont à coeur la conversion des catholiques romains, de lire quelques détails sur l'oeuvre que nous faisons parmi les Canadiens de langue française, qui habitent sur les bords des États Unis, du côté du Canada. . . ."*

40   Mercantile Library Association of Montreal, "Report of the speeches & proceedings at a special meeting of the Mercantile Library Association of Montreal held on Monday evening, April 8, 1850: to take into consideration the action of the board of direction in respect to the expulsion of the 'Christian Inquirer' from the news room," (Montreal: J. Potts, 1850), pp. 9-10.

41   *Ibid.*, p. 8.

42   AO, F51, Reel 3, "On Industry and Perseverance," p. 46.

43   AO, F51, Reel 3, "On the Influence of Mercantile Library Associations," p. 1.

44   AO, F51, Reel 3, "On Industry and Perseverance," p. 54.

45   See *Ibid.*, pp. 5-6.

46   See *Ibid.*, p. 37.

47   AO, F51, Reel 4, Memorandum by Edmund Morris, regarding the Morris family.

48   Edmund Morris explained: "Grandfather, going to the military settlement on the Rideau with the disbanded troops after the war in 1816, got the Indians to work for him. These Indians of the Ottawa Valley called him The Rising Sun – Shakeishkeik. From him my father learned to have a deep sympathy for the red men." In Edmund Morris, *The Diaries of Edmund Montague Morris*, p. 115.

49   *Montreal Gazette*, 17 Jan. 1849, p. 2.

50   Jean Friesen, "Alexander Morris."

51   AO, F51, Reel 4, Memorandum by Edmund Morris, regarding the Morris family.

52   *Montreal Gazette*, 17 Jan. 1849, p. 2.

53   Douglas Owram, *Promise of Eden*, pp. 16-17.

54   See, for instance, Aborigines' Protection Society, *Canada West and the Hudson's Bay Company: A Political and Humane Question of Vital Importance to the Honour of Great Britain, to the Prosperity of Canada, and to the Existence of the Native Tribes* (London: W. Tweedie, 1856). Copy held at LAC.

55   AO, F51, Reel 3, "To Brockville Horticultural Society."

56   *Ibid.*, pp. 2-3.

57   *Ibid.*, p. 8.

58   *Ibid.*, p. 7.

59   AO, F51, "On the Influence of the Mercantile Library Associations," third to last page.

60   Alexander Morris, *The Treaties of Canada*, p. 232.

Notes to Chapter Three

1   Alexander Morris, *Nova Britannia*; this view emerges most clearly in "The Hudson's Bay and Pacific Territories," a lecture given to the Mercantile Library Association of Montreal in late 1858.

2   AO, F51, Reel 4, Memorandum by Edmund Morris, regarding the Morris family. See also reel 2, W. J. Morris to Alexander Morris, 28 Nov. 1856. "[A]ll . . . things should be sacrificed to secure our father's comfort," Alexander told his brother.

3   AO, F51, Reel 2, Power of Attorney, William Morris to Alexander Morris, 1 March 1855.

4   AO, F51, Reel 1, Quit Claim from James Morris to Alexander Morris, 1 Dec. 1847.

5   See, for instance, AO, F51, Reel 1, James Dunlop to William Morris, 9 March 1848.

6   See also AO, F51, Reel 2, John Booth to Alexander Morris, 20 June 1859; and William Gibbard to Alexander Morris, 1 June 1858.

7   See, for instance, AO, F51, Reel 2, William Gibbard to Alexander Morris, 23 July 1858.

8   See, for instance, AO, F51, Reel 2, Alexander Morris to M. A. Hamilton, 6 Jan. 1859.

9   See, for example, AO, F51, Reel 3, Joseph Bawden, Kingston, to Alexander Morris, 16 Jan. 1873.

10   See AO, F51, Reel 2, David Campbell to Alexander Morris, 17 March 1857; and R. T. Greene to Alexander Morris, 25 July 1863.

11   See AO, F51, Reel 2, Opinion of O. Mowat, 20 Nov. 1858.

12   AO, F51, Reel 3, correspondence from Morris's siblings in the 1880s.

13   AO, F51, Reel 2, Apportionment of estate of the late William Morris, 5 April 1860.

14   AO, F51, Reel 2, John Booth to Alexander Morris, 20 June 1859.

15   Douglas Owram, *Promise of Eden*, pp. 43-46.

16   *Ibid.* p. 43.

17   AO, F51, Reel 3, draft of speech: "Thoughts about Agricultural and Manufacturing Interests of Canada," n.d, Likely written in the mid-1850s, before 1856.

18   *Ibid.*, p. 8.

19   *Ibid.*, pp. 3-4.

20   G. Blaine Baker, "Law Practice and Statecraft in Mid-Nineteenth-Century Montreal," p. 47.

21   *Ibid.*, p. 70.

22   *Ibid.*, pp. 55-56.

23   *Ibid.*, pp. 46-47, 59-60.

24   *Ibid.*, p. 49.

25   *Ibid.*, p. 61.

26   MA, MG4166, Container 1, file 00008, "Torrance and Morris Commonplace book," 1850-1881, pp. 38-39.

Notes to Chapter Four

1 Alexander Morris, "Canada and Her Resources: An Essay, to which, upon a Reference from the Paris Exhibition Committte of Canada, Was Awarded, by His Excellency Sir Edmund Walker Head, Governor General of British North America, the Second Prize" (Montreal: B. Dawson, 1855), pp. 21-22.

2 Jean Friesen, "Alexander Morris."

3 Alexander Morris, "Canada and Her Resources," preface.

4 *Ibid.*, preface and p. 7.

5 *Ibid.*, see pp. 71-82.

6 *Ibid.*, pp. 29, 40.

7 *Ibid.*, pp. 51-52.

8 *Ibid.*, p. 49.

9 *Ibid.*, p. 37.

10 *Ibid.*, p. 51.

11 *Ibid.*, pp. 52.

12 *Ibid.*, p. 57.

13 See Peter J. Smith, "The Ideological Origins of Canadian Confederation," *Canadian Journal of Political Science*, XX: 1 (March 1987), p. 19.

14 Alexander Morris, "To the Electors of the County of Renfrew," election poster, 1855.

15 *Ibid.*

16 AO, F51, Reel 4, Memorandum by Edmund Morris regarding the Morris family.

17 AO, F51, Reel 2, David Campbell to Alexander Morris, 17 March 1857.

18 Douglas Owram, *Promise of Eden*, p. 39.

19 *Ibid.*, p. 40.

20 *Ibid.*

21 *Ibid.*, p. 39.

22 Alexander Morris, "Nova Britannia," p. 1.

23 *Ibid.*, p. 39.

24 *Ibid.*, pp. 37-38.

25 Carl Berger, *The Sense of Power*, pp. 217-218.

26 Alexander Morris, "Nova Britannia," p. 49.

27 *Ibid.*, pp. 4-7, 28-29.

28 Alexander Morris, "The Hudson's Bay and Pacific Territories," p. 88.

29 Alexander Morris, "Nova Britannia," pp. 25-26.

30 Alexander Morris, "The Hudson's Bay and Pacific Territories," p. 64.

31 *Ibid.*, p. 66.

32 *Ibid.*, p. 76.

33 *Ibid.*, pp. 88-90.

34 Alexander Morris, "Nova Britannia," pp. 44, 46.

35 *Ibid.*, p. 32.

36 Alexander Morris, "The Hudson's Bay and Pacific Territories," see pp. 52-54.

37 *Ibid.*, pp. 55-56.

38 Alexander Morris, "Nova Britannia," pp. 28-29.

39 Alexander Morris, "The Hudson's Bay and Pacific Territories," p. 85.

40 Alexander Morris, "Nova Britannia," pp. 31-32.

41 Alexander Morris, "The Hudson's Bay and Pacific Territories," pp. 81, 83.

42 *Ibid.*, p. 85.

43 Alexander Morris, "Nova Britannia," pp. 29-30.

44 Alexander Morris, "The Hudson's Bay and Pacific Territories," pp. 56, 87-88.

45 *Ibid.*, p. 55.

46 *Ibid.*, p. 84, and Douglas Owram, *Promise of Eden*, p. 34.

47 Alexander Morris, "The Hudson's Bay and Pacific Territories," p. 88.

48 Alexander Morris, "South Lanark Election! The Nomination!" Election poster, 1861.

49 See J. I. Little, "Lewis Thomas Drummond," in *Dictionary of Canadian Biography Online*, www.biographi.ca/EN/ShowBio.asp?BioId=39613&query=drummond, and Edgar McInnes, *Canada: A Political and Social History* (Toronto: Rinehart, 1959), pp. 280-281. The *Parti rouge* was active in Canada East from 1848-67; it drew its doctrines from American republicanism and French radicalism, and never succeeded in drawing more than a small minority of electors to its banner.

50 See Alexander Morris, "Speech Delivered in the Canadian Assembly during the Debate on the Speech from the Throne, on Friday, 28th March, 1862," in *Nova Britannia*, pp. 94-96.

51 R. G. Babion, "Alexander Morris," p. 37.

52 AO, F51, Reel 4, Memorandum by Edmund Morris, regarding the Morris family.

53 R. G. Babion, "Alexander Morris," p. 44.

54 *Ibid.*, p. 63.

55 Alexander Morris, "Speech Delivered in the Legislative Assembly during the Debate on the Subject of Confederation of the North American Provinces" (Quebec: Hunter, Rose, 1865), p. 6.

56 *Ibid.*, pp. 14-15.

57 Alexander Morris, "Speech on the Resolutions for the Acquisition of the North West," 5 Dec. 1867, in *Nova Britannia*, pp. 140-142.

58   Alexander Morris, "Speech at Perth, on Re-election by Acclamation, after Accepting Office in the Dominion Government, as Minister of Inland Revenue," late 1869, in *Nova Britannia*, p. 145.

59   Alexander Morris, "Speech on the Resolutions for the Acquisition of the North West," pp. 141-142.

Notes to Chapter Five

1   AO, F51, Reels 2 and 3.

2   See AO, F51, Reels 2 and 3, especially correspondence from 1868-73.

3   Jean Friesen, "Alexander Morris."

4   *Ibid.* As Friesen puts it, the task of Chief Justice of Manitoba "would hardly seem suitable for a sick man."

5   *Ibid.*

6   MR, MS 837, John A. Macdonald to Alexander Morris, 16 Dec. 1872.

7   Jean Friesen, "Alexander Morris."

8   William Leggo, *The History of the Administration of the Right Honourable Frederick Temple, Earl of Dufferin* (Montreal: Lovell Printing and Publishing Company, 1878), pp. 557, 612-613.

9   Olive Patricia Dickason, *Canada's First Nations: A History of Founding Peoples from Earliest Times*. Third Edition (Oxford University Press, 2002), p. 275.

10   See Brian Walmark, "Alexander Morris and the Saulteaux" (M.A. Thesis, Lakehead University, 1994), p. 66; Ketchison Collection, "Correspondence, 1845-1911," INAC Library, Claims and Historical Research Collection, B.12., correspondence from late 1872 to late 1873; and LG, INAC Library, Claims and Historical Research Collection, B.13, correspondence from late 1872 to late 1873.

11   Brian Walmark, "Alexander Morris and the Saulteaux," p. 70.

12   *Ibid.*, p. 77.

13   *Ibid.*, p. 82.

14   *Ibid.*, p. 90.

15   *Ibid.*, p. 87.

16   Olive Patricia Dickason, *Canada's First Nations*, p.275

17   R. G. Babion, "Alexander Morris," p. 122.

Notes to Chapter Seven

1   Harold Cardinal and Walter Hildebrandt, *Treaty Elders of Saskatchewan*, p. 31.

2   Stephen Sliwa, "Treaty Day for the Willow Cree," *Saskatchewan History*, 47, 1 (1995), p. 5.

3   *Ibid.*, p. 4.

4   John S. Milloy, *The Plains Cree: Trade, Diplomacy and War, 1790 to 1870* (Winnipeg: University of Manitoba Press, 1990), p. 108.

5   "Sioux" is the French version of an Ojibwa word meaning "adders" or "snakes" — metaphorically, enemies. In their own dialects, they are known as Dakota, Lakota, and Nakota, depending on their territory. The band that Sitting Bull brought into Canada following the Battle of the Little Big Horn were Lakota. Their name in the Siouan dialect means "allies." See Donald Ward, *The People: A Historical Guide to the First Nations of Alberta, Saskatchewan, and Manitoba* (Saskatoon: Fifth House, 1995), p. 84.

6   The Blackfoot, similarly, are known to themselves as *Soyitapi*, "prairie people," and their confederacy was made up of three distinct nations, the Siksikah, the Blood, and the Piegan. *Ibid.*, p. 24.

7   John S. Milloy, *The Plains Cree*, pp. 61, 108. For a broader discussion, see also Dale R. Russell, *Eighteenth-Century Western Cree and their Neighbours* (Hull: Canadian Museum of Civilization, 1991).

8   See J. E. Foster, "Indian-White Relations in the Prairie West during the Fur Trade Period: A Compact?" in Richard Price (Ed.), *The Spirit of the Alberta Treaties* (Toronto: Institute for Research on Public Policy, 1979). Foster argues that the First Nations and the HBC developed a "compact relationship."

9   Arthur J. Ray et al., *Bounty and Benevolence*, p. 4.

10   *Ibid.*, pp. 7-8. Andrew Graham, an 18th-century HBC officer at York Factory, gives a vivid recollection of one such ceremony.

11   Treaty 7 Elders et al., *The True Spirit and Original Intent of Treaty 7*, p. 305.

12   Laura Peers, *The Ojibwa of Western Canada, 1780 to 1870* (Winnipeg: University of Manitoba Press, 1994), pp. 89-90.

13   Harold Cardinal and Walter Hildebrandt, *Treaty Elders of Saskatchewan*, p. 33.

14   *Ibid.*, pp. 35-36.

15   Delia Opekokew, "The Nature and Status of the Oral Promises in Relation to the Written Terms of the Treaties." *Public Policy and Aboriginal Peoples, 1965-1992*, no. 192, (1992), p. 21, INAC Library, E92 R702.

16   *Ibid.*, p. 20.

17   Indian Association of Alberta, "Comments on the Revision of the Constitution of Canada" (1978), INAC, E92 C6542, p. 2.

18 FSI, *Recognition and Entrenchment of Treaty and Aboriginal Rights and Indian Government Within the Canadian Confederation* (1980), INAC Library, E92 F43; see also Delia Opekokew, *The First Nations: Indian Government and the Canadian Confederation* (FSI, 1979), INAC Library, E92 O64.

19 Marlene Brant Castellano, "Education and Renewal in Aboriginal Nations: Highlights of the Report of the Royal Commission on Aboriginal Peoples," in Roger Neil, *Voice of the Drum: Indigenous Education and Culture* (Brandon: Kingfisher Publications, 2000), pp. 261-276.

20 Calendar of the Alexander Morris Papers, Ketchison Collection, "Correspondence, 1845-1911," INAC Library, Claims and Historical Research Collection, B.12, Alexander Morris to Alexander Campbell, 2 Aug. 1873.

21 David M. Arnot, *Statement of Treaty Issues: Treaties as a Bridge to the Future* (Saskatoon: Office of the Treaty Commissioner, 1998), p. 23. This petition was written with the assistance of W. J. Christie, former HBC officer and a Treaty 4 Commissioner.

22 J. R. Miller, *Skyscrapers Hide the Heavens: A History of Indian-White Relations in Canada*, Third Edition (Toronto: University of Toronto Press, 2000), p. 209.

23 Ketchison Collection, "Correspondence, 1845-1911," 5, 6, and 14 Aug. 1873.

24 John L. Tobias, "Canada's Subjugation of the Plains Cree," p. 521.

Notes to Chapter Eight

1   Arthur J. Ray et al., *Bounty and Benevolence,* p. 34.

2   *Ibid.*, p. 51.

3   Frank Tough, "Aboriginal Rights versus the Deed of Surrender," p. 227.

4   Arthur J. Ray et al., *Bounty and Benevolence,* p. 51.

5   Alexander Morris, *The Treaties of Canada*, pp. 13-24.

6   Cited in Wayne E. Daugherty, *Treaty Research Report: Treaty Three (1873)* (Treaties and Historical Research Centre, Self-Government, INAC, 1986), p. 63.

7   Arthur J. Ray et al., *Bounty and Benevolence*, chap. 5.

8   Alexander Morris, *The Treaties of Canada*, p. 28.

9   Wayne E. Daugherty, *Treaty Research Report: Treaty One and Treaty Two (1871)* (INAC, 1983), p. 6.

10 *Ibid.*, p. 14.

11 *Ibid.*

12 Alexander Morris, *The Treaties of Canada*, pp. 102, 109.

13 *Ibid.*, p. 109.

14 *Ibid.*, pp. 115, 117.

15   Harold Cardinal and Walter Hildebrandt, *Treaty Elders of Saskatchewan*, p. 34.

16   Alexander Morris, *The Treaties of Canada*, pp. 92-93.

17   See Rev. George McDougall's report to Alexander Morris, 23 Oct. 1875, in *Ibid,*, p. 173.

18   Alexander Morris, *The Treaties of Canada*, p. 93.

19   *Ibid.*, p. 286.

20   Wayne E. Daugherty, *Treaty Research Report: Treaty Three*, p. 7.

21   *Ibid.*, pp. 18-19.

22   *Ibid.*, p. 9.

23   *Ibid.*, p. 6.

24   *Ibid.*, p. 10.

25   Brian Walmark, "Alexander Morris and the Saulteaux," p. 85.

26   Wayne E. Daugherty, *Treaty Research Report: Treaty Three*, p. 20.

27   *Ibid.*, p. 22.

28   Alexander Morris, *The Treaties of Canada*, p. 47.

29   In Wayne E. Daugherty, *Treaty Research Report: Treaty Three*, pp. 21-22.

30   *Ibid.*, p. 22.

31   *Ibid.*, p. 30.

32   *Ibid.*, p. 32.

33   Alexander Morris, *The Treaties of Canada*, pp. 48-49.

34   Wayne E. Daugherty, *Treaty Research Report: Treaty Three*, p. 34.

35   *Ibid.*

36   Alexander Morris, *The Treaties of Canada*, pp. 48-49.

37   *Ibid.*, p. 49.

38   *Ibid.*, p. 74.

39   *Ibid.*, p. 51.

40   *Ibid.*, p. 72.

41   *Ibid.*, p. 50.

42   *Ibid.*, p. 51.

43   *Ibid.*, pp. 55-56.

44   *Ibid.*, p. 58.

45   *Ibid.*, pp. 60-61.

46   *Ibid.*

47   *Ibid.*, p. 61.

48 *Ibid.*

49 *Ibid.*, pp, 72, 74

50 *Ibid.*, pp. 66-67.

51 *Ibid.*, p. 69.

52 *Ibid.*, p. 71.

53 *Ibid.*, p. 72.

54 *Ibid.*

55 *Ibid.*, p. 56.

56 *Ibid.*, p. 72.

57 *Ibid.*, pp. 72-73.

58 *Ibid.*, p. 75.

59 *Ibid.*

60 *Ibid.*, p. 76.

61 *Ibid.*

62 *Ibid.*, p. 52.

63 *Ibid.*, p. 50.

64 *Ibid.*, p. 74.

65 Ketchison Collection, "Correspondence, 1845-1911," Morris to Alexander Campbell, 11 Aug. 1873.

66 Alexander Morris, *The Treaties of Canada*, p. 168.

67 Ketchison Collection, "Correspondence, 1845-1911," James McKeagney to John A. Macdonald, 1 May 1873.

68 John L. Tobias, "Canada's Subjugation of the Plains Cree," p. 520.

69 Ketchison Collection, "Correspondence, 1845-1911," Alexander Morris to Alexander Campbell, 2 Aug. 1873.

70 *Ibid.*, Alexander Morris to David Laird, 4 Dec. 1873.

71 *Ibid.*, Alexander Mackenzie to Alexander Morris, 6 Dec. 1873.

72 Report of Alexander Morris, 17 Oct., 1874, in *The Treaties of Canada*, p. 83.

73 See David Laird, "Our Indian Treaties," *Historical and Scientific Society of Manitoba,* 23 Feb. 1905, INAC Library, Claims and Historical Research Collection, X.53, p. 3.

74 See Irene M. Spry, "William Joseph Christie," *Dictionary of Canadian Biography Online,* www.biographi.ca/EN/ShowBio.asp?BioId=40153&query=christie); and *The Canadian Biographical Dictionary and Portrait Gallery of Eminent and Self-Made Men*, Ontario Volume (Toronto: American Biographical Publishing Co., 1880), pp. 208-211.

75   John L. Taylor, *Treaty Research Report: Treaty Four (1874)* (Ottawa: Treaties and Historical Research Centre, Department of Indian Affairs and Northern Development, 1987), p. 8.

76   Report of Alexander Morris, 17 Oct. 1874, in *The Treaties of Canada*, p. 80.

77   Alexander Morris, *The Treaties of Canada*, p. 96.

78   *Ibid.*, p. 101.

79   *Ibid.*, pp. 102-103.

80   *Ibid.*, pp. 104-105.

81   *Ibid.*, pp. 111-112.

82   *Ibid.*, pp. 100, 112, 115.

83   *Ibid.*, p. 112.

84   *Ibid.*, p. 123.

85   *Ibid.*, p. 89.

86   *Ibid.*, p. 90.

87   *Ibid.*, p. 116

88   *Ibid.*, p. 112.

89   *Ibid.*, p. 92.

90   *Ibid.*, p. 94.

91   *Ibid.*, p. 109.

92   *Ibid.*, pp. 100-101.

93   *Ibid.*, p. 112.

94   *Ibid.*, p. 115.

95   *Ibid.*

96   *Ibid.*, p. 118.

97   Report of Alexander Morris, 17 Oct. 1874, in *Ibid.*, p. 81.

98   *Ibid.*, pp. 122-123.

99   Marlene Brant Castellano, "Education and Renewal in Aboriginal Nations," pp. 261-276.

100   "The Qu'Appelle Treaty, Number Four," in Alexander Morris, *The Treaties of Canada*, p. 333.

101   *Ibid.*, p. 330.

102   See Delia Opekokew, "Position of the Federation of Saskatchewan Indians" (FSI, n.d.), p. 10. The present Aboriginal understanding of the intent of the treaties and the treaty text itself continue to be invoked in favour of expanded Aboriginal rights and self-government.

103 Report of W. J. Christie, 7 Oct. 1875, in Alexander Morris, *The Treaties of Canada*, p. 86.

104 Alexander Morris to David Laird, Minister of the Interior, Oct. 11, 1875, in *Ibid.*, p. 151.

105 Kenneth S. Coates and William R. Morrison, *Treaty Research Report: Treaty 5*, p. 12.

106 See HBCA, E.52/1, "Gilbert Spence Hackland Diary," 1875.

107 Kenneth S. Coates and William R. Morrison, *Treaty Research Report: Treaty 5*, p. 9.

108 Alexander Morris to David Laird, 11 Oct. 1875, in *The Treaties of Canada*, p. 152.

109 Alexander Morris, *The Treaties of Canada*, p. 143.

110 Kenneth S. Coates and William R. Morrison, *Treaty Research Report: Treaty 5*, p. 10.

111 See Edmund Morris, *The Diaries of Edmund Montague Morris*, Fitz-Gibbon's endnote 98, at p. 61.

112 Alexander Morris to David Laird, 11 Oct. 1875, in *The Treaties of Canada*, pp. 147-149.

113 *Ibid.*, p. 148.

114 *Ibid.*

115 *Ibid.*, p. 149.

116 *Ibid.*, pp. 150-151.

117 *Ibid.*, p. 149.

118 J. Lestock Reid to Alexander Morris, Oct. 14, 1876, in *Ibid.*, p. 167.

119 Report of Alexander Morris, 17 Nov., 1876, *Ibid.*, p. 153.

120 Alexander Morris to the Minister of the Interior, 27 March 1877; LAC, RG 10, Vol. 3636, file 6694-2.

121 John L. Taylor, *Treaty Research Report: Treaty Six (1876)* (Treaties and Historical Research Centre, INAC, 1986), p. 9.

122 See W. J. Christie memorandum, 13 April 1871, in Alexander Morris, *The Treaties of Canada*, pp. 170-171.

123 *Ibid.*

124 John L. Taylor, *Treaty Research Report: Treaty Six*, pp. 5-6.

125 *Ibid.*, pp. 6-7.

126 *Ibid.*, p. 6.

127 *Ibid.*, p. 8.

128 *Ibid.*

129 Report of Alexander Morris, 4 Dec. 1876, in *The Treaties of Canada*, p. 182.

130 See Fitz-Gibbon, in Edmund Morris, *The Diaries of Edmund Montague Morris*, p. 45, and p. 61, endnote 98.

131 Edmund Morris, *The Diaries of Edmund Montague Morris*, p. 116.

132   Alexander Morris, *The Treaties of Canada*, p. 233.

133   *Ibid.*, p. 210.

134   *Ibid.*, pp. 210-213.

135   *Ibid.*, p. 211.

136   *Ibid.*, p. 213.

137   See Peter Erasmus, *Buffalo Days and Nights*, as told to Henry Thompson (Calgary: Glenbow-Alberta Institute, 1976), p. 254.

138   Alexander Morris, *The Treaties of Canada*, p. 215.

139   For a complete list, see Report of Alexander Morris, 4 Dec. 1876, in *Ibid.*, p. 185.

140   Alexander Morris, *The Treaties of Canada*, p. 204.

141   Report of Alexander Morris, 4 Dec. 1876, in *Ibid.*, pp. 185, 191.

142   Chief Wahtahnee, in *Ibid.*, p. 243.

143   *Ibid.*, p. 241. Morris made similar remarks in his 4 Dec. 1876 report to Ottawa.

144   *Ibid.*, p. 204.

145   *Ibid.*, p. 217.

146   The text of the treaty can be found at www.indianclaims.ca/pdf/authorities/6%20eng.pdf.

147   Report of Rev. G. McDougall, 23 Oct. 1875, in Alexander Morris, *The Treaties of Canada*, p. 173.

148   Alexander Morris, *The Treaties of Canada*, p. 176.

149   Report of Alexander Morris, 4 Dec. 1876, in *Ibid.*, p. 184.

150   Peter Erasmus, *Buffalo Days and Nights*, p. 245.

151   *Ibid.*, p. 244.

152   Alexander Morris, *The Treaties of Canada*, pp. 223-224.

153   *Ibid.*, p. 224.

154   Peter Erasmus, *Buffalo Days and Nights*, p. 246.

155   Report of Alexander Morris, 4 Dec. 1876, in *The Treaties of Canada*, p. 196.

156   Peter Erasmus, *Buffalo Days and Nights*, p. 227.

157   Alexander Morris, *The Treaties of Canada*, p. 229.

158   Peter Erasmus, *Buffalo Days and Nights*, p. 240.

159   John L. Taylor, *Treaty Research Report: Treaty Six*, p. 10.

160   Alexander Morris, *The Treaties of Canada*, p. 285.

161   *Ibid.*, p. 198.

162   *Ibid.*, p. 183.

163   *Ibid.*, p. 513.

164   *Ibid.*, p. 202.

165   Report of Alexander Morris, 4 Dec. 1876, in *Ibid.,* p. 190. See also *Ibid.*, p. 234.

166   See, for instance, Helen Buckley, *From Wooden Ploughs to Welfare*, pp. 33, 35. While criticizing Morris for "attempting to imitate the poetic gifts" of the First Nations negotiators, Buckley nonetheless acknowledges that "Governor Morris impresses us as a man who genuinely liked Indian people and wished to help them."

167   Alexander Morris, *The Treaties of Canada*, p. 213.

168   Report of Alexander Morris, 4 Dec. 1876, in *Ibid.*, p. 191.

169   *Ibid.*, p. 238.

170   Peter Erasmus, *Buffalo Days and Nights*, p. 245.

171   *Ibid.*

172   *Ibid.*, p. 246.

173   *Ibid.*, p. 247.

174   *Ibid.*, p. 248.

175   *Ibid.*, pp. 248-249.

176   *Ibid.*, pp. 249-250.

177   *Ibid.*, pp. 250-251.

178   Alexander Morris, *The Treaties of Canada*, pp. 200-201.

179   *Ibid.*, p. 234.

180   *Ibid.*, p. 240.

181   *Ibid.*, pp. 206-207.

182   *Ibid.*, p. 208.

183   See G. Macdonald to Alexander Morris, 23 Oct. 1875, in *Ibid.*, p. 173.

184   Report of Alexander Morris, 4 Dec. 1876, in *Ibid.*, p. 187.

185   *Ibid.*, pp. 222-223.

186   *Ibid.*, pp. 241-242.

187   *Ibid.*, p. 237.

188   Report of Alexander Morris, 4 Dec. 1876, in *Ibid.*, p. 194.

189   *Ibid,*, p. 195.

190   *Ibid.*, p. 194.

191   *Ibid.*, p. 195.

Notes to Chapter Nine

1   LAC, RG 10, Vol. 3586, file 1137, Alexander Morris to Joseph Howe, 13 Dec. 1872.

2   *Ibid.*

3   *Ibid.*

4   LAC, RG 10, Vol. 3605, file 2903, Alexander Morris to Alexander Campbell, 23 June 1873, marked "Confidential."

5   *Ibid.*

6   Ketchison Collection, "Correspondence, 1845-1911," Morris to Alexander Campbell, 11 Aug. 1873.

7   *Ibid.*

8   LAC, RG 10, Vol. 3598, file 1356, Chief Henry Prince to Alexander Morris, 23 June 1873.

9   LAC, RG 10, Vol. 3598, file 1356, Abraham Cowley to Alexander Morris, 23 June 1873.

10 LAC, RG 10, Vol. 3598, file 1356, Alexander Morris to Alexander Campbell, 26 June 1873, marked "Confidential."

11 *Ibid.*

12 LAC, RG 10, Vol. 3605, file 2946, Report of Alexander Morris to the Minister of the Interior, 24 Jan. 1874.

13 *Ibid.*

14 *Ibid.*

15 LAC, RG 10, Vol. 3605, file 2903, Alexander Morris to Alexander Campbell, 23 June 1873, marked "Confidential."

16 LAC, RG 10, Vol. 3605, file 2946, Report of Alexander Morris to the Minister of the Interior, 24 Jan. 1874.

17 *Ibid.*

18 *Ibid.*

19 LAC, RG 10, Vol. 3605, file 2946, Order-in-Council, 9 March 1874.

20 See, for instance, LAC, RG 10, Vol. 3616, file 4511; and Vol. 3639, file 7415.

21 LAC, RG 10, Vol. 3609, file 3325, E. A. Meredith to Alexander Morris, 18 May 1874.

22 See LAC, RG 10, Vol. 3609, file 3325.

23 See LAC, RG 10, Vol. 3610, file 3456.

24 LAC, RG 10, Vol. 3621, file 4719, Rob Sinclair to the Minister of the Interior, 2 April 1875.

25 LAC, RG 10, Vol. 3621, file 4719, E. A. Meredith to J. A. N. Provencher, 22 April 1875.

26 LAC, RG 10, Vol. 3622, file 5013, Alexander Morris to the Minister of the Interior, 18 June 1875.

27   *Ibid.*

28   *Ibid.*

29   LAC, RG 10, Vol. 3583, file 1128, Alexander Morris to Alexander Campbell and Joseph Howe, Nov. 1872.

30   LAC, RG 10, Vol. 3611, file 3679, Alexander Morris to the Minister of the Interior, 13 July 1874.

31   LAC, RG 10, Vol. 3600, file 1567, Alexander Morris to the Secretary of State for the Provinces, 21 March 1873.

32   See LAC, RG 10, Vol. 3602, file 1848, Archibald Macdonald of the HBC post, Fort Ellice, to Alexander Morris.

33   LAC, RG 10, Vol. 3613, file 4049.5.

34   LAC, RG 10, Vol. 3603, file 2118, Alexander Morris to the Minister of the Interior, 10 Jan. 1874.

35   *Ibid.*, Alexander Morris to the Secretary of State for the Provinces, 7 June 1873.

36   See LAC, RG 10, Vol. 3605, file 2905, Alexander Morris to the Minister of the Interior, 4 August 1873; see also Vol. 3603, file 2118, "Copy of a Report of a Committee of the Honourable the Privy Council, approved by His Excellency the Governor General in Council on the 13th August 1873."

37   See LAC, RG 10, Vol. 3603, file 2118, Alexander Morris to the Minister of the Interior, 10 Jan. 1874; see also Vol. 3613, file 4048, Alexander Morris to the Secretary of State, 31 Oct. 1874.

38   LAC, RG 10, Vol. 3609, file 3289, "Fort Ellice Agency: General correspondence regarding an agreement reached between the government and the Sioux. 1874-1875." The file includes a transcription of discussions between Morris and the Sioux in 1875. The section of Morris's report is undated, but is likely from spring or summer 1875.

39   *Ibid.*

40   LAC, RG 10, Vol. 3623, file 5068, Alexander Morris to the Minister of the Interior, 10 Aug. 1875. See also Morris to the Minister, 9 Sept. 1875.

41   See LAC, RG 10, Vol. 3625, file 5493, Alexander Morris to the Minister of the Interior, 11 Oct. 1875; Vol. 3625, file 5494, Alexander Morris to the Minister of the Interior, 11 Oct. 1875, including enclosed letter from Morris to Sioux Chiefs, by care of Christie; and Vol. 3627, file 5957, Alexander Morris to the Minister of the Interior, 17 Feb. 1876.

42   LAC, RG 10, Vol. 3623, file 5045, E. A. Meredith to Alexander Morris, 3 Feb. 1876.

43   LAC, RG 10, Vol. 3623, file 5045, Alexander Morris to the Minister of the Interior, 25 Feb. 1876.

44   See LAC, RG 10, Vol. 3623, file 5068, David Laird to Alexander Morris, 26 April 1876; and Frank Decker to the Minister of the Interior, 2 Aug. 1876.

45   LAC, RG 10, Vol. 3598, file 1447, Report from Indian Agent Molyneux St. John, 24 Feb. 1873.

46   See LAC, RG 10, Vol. 3607, file 3008, Reports of Alexander Morris, March 1874.

47   See LAC, RG 10, Vol. 3607, file 3008, J. A. N. Provencher to the Minister of the Interior.

48   LAC, RG 10, Vol. 3608, file 3192, Alexander Morris to the Minister of the Interior, 25 April 1874, and 5 May 1874.

49   LAC, RG 10, Vol. 3611, file 3730, Alexander Morris to the Minister of the Interior, 24 July 1874.

50   *Ibid.*

51   *Ibid.*

52   *Ibid.*

53   *Ibid.*

54   *Ibid.*

55   LAC, RG 10, Vol. 3613, file 4042, Report of a conversation between Alexander Morris and Chief Mekis, 21 Sept. 1874.

56   LAC, RG 10, Vol. 3613, file 4042, Alexander Morris to the Secretary of State, 17 Oct. 1874. The change in reserve location was ultimately approved. *Ibid.*, Order-in-Council, 12 April 1875.

57   See LAC, RG 10, Vol. 3613, file 4057, Correspondence regarding complaints from the Indians of St. Peter's Reserve about unfulfilled treaty obligations and lack of communications with the Commissioner, among others, 1874.

58   See LAC, RG 10, Vol. 3613, file 4056, Report of a meeting of Indians with the Minister of the Interior, 15 Aug. 1874.

59   LAC, RG 10, Vol. 3615, file 4412, Alexander Morris to the Secretary of State, 29 Jan. 1875.

60   *Ibid.*

61   See LAC, RG 10, Vol. 3615, file 4412, Reply of the Department of the Interior to Alexander Morris, 19 May 1875.

62   LAC, RG 10, Vol. 3621, file 4767, various correspondence from the Department of the Interior to Alexander Morris.

63   LAC, RG 10, Vol. 3621, file 4767, Alexander Morris to the Minister of the Interior, 5 July 1875.

64   LAC, RG 10, Vol. 3624, file 5217-1, Alexander Morris to the Minister of the Interior, 10 Aug. 1875.

65   *Ibid.*

66   *Ibid.*

67 *Ibid.*

68 *Ibid.*

69 See LAC, RG 10, Vol. 3624, file 5217-1, Reply of the Department of the Interior to Alexander Morris, 4 Oct. 1875.

70 See LAC, RG 10, Vol. 3621, file 4767, Alexander Morris to the Superintendent of Indian Affairs, 27 Oct. 1875.

71 LAC, RG 10, Vol. 3624, file 5217-1, Reply of the Department of the Interior to Alexander Morris, 26 April 1876.

72 LAC, RG 10, Vol. 3624, file 5217-1, Alexander Morris to E. A. Meredith, 22 May 1876.

73 LAC, RG 10, Vol. 3624, file 5217-1, Alexander Morris to the Minister of the Interior, 8 July 1876; see also Vol. 3624, file 5217-1, Alexander Morris to David Laird, 23 June 1876.

74 LAC, RG 10, Vol. 3624, file 5217-1, Alexander Morris to the Minister of the Interior, 8 July 1876.

75 *Ibid.*

76 *Ibid.*

77 See LAC, RG 10, Vol. 3624, file 5217-1, Report of J. Lestock Reid, attachment in Alexander Morris to the Minister of the Interior, 14 July 1876. "I would mention in conclusion," Reid wrote, "that 'the Short Bear,' and the Chief of the White Mud Band expressed the utmost satisfaction and regard for the manner Your Excellency saw fit to settle the difficult question in connection with their lands, etc."

78 LAC, RG 10, Vol. 3624, file 5217-1, Alexander Morris to the Minister of the Interior, 14 July 1876.

79 See LAC, RG 10, Vol. 3624, file 5217-1, David Laird to Alexander Morris, 24 July 1876; and, this file, Report of the Minister of the Interior on the settlement of the outside promises, July 1876.

80 See LAC, RG 10, Vol. 3624, file 5217-1, Report of J. Lestock Reid.

81 LAC, RG 10, Vol. 3624, file 5217-1, Alexander Morris to the Minister of the Interior, 23 Oct. 1876.

82 *Ibid.*

83 See LAC, RG 10, Vol. 3624, file 5217-1, Report of J. Lestock Reid to Alexander Morris, 15 Nov. 1876, including a letter from Yellow Quill to Alexander Morris, 2 Nov. 1876. Reid also reported on the number of implements they and the Short Bears had received, as Morris had requested.

84 LAC, RG 10, Vol. 3624, file 5217-1, Alexander Morris to the Minister of the Interior, 6 Dec. 1876.

85 LAC, RG 10, Vol. 3624, file 5217-1, Alexander Morris to the Minister of the Interior, 6 Dec. 1876, including a report by J. Lestock Reid.

86   *Ibid.*

87   Robert C. Vipond, "David Mills," *Dictionary of Canadian Biography Online*, www.biographi.ca/EN/ShowBio.asp?BioId=41057&query=mills.

88   LAC, RG 10, Vol. 3624, file 5217-1, Deputy Minister of the Interior to Alexander Morris, 29 Dec. 1876.

89   LAC, RG 10, Vol. 3624, file 5217-1, Alexander Morris to the Minister of the Interior, 19 Jan. 1877.

90   *Ibid.*

91   *Ibid.*

92   *Ibid.*

93   *Ibid.*

94   LAC, RG 10, Vol. 3624, file 5217-1, Alexander Morris to the Minister of the Interior, 19 Feb. 1877.

95   *Ibid.*

96   *Ibid.*

97   *Ibid.*

98   *Ibid.*

99   *Ibid.*

100 LAC, RG 10, Vol. 3624, file 5217-1, Alexander Morris to the Secretary of State, 19 Feb. 1877.

101 LAC, RG 10, Vol. 3624, file 5217-1, Alexander Morris to the Minister of the Interior, 1 June 1877.

102 LAC, RG 10, Vol. 3624, file 5217-1, Reply of the Department of the Interior to Alexander Morris, 12 June 1877.

103 See LAC, RG 10, Vol. 3604, file 2790, various correspondence from Alexander Morris to the Minister of the Interior, July 1874.

104 LAC, RG 10, Vol. 3623, file 5067, Alexander Morris to the Minister of the Interior, 5 July 1875; letter from Robert Phair attached.

105 LAC, RG 10, Vol. 3624, file 5127, Alexander Morris to the Minister of the Interior, 19 July 1875.

106 *Ibid.*

107 *Ibid.*

108 See LAC, RG 10, Vol. 3622, file 5007, Alexander Morris to David Laird, 10 July 1875.

109 LAC, RG 10, Vol. 3622, file 5007, W. J. Christie to the Minister of the Interior, 16 July 1875.

110 LAC, Vol. 3622, file 5007, David Laird to W. J. Christie, 27 July 1875.

111   LAC, RG 10, Vol. 3622, file 5007, W. J. Christie to E. A. Meredith, Deputy Minister of the Interior, 28 July 1875.

112   See, for instance, LAC, RG 10, Vol. 3622, file 5007, Departmental instruction to W. J. Christie, 27 July 1875.

113   See LAC, RG 10, Vol. 3635, file 6587, David Laird to J. A. N. Provencher, June 1876.

114   See LAC, RG 10, Vol. 3635, file 6587, E. A. Meredith to Alexander Morris, 26 June 1876; the discussion is in relation to Treaty 5.

115   See LAC, RG 10, Vol. 3632, file 6379, Angus McKay to E. A. Meredith, 18 Aug. 1876; see also Vol. 3622, file 6379, various correspondence.

116   See LAC, RG 10, Vol. 3622, file 5007, E. A. Meredith to W. J. Christie, 3 Aug. 1875; E. A. Meredith to W. F. Forsyth, 3 Aug. 1875; and W. J. Christie to E. A. Meredith, 12 Aug. 1875.

117   LAC, RG 10, Vol. 3632, file 6418, Report of William Wagner to the Minister of the Interior, Jan. 1876.

118   See *Ibid.*, file 6260, "Gen. corres. re arrangements to be made for supplies, clothing, presents, etc. for the proposed Treaty 6 at Fort Carlton, SK. 1876-1877."

119   See, for instance, LAC, RG 10, Vol. 3634, file 6435; and Vol. 3634, file 6436.

120   LAC, RG 10, Vol. 3625, file 5489, Alexander Morris to the Minister of the Interior, 23 Oct. 1875.

121   *Ibid.*

122   See LAC, RG 10, Vol. 3609 file 3230, Rev. E. R. Young to Alexander Morris, 18 March 1874; and LAC, RG 10, Vol. 3636, file 5732, Alexander Morris to the Minister of the Interior, 18 Dec. 1875.

123   LAC, RG 10, Vol. 3636, file 6765, Alexander Morris to the Minister of the Interior, 12 July 1876.

124   *Ibid.*

125   LAC, RG 10, Vol. 3635, file 6587, Alexander Morris to the Minister of the Interior, 7 June 1876.

126   *Ibid.*, Alexander Morris to Thomas Howard and J. Lestock Reid, 14 July 1876.

127   *Ibid.*, various correspondence between Alexander Morris and David Laird, July 1876. Morris succeeded in securing an additional $500 for adhesions from a reluctant Laird.

128   See, for instance, LAC, RG 10, Vol. 3636, file 6694-2, Alexander Morris to the Minister of the Interior, 3 May 1876.

129   See LAC, RG 10, Vol. 3638, file 7139, Alexander Morris to the Minister of the Interior, 13 Oct. 1876.

130   *Ibid.*, Memo, Rob Sinclair, 14 Oct. 1876.

131   LAC, RG 10, Vol. 3638, file 7305, Indian Branch Memorandum, 30 Nov. 1876.

132 *Ibid.*, Alexander Morris to the Minister of the Interior, 17 Nov. 1876.

133 LAC, RG 10, Vol. 3636, file 6694-2, Indian Branch Memorandum, 31 Jan. 1877; see also Lawrence Vankoughnet to the Superintendent General of Indian Affairs, 12 Feb. 1877.

134 LAC, RG 10, Vol. 3636, file 6694-2, Department of the Interior to Alexander Morris, 1 March 1877.

135 *Ibid.*

136 Alexander Morris, *The Treaties of Canada*, p. 217.

137 LAC, RG 10, Vol. 3636, file 6694-2, Indian Branch Memorandum, 31 Jan. 1877.

138 *Ibid.*, Order-in-Council, 10 Feb. 1877.

139 *Ibid.*, Alexander Morris to the Minister of the Interior, 27 March 1877.

140 *Ibid.*

141 *Ibid.*

142 *Ibid.*

143 *Ibid.*

144 *Ibid.*

145 *Ibid.*

146 *Ibid.*

147 *Ibid.*

148 *Ibid.*, James McKay to the Minister of the Interior, 28 March 1877.

149 LAC, RG 10, Vol. 3627, file 5972, Rob Sinclair to the Minister of the Interior, 3 Feb. 1876, marked "Private."

150 *Ibid.*

151 LAC, RG 10, Vol. 3625, file 5506, Alexander Morris to the Minister of the Interior, 18 Feb. 1876.

152 *Ibid.*

153 *Ibid.*

154 *Ibid.*

155 LAC, RG 10, Vol. 3634, file 6464, Order-in-Council prepared by the Minister of the Interior, 12 May 1876.

156 *Ibid.*, E. A. Meredith, Confidential Memorandum, 11 Jan. 1877.

157 *Ibid.*

158 LAC, RG 10, Vol. 3646, file 7966, Alexander Morris to the Minister of the Interior, 2 April 1877.

159   LAC, RG 10, Vol. 3645, file 7806, Alexander Morris to the Minister of the Interior, 1 March 1877.

160   *Ibid.*, J. A. N. Provencher to the Minister of the Interior, 9 May 1877.

161   LG, INAC Library, Claims and Historical Research Collection, B.13, Chief Côté to Alexander Morris, March 1875.

162   Harold Cardinal and Walter Hildebrandt, *Treaty Elders of Saskatchewan*, p. 28.

163   Jean Friesen, "Magnificent Gifts," p. 50.

164   LG, INAC Library, Claims and Historical Research Collection, B.13, 7 Oct. 1875.

165   Helen Buckley, *From Wooden Ploughs to Welfare*, pp. 28-66.

166   LG, INAC Library, Claims and Historical Research Collection, B.13, W. J. Christie to Alexander Morris, 7 Oct. 1875.

167   John L. Tobias, "Canada's Subjugation of the Plains Cree," p. 525.

168   *Ibid.*, p. 534.

169   *Ibid.*, pp. 547-548.

Notes to Chapter Ten

1   Alexander Morris, "Speech at the Banquet to Lord Dufferin, at Winnipeg," 29 Sept. 1877, in *Nova Britannia*, pp. 185-186.

2   *Ibid.*, p. 186.

3   *Ibid.*, p. 187.

4   R. G. Babion, "Alexander Morris," p. 139.

5   MR, MS 837, newspaper clipping from the London *Daily Free Press*, n.d.

6   See Manitoba Archives, MG12B4, "Personal Papers."

7   R. G. Babion, "Alexander Morris," pp. 163-165.

8   *Ibid.*, pp. 151-152.

9   LAC, RG10, Vol. 3613, file 4518, Fr. Lacombe to Alexander Morris, 13 Feb. 1875. "*[L]es traités déjà fait ici ont été pour la satisfaction de tous. Tout le monde connait trop bien votre justice quand il s'agit surtout du pauvre sauvage. . . . Je suis sûr que vous voulez le bien de ces sauvages, puis que dans les premières années de votre vie publique, déjà vous plaidiez si bien la cause du pauvre enfant des bois et des prairies. . . .*"

10   LAC, RG10, Vol. 3613, file 4518, Attachment in Alexander Morris to the Secretary of State, 25 Feb. 1875. "*[V]euillez me permettre d'avouer à Votre Excellence que pour ma part, je pense que l'arrivé des Blancs parmi les Sauvages, avec tout ce qu'ils leurs ont apporté des douceurs de la civilisation, a toujours été un grand malheur pour les tribus Indiennes. . . . [L]es sauvages, qui n'ont jamais vu les Blancs sont moins malheureux pour la vie corporelle que ceux auxquels on a appris des besoins qu'ils ne connaissaient pas auparavant.*"

11 See Edmund Morris, *The Diaries of Edmund Montague Morris,* pp. 35, 66, 68, 70, 92.

12 LAC, RG 10, Vol. 6761, file 420-303, Letter from the Union Council of the old North West Angle Treaty Number 3 to King George VI of England, n.d., received some time before 11 Dec. 1937.

13 Brian McNab, "Treaties and an Official Use of History," *Canadian Journal of Native Studies,* Vol. 13, no. 1 (1993), pp. 139-143.

14 John L. Taylor, *Treaty Research Report: Treaty Four,* endnotes 1 and 15, pp. 17-18.

15 NIB, "Brief for the Foreign and Commonwealth Affairs Committee of the British House of Commons," in *Brief to the Special Joint Committee of the Senate and of the House of Commons on the Constitution of Canada* (16 Dec. 1980), p. 10, endnote 4.

16 Edmund Morris, *The Diaries of Edmund Montague Morris,* p. 76.

17 HBC, E.52/1, "Gilbert Spence Hackland Diary," 1875.

18 Peter Erasmus, *Buffalo Days and Nights,* pp. 214; John L. Taylor, *Treaty Research Report: Treaty Six,* p. 14.

19 See, for instance, G. McDougall to Alexander Morris, 23 Oct. 1875, in *The Treaties of Canada,* p. 174.

20 NIB, "Brief for the Foreign and Commonwealth Affairs Committee of the British House of Commons," p. 10, endnote 4.

21 Alexander Morris, *The Treaties of Canada,* p. 11.

22 *Ibid.,* preface.

23 Report of Alexander Morris, 17 Oct. 1874, in *Ibid.,* p. 83.

24 Report of Alexander Morris, 4 Dec. 1876, in *Ibid.,* pp. 195-196.

25 LAC, RG 10, Vol. 3624, file 5217-1, Alexander Morris to the Minister of the Interior, 19 Feb. 1877.

26 Alexander Morris, *The Treaties of Canada,* p. 131.

27 *Ibid.*

28 *Ibid.,* pp. 143-167.

29 See, for instance, *Ibid.,* p. 176, in which Mills comes off as having praised Morris's work.

30 *Ibid.,* p. 285.

31 *Ibid.,* p. 288.

32 *Ibid.,* pp. 286-287.

33 *Ibid.,* p. 287.

34 *Ibid.,* pp. 287-288.

35 *Ibid.,* pp. 288-289.

36 *Ibid.,* pp. 289-290.

37   *Ibid.*, p. 291.

38   *Ibid.*, p. 295.

39   *Ibid.*, p. 294.

40   *Ibid.*, pp. 294-295.

41   *Ibid.*

42   *Ibid.*, pp. 296-297.

Note to Conclusion

1   LAC, RG 10, Vol. 3624, file 5217-1, Alexander Morris to the Minister of the Interior, 19 Feb. 1877.

Bibliography

Archival Sources

Alexander Morris Papers. Ketchison Collection. "Correspondence, 1845-1911," Indian and Northern Affairs (INAC) Library, Claims and Historical Research Collection, B.12.

Archives of Ontario. Fonds F51. "Alexander Morris family fonds."

HBCA. E.52/1. "Gilbert Spence Hackland Diary." 1875.

Legislative Library of Manitoba. Heritage Files. A. Morris file.

LAC. MG26-A. Prime Ministers' fonds. John Alexander Macdonald papers.

LAC. MG27-IC8. Alexander Morris fonds.

LAC. RG10. Black Series.

Lieutenant-Governor's collection, 1872-1877. INAC Library, Claims and Historical Research collection, B.13.

Manitoba Archives. MG12B4. "Personal Papers."

MA. MG4166. Container 1.

MR. MS 837.

Morris, Alexander. "An Incident in the Rebellion in Canada in the Years 38-9." Essay submitted to Rob Buchanan, 14 April 1843. Goodwin-Haines Collection, William Lyon Mackenzie Papers, McLaughlin Library, University of Guelph.

NIB. "Brief for the Foreign and Commonwealth Affairs Committee of the British House of Commons." In NIB, *Brief to the Special Joint Committee of the Senate and of the House of Commons on the Constitution of Canada*. Ottawa: The Brotherhood, 16 December 1980. Human Rights Centre, University of Ottawa. Can I Submissions/17.

"Petition by the Indian People of Canada to Her Majesty Queen Elizabeth II." Ottawa: November 1980. Congress of Aboriginal Peoples Archives.

Printed Primary Sources

Aborigines' Protection Society. *Canada West and the Hudson's Bay Company: A political and humane question of vital importance to the honour of Great Britain, to the prosperity of Canada, and to the existence of the Native tribes.* London: W. Tweedie, 1856. LAC.

British American League. "Minutes of the Proceedings of a Convention of Delegates of the British American League." Kingston: Chronicle and News, 1849. LAC.

Erasmus, Peter. *Buffalo Days and Nights*, as told to Henry Thompson. Irene Spry, ed. Calgary: Glenbow-Alberta Institute, 1976.

Federation of Saskatchewan Indians. "Recognition And Entrenchment of Treaty and Aboriginal Rights And Indian Government Within The Canadian Confederation," 1980. INAC Library, E92 F43.

Indian Association of Alberta. "Comments on the Revision of the Constitution of Canada." Edmonton: Indian Association of Alberta, 1978. INAC Library, E92 C6542.

The Juvenile Presbyterian. Montreal: The Lay Association. LAC collection includes years 1856-1858 and 1861.

Laird, David. "Our Indian Treaties." *Historical and Scientific Society of Manitoba*, February 23, 1905. INAC Library, Claims and Historical Research collection, X.53.

Mercantile Library Association of Montreal. *Annual Report of the Mercantile Library Association of Montreal, 1847-1848.* Montreal: Lovell and Gibson, 1848. LAC.

_____. "Report of the speeches & proceedings at a special meeting of the Mercantile Library Association of Montreal held on Monday evening, April 8, 1850: to take into consideration the action of the board of direction in respect to the expulsion of the 'Christian Inquirer' from the news room." Montreal: J. Potts, 1850.

Montgomerie, H. E. and Alexander Morris. *The Question Answered: "Did the Ministry Intend to Pay Rebels?" in a letter to His Excellency the Right Honourable the Earl of Elgin and Kincardine, K. T., Governor General of British North America, by a Canadian Loyalist.* Montreal: Armour & Ramsay, 1849.

Montreal Gazette. 17 January 1849.

Morris, Alexander. "Canada and Her Resources: an essay, to which, upon a reference from the Paris Exhibition Committee of Canada, was awarded, by His Excellency Sir Edmund Walker Head, Governor General of British North America, the Second Prize." Montreal: B. Dawson, 1855.

_____. "To the Electors of the County of Renfrew." Election poster, 1855.

_____. "To the Electors of the South Riding of Lanark." Election poster, 1869.

Morris, Alexander. *Nova Britannia; or Our New Canadian Dominion Foreshadowed.* Toronto: Hunter, Rose & Co., 1884.

_____. "Speech delivered in the Legislative Assembly during the debate on the subject of Confederation of the North American provinces." Quebec: Hunter, Rose, & Co., 1865.

_____. "South Lanark Election! The Nomination!" Election poster, 1861.

_____. *The Treaties of Canada with the Indians of Manitoba and the North West Territories, Including the Negotiations on Which They Were Based, and Other Information Relating Thereto.* Toronto: Belfords, Clarke & Co., 1880; reprint, Saskatoon: Fifth House Publishers, 1991.

Morris, Edmund. *The Diaries of Edmund Montague Morris: Western Journeys, 1907-1910.* Mary Fitz-Gibbon (Ed.). Toronto: Royal Ontario Museum, 1985.

Secondary Sources

Allin, Cephas D. "The British North American League, 1849." Paper read before the Ontario Historical Society. Toronto: 1915.

Arnot, David M. *Treaties as a Bridge to the Future: The Saskatchewan Model,* Twenty-Third Viscount Bennett Memorial Lecture, University of New Brunswick, 7 Nov. 2000. Saskatoon: Office of the Treaty Commissioner, 2000.

Arnot, David M. *Statement of Treaty Issues: Treaties as a Bridge to the Future.* Saskatoon: Office of the Treaty Commissioner, 1998.

Babion, R. G. "Alexander Morris: his place in Canadian history." M.A. thesis, Queen's University, Kingston, 1945.

Baker, G. Blaine. "Law Practice and Statecraft in Mid-Nineteenth-Century Montreal: The Torrance-Morris Firm, 1848 to 1868," in C. Wilton (Ed.). *Beyond the Law: Lawyers and Business in Canada, 1830 to 1930.* Toronto: Butterworth, 1990.

Berger, Carl. *The Sense of Power: Studies in the Ideas of Canadian Imperialism, 1867-1914.* Toronto: University of Toronto Press, 1970.

Bridgman, H. J. "William Morris," *Dictionary of Canadian Biography Online.* John English and Réal Bélanger (Eds.). University of Toronto/Université Laval, 2000. Library and Archives Canada. www.biographi.ca/EN/ShowBio.asp?BioId=38218 &query=morris.

Buckley, Helen. *From Wooden Ploughs to Welfare: Why Indian Policy Failed in the Prairie Provinces.* Montreal: McGill-Queen's University Press, 1992.

The Canadian Biographical Dictionary and Portrait Gallery of Eminent and Self-Made Men. Ontario Volume. Toronto: American Biographical Publishing Co., 1880.

Canadian Broadcasting Corporation. "Historic pictograph is First Nations view of treaty talks." 22 February 2007. Online at http://www.cbc.ca/canada/ saskatchewan/story/2007/02/22/pasqua-pictograph.html.

Cardinal, Harold and Walter Hildebrandt. *Treaty Elders of Saskatchewan: Our Dream Is that Our Peoples Will One Day Be Clearly Recognized as Nations.* Calgary: University of Calgary Press, 2000.

Castellano, Marlene Brant. "Education and Renewal in Aboriginal Nations: Highlights of the Report of the Royal Commission on Aboriginal Peoples," in Roger Neil. *Voice of the Drum: Indigenous Education and Culture.* Brandon, Manitoba: Kingfisher Publications, 2000.

Chalmers, John W. *Laird of the West.* Calgary: Detselig Enterprises Ltd., 1981.

Christensen, Deanna. Ahtahkakoop. *The Epic Account of a Plains Cree Head Chief, His People, and Their Struggle for Survival, 1816-1896.* Shell Lake, Saskatchewan: Ahtahkakoop Publishing, 2000.

Coates, Kenneth S. and William R. Morrison. *Treaty Research Report: Treaty 5 (1875).* Treaties and Historical Research Centre, INAC, 1986. Accessed online at http: //www.ainc-inac.gc.ca/pr/trts/hti/t5/tre5_e.pdf.

Cochrane, William (Ed.). *The Canadian Album. Men of Canada; or, Success by Example, in Religion, Patriotism, Business, Law, Medicine, Education and Agriculture.* Vol. III. Brantford, Ont.: Bradley, Garretson & Co., 1894.

Daugherty, Wayne E. *Treaty Research Report: Treaty One and Treaty Two (1871).* Treaties and Historical Research Centre, Research Branch, Corporate Policy, INAC, 1983. Accessed online at http://www.ainc-inac.gc.ca/pr/trts/hti/t1-2/tre1-2_e.pdf.

_____. *Treaty Research Report: Treaty Three (1873).* Treaties and Historical Research Centre, Self-Government, INAC, 1986. Accessed online at http://www.ainc-inac.gc.ca/pr/trts/hti/t3/tre3_e.pdf.

Dickason, Olive Patricia. *Canada's First Nations: A History of Founding Peoples from Earliest Times.* Third Edition. Oxford University Press, 2002.

Fitz-Gibbon, Mary (Ed.), *The Diaries of Edmund Montague Morris: Western Journeys, 1907-1910* (Toronto: Royal Ontario Museum, 1985), p. 1.

Foster, J. E. "Indian-White Relations in the Prairie West during the Fur Trade Period: A Compact?" in Richard Price (Ed.). *The Spirit of the Alberta Treaties.* Toronto: Institute for Research on Public Policy, 1979.

Friesen, Jean. "Alexander Morris." *Dictionary of Canadian Biography Online,* www.biographi.ca/EN/ShowBio.asp?BioId=39842.

Friesen, Jean. "Magnificent Gifts: The Treaties of Canada with the Indians of the Northwest, 1869-76." *Transactions of the Royal Society of Canada,* series V, vol. I, 1986.

Haig-Brown, Celia and David A. Nock, Eds. *With Good Intentions: Euro-Canadian and Aboriginal Relations in Colonial Canada*. Vancouver: University of British Columbia Press, 2006.

Innes, Rob. "'I Do Not Keep the Lands nor Do I Give Them Away:' Did Canada and the Plains Cree Come to a Meeting of the Minds in the Negotiations of Treaty Four and Six?" *Journal of Indigenous Thought* 2, no.2, 1999.

Jones, Dorothy V. "British Colonial Indian Treaties," in *Handbook of North American Indians*, Vol. 4, *History of Indian-White Relations*, Wilcomb E. Washburn (Ed.). Washington: Smithsonian Institution, 1988. pp. 185-194.

Laird, David. "Our Indian Treaties," *Historical and Scientific Society of Manitoba*, 23 Feb. 1905, INAC Library, Claims and Historical Research Collection, X.53.

Leggo, William. *The History of the Administration of the Right Honourable Frederick Temple, Earl of Dufferin*. Montreal: Lovell Printing and Publishing Company, 1878.

Little, J. I. "Lewis Thomas Drummond." *Dictionary of Canadian Biography Online*. www.biographi.ca/EN/ShowBio.asp?BioId=39613&query=drummond.

McEvoy, J. P. "Case Comment: *Marshall v. Canada*: Lessons from Wisconsin." *National Journal of Constitutional Law*, vol. 12, (2000-2001).

McInnes, Edgar. *Canada: A Political and Social History*. Toronto: Rinehart, 1959.

McNab, Brian. "Treaties and an Official Use of History." *Canadian Journal of Native Studies*, vol. 13, no. 1, 1993.

Miller, J. R. "'I will accept the Queen's hand': First Nations Leaders and the Image of the Crown in the Prairie Treaties," in J. R. Miller. *Reflections on Native-Newcomer Relations. Selected Essays*. Toronto: University of Toronto Press, 2004.

_____. "Owen Glendower, Hotspur, and Canadian Indian Policy." *Ethnohistory* 37, 4 (Fall 1990).

_____. *Skyscrapers Hide the Heavens: A History of Indian-White Relations in Canada*, Third Edition. Toronto: University of Toronto Press, 2000.

Milloy, John S. *The Plains Cree: Trade, Diplomacy and War, 1790 to 1870*. Winnipeg: University of Manitoba Press, 1990.

Morgan, Henry James (Ed.). *The Canadian Men and Women of the Time: A Handbook of Canadian Biography of Living Characters*. Second edition. Toronto: William Briggs, 1912.

Moyles, R. G. and Doug Owram. *Imperial Dreams and Colonial Realities. British Views of Canada, 1880-1914*. Toronto: University of Toronto Press, 1988.

Native Council of Canada. *Native People and the Constitution of Canada: Report of the Metis and Non-Status Indian Constitutional Review Commission*. Commissioner H. W. Daniels. Ottawa: Mutual Press, 1981.

Opekokew, Delia. *The First Nations: Indian Government and the Canadian Confederation.* FSI, 1979. INAC Library, E92 O64.

Opekokew, Delia. "The Nature and Status of the Oral Promises in Relation to the Written Terms of the Treaties." *Public Policy and Aboriginal Peoples, 1965-1992,* no. 192, (1992). INAC Library, E92 R702.

_____. "Position of the Federation of Saskatchewan Indians in the Confirmation of Aboriginal and Treaty Rights in the Canadian Constitution and/or Legislation." FSI, n.d. INAC Library.

Owram, Douglas. *Promise of Eden: The Canadian Expansionist Movement and the Idea of the West, 1856-1900.* Toronto: University of Toronto Press, 1980.

Patterson, G. H. "John Charles Dent." *Dictionary of Canadian Biography Online.* www.biographi.ca/EN/ShowBio.asp?BioId=39595&query=dent.

Peers, Laura. *The Ojibwa of Western Canada, 1780 to 1870.* Winnipeg: University of Manitoba Press, 1994.

Ray, Arthur J. et al. *Bounty and Benevolence: A History of Saskatchewan Treaties.* Montreal: McGill-Queen's University Press, 2000.

Robb, Andrew. "David Laird." *Dictionary of Canadian Biography Online.* www.biographi.ca/EN/ShowBio.asp?BioId=41625&query=laird.

Rose, Geo. Maclean (Ed.). *A Cyclopaedia of Canadian Biography: Being Chiefly Men of the Time.* Toronto: Rose Publishing Co., 1886.

Russell, Dale R. *Eighteenth-Century Western Cree and their Neighbours.* Hull, Quebec: Canadian Museum of Civilization, 1991.

Sliwa, Stephen. "Treaty Day for the Willow Cree." *Saskatchewan History,* 47, 1, 1995.

Smith, Peter J. "The Ideological Origins of Canadian Confederation." *Canadian Journal of Political Science* XX, 1 (March) 1987.

Spry, Irene M. "William Joseph Christie." *Dictionary of Canadian Biography Online.* www.biographi.ca/EN/ShowBio.asp?BioId=40153&query=christie.

Staples, Lila. "The Honourable Alexander Morris: The Man; His Work." *Canadian Historical Association Report,* 1928.

Taylor, John L. *Treaty Research Report: Treaty Four (1874).* Ottawa: Treaties and Historical Research Centre, INAC, 1987. www.ainc-inac.gc.ca/pr/trts/hti/t4/tre4_e.pdf.

Taylor, John L. *Treaty Research Report: Treaty Six (1876).* Ottawa: Treaties and Historical Research Centre, INAC, 1986. www.ainc-inac.gc.ca/pr/trts/hti/t6/tre6_e.pdf.

Titley, Brian. *The Frontier World of Edgar Dewdney.* Vancouver: University of British Columbia Press, 1999.

Tobias, John L. "Canada's Subjugation of the Plains Cree, 1879-1885." *Canadian Historical Review* LXIV, 4, 1983.

Tough, Frank. "Aboriginal Rights versus the Deed of Surrender: The Legal Rights of Native Peoples and Canada's Acquisition of the Hudson's Bay Company Territory." *Prairie Forum* 17, no. 2, 1992.

Treaty 7 Elders and Tribal Council, et. al. *The True Spirit and Original Intent of Treaty 7*. Montreal: McGill-Queen's University Press, 1997.

Vipond, Robert C. "David Mills." *Dictionary of Canadian Biography Online.* www.biographi.ca/EN/ShowBio.asp?BioId=41057&query=mills.

Walmark, Brian. "Alexander Morris and the Saulteaux: The Context and Making of Treaty Three, 1869-1873." M.A. Thesis, Lakehead University, 1994.

Ward, Donald. *The People: A Historical Guide to the First Nations of Alberta, Saskatchewan, and Manitoba*. Saskatoon: Fifth House, 1995.

Weaver, John C. *The Great Land Rush and the Making of the Modern World, 1650-1900*. Montreal: McGill-Queen's University Press, 2003.

Wheaton, Cathy. "The Role of Treaties in the History of Saskatchewan Indian Politics, 1910-1992." *Journal of Indigenous Thought* 2, no. 2 (Fall) 1999.

Index

Page numbers in italics indicate a caption.

---

* The term "Indian" was in common use in Morris's time and that usage has been reflected here.

Americans 85-6, 128;
  outlaws 79-80, 85;
  traders 15, 62-3, 80, 95, 108, 109-10

the Angle [site of Treaty Three] 69, 70-1,
  73, 81, 82, 84, 125, 133, 146-7

annexation: of the North West 11-12,
  41-6, 47-8, 49, 163, 173-4;
  of Canada by the US 21, 79-81, 164

anti-American sentiment 20-1, 35

anti-French-Canadian sentiment 20, 21,
  23-4

annuities 15, 65, 68, 70-1, 72-3, 75, 84,
  89, 121, 123, 126, 132-4, 136, 137, 139,
  147, 150-1, 155, 158, 174-5;
  refused by Indians 63, 68, 131

Archibald, Adams 52, 66-7, 70-1, 95,
  131-2, 140

assimilation 40, 47, 163;
  of the Indians 15, 85, 129, 131;
  of the French Canadians 21, 43, 51

Assiniboine River 44, 54, 128, 129, 136,
  138

Assiniboine peoples 59, 95

Atâhkakohp (Star Blanket) 101, 107-9,
  162, 165

B

Badger 108

Badgley, William 22

Baldwin, Robert 23

Battle River 102, *103*

Beardy, Chief 101

Bell, Charles N. 95

Berens, Chief Joseph 149-50;
  band 146

Berens River 90

Bidwell, Marshall Spring 21

Big Child. *See* Mistawâsis

Blackfoot 108, 110;
  and the Cree 58-9, 95, 108, 165

Blackstone, Chief 72

Breland, Pascal 51

British North America League 23-4

British North American union 23, 24,
  38, 40-1, 42-3

Brokenhead band

Brown, George 41-2, 47

buffalo: diminishing 59, 62, 70, 80, 85,
  95, 96-7, 99, 108-9, 153;
  preservation of 111;
  and the Métis 171

C

Campbell, Alexander: Minister of the
  Interior 62, 70, 121-2

Canada: annexation by the US, risk of
  21, 79-81, 164;
  Lower 35, 36, 37;
  potential for agriculture 32, 34-6, 38,
  39, 41-4, 48, 54, 80, 90, 94, 96, 173,
  land of lesser agricultural value 70,
  89, 90, 144;
  union of the Canadas 11, 21, 22, 23,
  42, 43, 46-7;
  Upper 19, 20, 32, 34-7, 39, 48

"Canada and her Resources" 38, 42, 90

Canadian government 10-11, 15-16, 50,
  65-6, 69, 74, 80, 109, 119, 145, 163,
  173

cattle 83, 92, 99, 121;
  Morris on 110-11, 130, 139, 152;
  not delivered as promised 139, 147-8,
  159;
  requested 63, 72-3

census 155;
  Métis (1871) 52-3

M

Macdonald, John A. 11, 18, 23, 42, 47, 49, 51;
appointed Morris Lieutenant Governor 51;
role in Morris's law career 21-2;
and treaty implementation 63, 160, 164

Macdonell, Allan 42

MacKenzie, Alexander (explorer) 44

Mackenzie, Alexander (prime minister) 80

Mackenzie, William Lyon 21

Mandan peoples 59

Manitoba: creation of 49

Manitoba Act (1870) 52-3

Manitoulin Island Treaty 60, 65

Mawedopenais 73, 74-8, 79, 125

McDougall, Rev George 96, 101

McDougall, William 48

McGee, Thomas D'Arcy 51

McKay, Angus, 147

McKay, James 16, 71, 73, *89*, 122, 133, 154, 159, 167;
Commissioner 88, 91-2, 100, 104
interpreter 74, 91-2, 119, 128, 136, 139

McKenzie (sic) *see* Mackenzie, W.L.

medals: treaty 68-9, *69*, 74, 91, 92, 110, 139, 169;
silver 68-9, 79, 87, 133-4

medicine chest clause 99, 100, *114*

Mekis, Chief 134

Mercantile Library Association of Montreal 25-6, 27, 36, 42

Meredith, Edmund Allen: Deputy Minister of the Interior 16, *124*, 126, 130, 132, 137-8, 140-1, *141*, 145-6, 147, 154, 158

Métis 15, 50-4, 58, 62, 76-4, 76, 102, *105*, 128, 147, 171;
census (1871) 52-3;
as Indian agents 119, 123-4;
and Indian relationship 58, 62, 73-4, 80, 95;
land claims 50-1, 52-3, 95, 111, 171;
scrip 53;
treaty 74, 76, 111

military aid 60, 71, 80, 96

Mills, David 16,
as uninvested in the government's treaty promises 140-1, *141*, 142-4, 147, 152, 154, 165, 168;
Minister of the Interior 140, *141*, 143-7, 168-9, 171, 176

mineral rights 73-4, 79, 90, 164

Minister of the Interior. *See* Campbell; Laird; Mills

missionaries 26, 29, 48, 90, 99, 101, 111

Mistawâsis (Big Child) 98-9, 101, 107-9, *162*, 165

Montgomerie, Hugh E. 23-4, 35

Montreal: site of Morris's early life 19, 21-2, 25-7, 32, 36;
1849 riots in 23-4

Morris, Alexander *50*;
anti-American sentiments 20-1, 35;
appreciation of nature 20, 28-30, 35, 38, 39-40, 49, 96-7
Chief Justice 49-51;
children 22, 51-2, brought along to negotiations 71, 90, 96;
death of 165-6;
early life 16, 20-5, 27-8, 40, 173;

Reid, J. Lestock 93, 139, 150-1

religion 43, 45, 51-2;
Indians' 104;
Morris's, *which see. See also*
Christianity, Presbyterian

representation-by-population 46-7

reserve lands 73-4, 90-1, 93, 100, 107,
109, 132-9, 142-6, 170;
improper explanation of reserve
system to Indians 66;
as place of confinement 100, 129,
160;
selection of 74, 91-2, 100, 123, 136-8,
144, 175

Riel, Louis 51-2

Robinson Treaties (1850) 60-1, 65

Ross, Alexander 60

Royal Proclamation (1763) 65

Rupert's Land: sale of 62, 65, 95, 142

Russell, Lord John 24

S

Saskatchewan River 90, 92, 128, 129, 164

Saulteux peoples *see* Ojibwa

schools 70-1, 72-3, 109, 140, 164, 171;
on reserve 119, 125, 135, 159

Scotland, AM's ties to 17, 20, 25

scrip 53

Senum, Chief James 99, 152

seed. *See* agriculture

Seekahskootch, Chief 107

seigneurial tenure 22, 37, 47

self-government 39, 43, 48, 110, 140;
First Nations 62, 87-8, 110, 129, 160

Selkirk Treaty 60, 65

settlement. *See* development

She-she-gence, Chief 159

Short Bear (Young Chief) 137, 138-9,
140

Simpson, George 43

Simpson, Wemyss 63, 66-7, 69-71, 74,
80, 131

Sinclair, Rob 126, 150, 154-5

Sioux 59, 60, 119, 121-2, 146-7, 53;
Morris and 128-31;
refugees from the US 121, 126, 128

Six Nations 109

smallpox 62, 95, 99

Smith, Donald 164

Smyth, Selby 96

social formation 10-12, 158, 173

St. John, Molyneux 71, 131, 132-33

Stanley, George F.G. 14, 15, 65-6,

Star Blanket. *See* Atâhkakohp

starvation 63, 90, 95, 130, 132, 148;
as a policy 138, 160

subjugation: treaties as instruments of
14

Swampy Cree 90, 92, 95

Sweetgrass, Chief 57, 62-3, 95, 101, 104,
107

T

Taché, Bishop Alexandre 51

Teeteequaysay, Chief 99

Thickfoot 92

Thoma, Joseph 102

Torrance, Frederick William 36-7

transportation 34, 36, 39-40, 49, 54, 71,
90, 91, 111, 123, 138;
waterways 39-40, 69-70.
See also railways

treaty terms explained 14, 74, 91, 92, 97-8, 105, 138

treaty text 66, 73, 74, 87-9, 92, 99, 100, 131, 146, 151, 154, 166-7, 170, 175, *see also* outside promises;
copies given to the chiefs 87, 110

trust 59, 67, 87, 105-6, 119, 143;
as necessary in treaty negotiation 17, 81, 85, 105, 143-4;
Indians' trust in treaty process and commissioners 61-2, 65, 75-6, 90, 99, 101-2, 107-8, 133, 134, 137, 139, 140, 142, 151

U

United States 44;
as perceived threat to Canada 20-1, 35, 42-3, 47-8, 60, 79-80, 164;
treaty process in 18, 48, 70, 97, 108, 130, 153, 170

University of Manitoba 51

V

Vankoughnet, Lawrence 151, 169
Vankoughnet, Phillip M. 23, 42

W

Wagner, William 148-9
War of 1812 19, 109
Waywayseecappo, Chief 149
White Mud band 137-9
Winnipeg 54, 90, 93, 122, 126, 164;
Lake 88-9, 91, 167
Woodland Ojibwa 70
Wood Mountain 128
world view 11, 12, 158
Wuttunee, Chief *103*

Y

Yellow Quill, Chief 133-4, 136, 137-40, 142, 145, 168
Young Chief (Short Bear) 137, 138-9, 140

ROBERT J. TALBOT is originally from the Treaty 4 area, having grown up in Regina. He first became interested in the numbered treaties while an undergraduate student, when a chance encounter with former Federation of Saskatchewan Indian Nations president Perry Bellegarde convinced him that the treaties were more significant than his high school history texts had let on.

Mr. Talbot is an Ottawa-based historian with an extensive interest in Aboriginal/governmental relations. He has been a researcher for Indian and Northern Affairs Canada and Canadian Heritage, has presented papers on Aboriginal and Canadian history at a number of important academic conferences, and has published in *Mens: Revue de l'histoire intelectuelle de l'amérique française* on the topic of anglophone-francophone relations in Canada. He is currently working toward the completion of a PhD in history at the University of Ottawa, where he has also taught Canadian history.